Praise for *Ask a Historian*

'This rewarding rom ways of
the past is an immer lively,
engaging style acces ges . . .
One of Jenner's real enre of
public history that fuses scholarly research with humour, and
it is intended to entertain as much as it is to educate. For this
he is to be congratulated'

James Daybell, *BBC History Magazine*

'Jenner uses all the questions you never dared to ask about
history as an excellent excuse to rummage around in some
funny, fascinating, and downright peculiar corners of the past.
Every page contains delights, and you will be illuminated and
entertained in equal measure'

Lindsey Fitzharris, author of *The Butchering Art*

'Endlessly entertaining and utterly addictive, this book
provides a cornucopia of historical delights. The eclectic,
sometimes bizarre range of questions showcase the author's
encyclopaedic knowledge and engaging, humorous style to
perfection. The result is everything you need to know about
history - and much more besides'

Tracy Borman, author of *Thomas Cromwell*

'If history informs our future, Greg Jenner is one of the best
informants out there. He is a natural storyteller, conveying
complex ideas and events with pep, verve and wit. For anyone
who regularly asks the question 'Why?', this book is for you'

Susie Dent, author of *Word Perfect*

ASK
A
HISTORIAN

ASK
A
HISTORIAN

50 Surprising Answers to Things
You Always Wanted to Know

GREG JENNER

WEIDENFELD & NICOLSON

First published in Great Britain in 2021 by Weidenfeld & Nicolson,
This paperback edition first published in Great Britain in 2022
by Weidenfeld & Nicolson,
an imprint of The Orion Publishing Group Ltd
Carmelite House, 50 Victoria Embankment
London EC4Y 0DZ

An Hachette UK Company

1 3 5 7 9 10 8 6 4 2

A CIP catalogue record for this book is
available from the British Library.

ISBN (Mass Market Paperback) 978 1 4746 1862 5
ISBN (eBook) 978 1 4746 1863 2
ISBN (Audio) 978 1 4746 1864 9

Typeset by Input Data Services Ltd, Somerset

Printed and bound in Great Britain by Clays Ltd, Elcograf S.p.A.

www.weidenfeldandnicolson.co.uk
www.orionbooks.co.uk

To my wonderful wife, Kate, who has been my steadfast companion and champion throughout

Contents

Introduction

Hello, how are you? Keeping well, I hope. Obviously, I don't know when you're reading this, but I'm writing it on 23 December 2020. Ordinarily, I'd be driving to Kent to celebrate Christmas with my family tomorrow evening (I'm half-French, so we traditionally do it on Christmas Eve, and then drive back on Christmas morning to spend time with my wife's family). Sadly, this year hasn't been like the others. The Covid-19 pandemic has robbed so much from so many, and lockdown means many millions of people aren't seeing their loved ones at this special time of year. The majority of the country has had to socialise through the technological gateway of screens and speakers, and, while it's effective enough, I'm definitely not alone in yearning for face-to-face interactions with friends, family, colleagues, and strangers.

I am a natural chatterbox. I love to talk, and listen, and laugh. As a podcaster, I've been privileged in my opportunities to keep talking and laughing throughout this accursed year. But I've profoundly missed real human interactions, and one of my favourite things that was snatched away by the virus was the chance to meet people around the UK. You see, when I first agreed to write this book, I planned to gather up your historical questions in person, while touring my previous book, *Dead Famous: An Unexpected History of Celebrity*. I was going to come to your town, excitedly waffle on about celebrity for an hour, and then throw open the Q&A so that you could ask me absolutely anything. I'd have done my best to answer the questions live on stage, but would then have answered them properly in a book. This book.

Well, that didn't happen. *Dead Famous* had the unfortunate luck of launching one week into a global emergency, during which bookshops closed, events were cancelled, and the publishing industry went into temporary meltdown. It was somewhat less than ideal, and the lack of promotional events meant I had no audience questions for *Ask a Historian*. So, I had to change tack. The queries I've answered in the upcoming pages have instead been sourced from an online questionnaire, with the exception of some memorable classics that I'd been asked in previous years. I promise you with hand on heart that these are all genuine questions from members of the public (though I have a sneaky suspicion that one of the most difficult might have come from my literary agent, Donald), and I've included each questioner's name when they were happy to share them.

I am a public historian. My job is to encourage a love of historical learning, and I find it fascinating to see what people want to know. I also enjoy the sudden jolts of self-awareness when they chuck tricky questions at me, and I realise I don't know how to answer them. Doing audience Q&As on stage is always risky, because I have no idea what lethal grenade is being lobbed my way. Having read a couple of thousand books in my career, I'm usually able to give a vaguely coherent response, but every now and then I get totally blown away.

The best questions are often from small children whose intellectual creativity hasn't been drummed out of them yet. My fave was a young girl who asked, 'Did Jesus Christ know about dinosaurs, and was he sad that they had all died?' This produced a wonderful effect in the room; the audience initially burst into laughter – 'Ah, aren't children adorable!' – only for the chuckles to gradually morph into a muffled chorus of muttering, as the realisation dawned that this little girl had posed a theological quandary difficult enough to fluster even the Pope. I don't recall how I answered it, but I'm pretty sure I didn't cover myself in glory, presumably making some waffly admission that the Bible is somewhat unclear on divine dino-remorse.

Wading through the questions submitted for this book, there were a couple that were equally flummoxing. The best was the marvellous: *Did anyone ever paint a tunnel on a wall and fool someone into running/driving into it?'* The questioner was anonymous, so I can only presume it came from Road Runner who was plotting another humiliation for Wile E. Coyote. Intrigued, I looked at early Hollywood history to see whether Cecil B. DeMille had ever built a movie set in the desert, only for some unfortunate drunk driver to smash into it. Sadly, I couldn't find anything. And it felt overly tangential to pivot instead to the use of military decoys in the Second World War, when the Allies made fake armies of inflatable tanks and dummy planes in order to throw the Nazis off the scent of D-Day. Alas, Road Runner's question defeated me. Beep, beep.

The successful questions which you're about to encounter are a brilliant mix of the familiar, the important, and the charmingly obscure. I was really heartened that people wanted to know about global history, as well as the usual Nazis and Tudors (wow, people *really* love Anne Boleyn!), and I enjoyed catching up on the latest archaeological research for some of the questions about Stone Age life. Occasionally, people made the reckless mistake of asking for my own personal opinions. Thankfully, my patient editor, Maddy, gently intervened when my impassioned rants veered wildly off course and turned into epic essays with TOO! MANY!! EXCLAMATION!!! MARKS!!!!

In general, I've tried to keep the tone light, cheerful, and informative. I hope each answer does a decent job of outlining what you need to know, but my even bigger hope is that you'll take a look at the recommended reading list and will use it to embark upon an even more fulfilling journey of discovery. The wonderful thing about asking questions is the answers often contain the seeds of yet more questions, producing a lovely feedback loop of constant curiosity. Ideally, this book won't just satisfy your historical appetite, but increase it too. In which case, allow me to raise a toast: here's to a lifetime of asking: 'Yeah, but *why* . . .?'

Thanks for taking the time to read this. I hope you enjoy the book.

Best wishes,
Greg

CHAPTER 1:

FACT OR FICTION?

1. **Did Anne Boleyn have three nipples? My history teacher said this was used as evidence of witchcraft against her at her trial.**
Asked by MH-B

I probably get asked about Anne Boleyn more than any other person. She is one of the most famous women in British history, having been the second of Henry VIII's six wives and the first to have been executed. Her gradual rise, and then sudden dramatic fall, has been a compelling story for five centuries, and every new generation of writers seems to want to chuck more fuel on the roaring flames of her notoriety. I'm afraid, MH-B, your teacher had fallen for something rather dubiously modern.

Speaking as someone who works in broadcasting, Boleyn is ratings gold dust; I'm writing this in November 2020, and, in the past twelve months alone, there have been three major TV documentaries about her, two on the same channel - in fact, that same channel has just announced that a third drama-documentary about her will air next year. We are a nation obsessed, as Dr Stephanie Russo demonstrates in her excellent book, *The Afterlife of Anne Boleyn: Representations of Anne Boleyn in Fiction and on the Screen,* which recounts all the ways she's been reinterpreted over the centuries.

The problem is, so much of what we enjoy about Anne Boleyn's story is either dodgy guff, or was politicised misinformation designed to destroy her reputation during a trumped-up treason trial. Despite countless biographies, novels, TV dramas, films, and documentaries, the real woman is strangely elusive, and you can very easily make the oppositional cases for her as being both unfortunate victim, crushed by powerful men, or conniving femme fatale who got her comeuppance. What we can say with certainty is that at no point in her lifetime was she accused of witchcraft, or of possessing a third nipple.

These unfounded rumours are built on the poisonous stories spread some fifty years after her death by the rebel Catholic priest Nicholas Sander. He loathed the Protestant Queen Elizabeth I, and it just so happened that Anne was Elizabeth's mother; by attacking the one he thus diminished the other. Sander had been a little kid when Anne's head was sliced off by a French swordsman in 1536, but as an adult he lived a life of Catholic exile in Rome, Madrid, and Ireland, doing what he could to launch rebellions and undermine Elizabeth's monarchical integrity. His book *Of the Origin and Progression of the English Schism* was regularly reprinted from 1586 onwards, with at least fifteen editions known before 1700, and these works influenced European writers with an axe to grind against the Protestant English. As the seventeenth century writer Peter Heylin pithily noted, he should have been called Nicholas *Slander* instead.

According to Sander, Anne Boleyn was 'rather tall of stature, with black hair and an oval face of sallow complexion, as if troubled with jaundice. She had a projecting tooth under the upper lip, and on her right hand, six fingers. There was a large wen [a swollen cyst or boil] under her chin, and therefore to hide its ugliness, she wore a high dress covering her throat . . . She was handsome to look at, with a pretty mouth, amusing in her ways, playing well on the lute, and was a good dancer.' In short, Sander claims Anne Boleyn may have had the charms and graces of a beauty, but she made Nanny McPhee look like Miss Universe by comparison.

Where did he get this stuff from, given he never saw her? The lumpy neck crops up in a couple of malicious sources of the time, including letters to Belgium from a gossipy diplomat, and the rumour was repeated later too, but we have pretty good reason to be suspicious of such claims. Despite having played the long game in wooing King Henry VIII, Anne Boleyn wasn't actually considered the hottest woman at court; her charms were more mental and personal than physical, but nor was she unattractive either. Any evidence of physical abnormalities is likely overstated, if not fully invented.

As for the sixth finger, now a staple 'fact' in many modern novels and websites, this seems to have come from a comment made by George Wyatt, again several decades after Anne's death. He writes: 'There was found, indeed, upon the side of her nail upon one of her fingers, some little show of a nail, which yet was so small, by the report of those that have seen her, as the workmaster seemed to leave it an occasion of greater grace to her hand, which, with the tip of one of her other fingers, might be and was usually by her hidden without any least blemish to it.' Hmmm, not so much a sixth finger as a tiny wart, then.

You'll notice we haven't had so much as a sniff of a third nipple, or black cats and bubbling cauldrons, and you'd think such lurid rumours would've swiftly found their way into the trial evidence brought against Anne by King Henry's chief minister, Thomas Cromwell. As it was, she was accused not of sorcery or demonic worship, but rather the much more straightforward crimes of treason, incest, and adultery. She was alleged to have been regularly romping with five men: Henry Norris, William Brereton, Francis Weston, a musician named Mark Smeaton, and – most scandalous of all – her own brother, George Boleyn.

Only Smeaton admitted to the charges, this being an unreliable confession extracted through brutal torture. The others protested their innocence, as did Anne herself, but adultery wasn't a capital offence; not even King Henry could get away with executing his wife for allegedly two-timing him. Cromwell needed something juicier, and so he ramped up the alleged offence to outright treason, claiming Anne planned to murder the King and marry one of her lovers instead. Two years earlier, King Henry had passed a law declaring it treasonous to even discuss the possibility of his death. Even if she hadn't been trying to hasten it along, it's plausible this is where Anne was caught out.

The trial was a foregone conclusion – historians have often noticed that Henry had already sent for that French swordsman before Anne even knew she was on trial – and all six of the accused were immediately executed with ruthless expediency. It's an extraordinary story of court intrigue and brutal politics, but it's one devoid of any magical or witchy hue.

The simple truth is that the sixteenth-century criticism of Anne was sexual; she was attacked from various sides, often by foreign ambassadors, as a promiscuous and sordid seducer who they suggested might have used elixirs and love potions to get Henry to fall in love with her. Henry himself is supposed to have angrily declared he had been the victim of bewitchment, charms, and *sortileges** – but this was a man yelling that he'd been tricked into marrying a wrong 'un, not that she was in league with Satan. Various novelists and biographers have toyed with these unfounded claims ever since, asking whether those accusations of using 'charms' and 'incantations' might lead us into a more sinister charge of black magic and devil worship. The trial records prove otherwise – Cromwell and his gathered jury didn't give a hoot about such things, and they were desperately looking for literally any excuse to kill her.

The witch stuff is much more of a twentieth-century invention, first introduced in the 1920s by the anthropologist Margaret Murray, who argued Anne Boleyn, Joan of Arc, and a few other historical heavy-hitters had actually belonged to an ancient, secret pagan cult. This was, of course, absolute tosh. For weary historians trying to fight bad history, it didn't help when the enormously popular *Harry Potter* films showed a portrait of Anne mounted on the wall at Hogwarts. Honestly, if she'd been a graduate of such an illustrious educational facility, you'd think Anne might have been able to pull off a cheeky *Expelliarmus* spell on the executioner's sword before legging it out of the Tower.

It's easy to see how this trope of a witchy Anne has emerged; while pop culture delights in stories of witches – from cackling, green-skinned hags to wand-wielding, teenage goths with perfect skin – one of the most influential traditions in twentieth-century feminist scholarship was to explain the European Witch Craze of the 1540s–1690s as a misogynistic

---

* We get this from a gossipy ambassador who didn't even speak English, and didn't name his source, so it's not exactly rock-solid proof.

enterprise designed to crush female power. This chimes nicely with the narrative of Thomas Cromwell being Anne's architect of destruction, using lies to bring down a meddlesome queen with too many womanly opinions. But, let me reiterate it for clarity: in a trial that we can fairly label a political witch-hunt, during an era famed for *actual* witch-hunts, Anne Boleyn wasn't tried for witchcraft. In fact, the word wasn't even mentioned once.

Though Anne Boleyn possessed no third nipple, the idea that such a thing could be sinister does have a genuine Early Modern heritage; back in the 1600s it was sometimes interpreted as a mark of the Devil upon a body, a sign that a woman or a man (yes, men could be witches too!) was in league with dark forces. Supposedly, a witch might be able to suckle their demonic familiar, often said to be a black cat, through this bonus boob. From this we presumably get the idiomatic phrase 'as cold as a witch's tit', because anything used to suckle evil was presumed devoid of maternal warmth. Personally, I take this as proof that Satan shares my love of ice cream, so I'm warming to the guy.

So, MH-B, I'm afraid your teacher was confusing fact with fiction, which is quite easy to do with someone as gossiped about as Anne Boleyn; but, just to be clear, she didn't have three nipples, six fingers, or five lovers, and you'd think her story would be interesting enough as it is. But I suppose writers are always looking for a fresh angle. We've already had Anne Boleyn the witch, and in 2010 she became a vampire queen in a novel by S. Cinsearae, so it's only a matter of time before she's an alien robot intent on wiping out the Earth. And with Henry VIII for a husband, frankly, who would blame her?

2. Is it true that a dead Pope was put on trial?
Asked by Steph

Well, Steph, the short answer is yes. The long answer?
ABSO-BLOODY-LUTELY YES!

Let me take you by the hand and welcome you to the chaos of the ninth century. On the face of it, these were shiny, golden times for Western Europe – the mighty Emperor Charlemagne was bossing it in his new Frankish Empire, England enjoyed the reforming talents of Alfred the Great, and it was an era of intellectual flourishing in libraries and monasteries. And yet, it was also when everything was basically on fire. From the north, Vikings were marauding up and down the rivers and seas – they hit Paris in 845 CE, and then smashed into Yorkshire in the 860s. In the south, a powerful Arab army sacked Rome in 846 CE. In the east, the Magyars waited until the 890s before sweeping westwards from Hungary and reaching as far as Bavaria.

Into this maelstrom we must add the Papacy. As the political and theological chief executives of the Church, Popes were meant to be stabilising forces, but proved to be anything but. Indeed, if the 800s were bad, the 900s are where it went spectacularly wrong. The biggest problem was numerous Popes being completely incapable of staying alive. As the legal historian Donald E. Wilkes Jr pointed out, between 872 and 965 CE there were twenty-four different Popes in ninety-four years. That was pretty bad. But 896–904 CE saw a frantic game of musical chairs in which a staggering NINE different Popes ruled in a mere eight years. Bear in mind that there were nine Popes in the entire twentieth century!

You might be wondering if this rapid turnover was just bad luck, caused by recurrent bouts of plague, or was perhaps the result of too many artery-clogging trans-fats in the papal canteen? Alas not. Over the course of that chaotic century, seven of the twenty-four Popes weren't doddery dudes with dodgy tickers, but were healthy men murdered by their rivals. Yes, papal politics in this period was ruthless and brutal, leading historians to label it the 'nadir of the Papacy'.

The primary cause of the chaos in the 900s was a power struggle between rival families, most notable among them being the counts of Tusculum, also known as the much-harder-to-say Theophylact family. They rose to prominence in 904 CE, when Marozia – teenage daughter of Count Theophylact – became the underage lover of Pope Sergius III, who'd ordered the strangulation of his two predecessors. What a nice man: a murderer and a creep! We'll get back to him later.

For some historians, Sergius III is when things really, really went downhill; not least because Marozia bore him an illegitimate son who he then made his successor. It's understandable why the historian Eamon Duffy described this era in the Papacy's history as a time in which: 'The Chair of St. Peter became the prize of tyrants and brigands and a throne fouled by fierce tides of crime and licentiousness . . . a ticket to local dominance for which men were prepared to rape, murder, and steal.' But seven years before this shameful crisis, Pope Stephen VI had already lowered the bar to ankle height with his infamous 'Cadaver Synod', when – as our question-setter, Steph, framed it – a dead Pope really was put on trial.

In January 897, having been Pope for a mere seven months, Pope Stephen ordered that the corpse (*cadaver*) of a previous Pope, called Formosus, be dug up out of his grave and tried for various crimes, at a special council meeting (*synod*). The name Formosus translates as 'handsome' in Latin, but there was nothing pretty about a rotting human being dragged from the ground, dressed up in papal robes, and plonked into a throne, ready for cross-questioning.

Yes, this was a show trial beyond parody, because the dead guy was formally interrogated. Unsurprisingly, he didn't have much to say for himself; instead, a teenage cleric stood behind his fetid body and played the bizarre role of corpse ventriloquist/defence lawyer, while Pope Stephen yelled accusations at the decaying heap of bones and flesh. Also involved in the proceedings was Sergius, who was still a bishop at that point.

Needless to say, Formosus was found guilty of whatever random crimes Stephen concocted. He was stripped of his papal attire and had his three fingers - with which he had blessed people - snapped off. He was then reburied in a commoner's grave. It seems Stephen quickly regretted this decision, perhaps fearing that Formosus would be dug up by his supporters and his bones turned into holy relics. He issued a new order that Formosus be re-excavated and chucked into the River Tiber instead. According to the story, this plan failed - either a monk or a fisherman retrieved Formosus from the water. Bad luck, Stephen!

And his luck only worsened from there. Stephen had frankly embarrassed himself and the Papacy with this bizarre behaviour. He'd also made an enemy of the pro-Formosus gang, who soon organised a successful countercoup. They stripped Stephen of his vestments, relegated him to mere monk status, hurled him in prison, and had him strangled to death. He'd barely held the job for a year, but that proved surprisingly long-lasting compared to what came next.

Presumably, one of the architects of the coup was the man who replaced him, the newly enthroned Pope Romanus, whose main claim to fame was immediately suffering his own humiliating demotion back to monk status after a mere four months in the gig. He was hopeless, and Rome was Popeless, but we're not sure whether he was bumped off too, or if he just went into embarrassing retirement. To fill the vacancy, along came the much more impressive Pope Theodore II, who ordered that Pope Formosus' bones be retrieved from that fisherman/monk, and reburied with full honours. Theodore reversed the Cadaver Synod and was described as wise, charitable, and temperate. He was exactly what the Papacy needed in this moment of crisis, so no prizes for guessing what happened to him . . .

Yup, Theodore mysteriously died twelve days into the job (another source says twenty-one days, but twelve is funnier). Another murder, you might ask? I couldn't possibly comment. So, next up was Pope John IX, who lasted exactly two years. Then it was Pope Benedict IV, who managed three and a half years before he suspiciously carked it too. Along came Pope Leo V, whose seven-month cameo ended with his being violently throttled to death, and then it was the turn of Pope Christopher who suffered the exact same fate, only much quicker. Was the rapid double-murder a coincidence? It doesn't take Detective Columbo to figure out where the blame lay.

The guilty man was our infamous Sergius, who popped on his papal robes and immediately reversed the reversal when it came to Pope Formosus' posthumous trial. Having taken part in the bizarre proceedings, Sergius was determined to once again besmirch his dead rival's reputation. He then shacked up with the aforementioned teenage countess Marozia, appointed his illegitimate son as his successor, and set about demeaning the office of the Papacy so intently that historians credited him with kickstarting an era ungenerously dubbed the 'papal Dark Ages'. Following in his filthy wake was Pope John X (914-928) – who watched his brother's murder in a cathedral before later getting the strangulation treatment – and, in 964, Pope John XII achieved the perfect soap opera death by being killed by his mistress's jealous husband after he'd walked in on them shagging.

In short, being Pope in the late 800s and 900s was about as dangerous as being a fighter pilot in the First World War, and a lot less reputable. At least pilots didn't have the indignity of being dug out of their graves and put on trial by their successor.

At least, not yet . . .

3. Who is the richest person that ever lived and what made him or her so rich?
Asked by Nana Poku

Being a historian is hard. There's the learning of foreign and/or dead languages; the remembering of archaic legal terms; the decoding of scrawled handwriting; the contextualising of long-forgotten slang and jokes; the traipsing off to faraway archives; the frustration of lacking key sources, or of having way too many; and the constant nagging doubt that there's both too much to know and so much we'll never know. Frankly, historians are a bunch of masochists. But one of the trickiest things we try to do is figure out the modern value of old money, because we get a huge range of values depending on whether we measure the value of goods, the size of the economy, or the average wages of the time.

For example, in my book *Dead Famous*, which was about the history of celebrity, I tried to work out the modern value of Charles Dickens' box-office takings during his second American tour in 1867. We know that he raked in £45,000, but was that a lot? It doesn't sound like a lot. Decades of inflation means that £45k is nothing to be sniffed at – it now gets you a shiny BMW 5 series (and please feel free to donate to my crowdfunder, so I can afford one) – but it's nothing like a twenty-first-century fortune. You can't buy a speedboat on £45k; at best, you're basically looking at a fancy pedalo with some really nice cushions.

But what did £45k mean to Dickens in 1867? Previous biographers have converted it into £3 million. Very healthy. But they used the value of goods in 1867 as their economic litmus test – apparently, he earned enough to buy 3,000 horses, which, having never bought a horse, strikes me as a lot of horses. But touring America was his job, and he did it to make money, so surely the better measure was to compare it with average personal income for the era? After all, people were buying $2 tickets to see him, paid out of their wages, and they weren't showing up to the box office looking to swap a horse for a front-row seat. Using wages as the economic measure produced a startlingly different result – Dickens' box-office windfall wasn't equivalent to 3 million quid in our money, it was *30* million! Proper speedboat dosh, that.

I bring this up because it reveals how wildly open to interpretation historicising wealth can be. That brings me on to our original question from Nana Poku: *'who was the wealthiest human of all time?'* It's a fun query to pose, but a hard one to answer. Whatever I say will need to have a massive, flashing, neon-coloured question mark hovering overhead.

At the time of writing this, the wealthiest human on the planet is Elon Musk, whose personal worth has expanded to a ridiculous $185 billion. You'd think, therefore, that he'd be the clear winner in this competition, but it really depends on what we do with the old Dickens conundrum. So, let's assert some boundaries. In searching for history's wealthiest human, are we looking for 'who had the most private wealth?' or 'who had control over the biggest economy?' because they're really different.

The simplest answer to the first question is probably John D. Rockefeller - the American oil tycoon. On his death in 1937, his obituary declared he'd accrued a fortune of about $1.5bn in a time when a new Ford motorcar cost about $750. If we do a simple calculation of inflation over the past eighty-five years, Rockefeller comes in at a disappointing figure of $22bn. But if we then perform a sneaky economist's trick, and adjust to reflect the ratio of his wealth compared to the entire American GDP, suddenly Big Johnny Rockefeller's 2 per cent share of the economy bumps him way up to $420bn in modern money - an eye-watering figure to make Elon Musk look like a Dickensian street urchin begging in the gutter. The problem, of course, is the $400bn chasm between those two sums; we're either saying Rockefeller would be roughly thirtieth in the *Forbes* rich list today, or we're saying he's the number one of all time. That's quite the discrepancy, isn't it?

All right, let's leave Rockefeller. Who else might steal the crown? Well, we can turn to the German banker Jakob Fugger, whose epithet was, fittingly enough, Jakob the Rich. His family's vast wealth was initially accrued through the Italian cloth trade, but the real boon to their fortunes came in the 1490s when they asserted their stranglehold on the mining of precious copper. This turned him into Mr Moneybags, and he became the personal banker of the Habsburg imperial dynasty, to the point that some of the most significant political events of the early sixteenth century were funded from his ravine-deep pockets.

And when the Holy Roman Emperor Maximilian died in 1519, Fugger manipulated the two rival claimants to the throne into a bidding war for his banking services, cranking up the size of the loan they'd have to borrow from him, before buying off the electors to secure the election of Maximilian's grandson, Charles I of Spain. This made Charles the ruler of two separate military superpowers, the Spanish Empire (with its territories in the Netherlands and the New World) and the Holy Roman Empire. It was a dynastic mega-alliance that reshaped the political fate of Europe. So, just how rich was Fugger? Well, upon his death in 1525, he'd squirrelled away over 2 million guilders (the coinage at the time) which five centuries of inflation converts into only a few billion (boring!). But if we measure Fugger's share of the wider European economy, he emerges level with Rockefeller.

Things get even trickier if we allow monarchs, emperors, and political leaders to join the competition. Did they control their own private wealth, or were they merely administering massive economies? We can list a great many emperors whose vast, fertile lands and lucrative trade routes brought in astonishing levels of revenue - Akbar the Great of Mughal South Asia, Darius the Great of Persia, Alexander the Great of Macedon, Ramesses the Great of Egypt, any number of Chinese emperors, etc. But did that money belong to them, or to their governments? I'd lean towards the latter. But in the interests of full disclosure, and because it's a particularly fascinating story, let me introduce you to perhaps the wealthiest of them all – Mansa Musa, ruler of Mali, in West Africa, from roughly 1312 until 1337.

Musa's empire was huge, much bigger than modern Mali's borders, and its incredible wealth was built upon salt mining, the abhorrent cruelty of human enslavement, and – most famously – gold mining. Much of the gold that we see in medieval European art, or in the royal crowns worn in coronation ceremonies, came from Mali. The reason we know a fair bit about Mansa Musa is because he was a devout Muslim who undertook the holy pilgrimage (Hajj) to Mecca, in what is now Saudi Arabia. But Musa didn't do things by halves, and nor did he pack light. Instead, he embarked on a massive expedition joined by tens of thousands of servants.

This enormous army popped into Cairo for a nice mini-break, as Musa was a cultured man who fancied a spot of sightseeing. Having brought 21 tonnes of gold with him, and feeling rather generous, he accidentally crashed the Egyptian economy by giving away so much treasure that the price of gold lost its value for two decades! Arab historians basically described him as a real-life Prince Ali from Disney's *Aladdin*, rolling into town with an impossibly glitzy parade. Having reached Mecca, he returned home via Cairo, where he recruited a gaggle of brilliant architects, poets, scholars, and theologians to expand and beautify his empire, most notably the city of Timbuktu, with its celebrated library. All in all, modern historians often call Mansa Musa the richest person of all time, with a fortune of something like $400bn in modern money.

So, we have something of a three-way tie at the top – Musa, Fugger, and Rockefeller. But I want to add another emperor into the contest, because I think this one exploits a cheeky loophole.

Rome's first emperor was Caesar Augustus; his name was originally Octavian, but, upon the murder of Julius Caesar, he was declared to be Caesar's adopted heir, and so inherited not only supreme political power – plus the loyalty of battle-hardened troops – but also Caesar's private wealth. Bear in mind that Caesar had conquered Gaul, so that was some serious real estate. Octavian therefore became both the first emperor of the Roman state – with all its enormous tax and trade revenues, totalling perhaps 2 billion sesterces – and also a mega-minted private citizen whose personal property was then further bolstered by the conquest of Egypt, following his crushing of Mark Antony and Cleopatra at the Battle of Actium. Astonishingly, naval victory didn't just win him glory. This ancient kingdom, with its fertile lands, seems to have slid straight into his personal property portfolio, making Octavian its new private landlord.

The guy was loaded. Indeed, in the early days of his reign, he apparently paid for the maintenance of Caesar's old army from his own wallet. And I'm not sure if you've ever tried to hire an army, but they don't come cheap. Professor Walter Scheidel, who is an expert in ancient economics, notes that Augustus also leveraged his supreme power to menace and cajole other wealthy citizens into naming him in their wills, forcing them to enrich him from their deathbeds. And if people pissed him off, he had no qualms in exiling or executing his enemies, and stripping them of their assets in the process.

Professor Scheidel estimates Augustus' total income, across two decades of extortion and extraction, was an eye-watering 1.4 billion sesterces. And, before you ask, estimating the value of a sestertius coin is another head-scratcher – money back then was based on the price of the metal, whereas ours is a fiat currency (nothing to do with unreliable Italian cars, it's simply a government-set value). A single brass sestertius coin might have been worth as little as 50 pence now, or it might have been several quid. It really depended on what you were buying – bread was cheap, a Roman would get two loaves for a single coin, but clothes were expensive. Nevertheless, having 1.4 billion coins jingling in your toga pocket was pretty good going.

We don't know how much Augustus inherited in total from Caesar, but we can see from his *Res Gestae* (a boastful list of his achievements) that he paid for many building pro- jects from his own purse, including a mid-sized personal palace (nice!) and a temple to Apollo. He also doled out hundreds of millions of sesterces as gifts and favours to his loyal entourage, so he wasn't just hoarding it all like some fairy-tale dragon. Annoyingly, this makes his wealth some- what tricky to estimate, but it's plausible that Caesar Augustus was the wealthiest person of all time by combining two gargantuan revenue streams: his personal finances and the resources of the Roman imperial state. But, if I'm honest, I'm much too cowardly to stick my neck out and declare him the winner.

Besides, if things keep going the way they are, soon Elon Musk might solve my problem for me. Maybe he'll buy me that BMW, if I ask nicely?

4. Are you fed up with people saying, 'Atlantis proves aliens are real'?
Asked by Anonymous

Yes! Next question . . .

Hang on a sec, my editor is calling me . . . Oh, apparently, one-word answers come off as a bit rude. My bad. OK, multiple-word answer, here we go!

As a public historian, I spend a lot of time on Twitter and YouTube, tracking how people engage with historical ideas. One of the most alarming recent trends is the growing number of people who think aliens built the pyramids, or were the original inhabitants of Atlantis. Every year, researchers at Chapman University, in California, run the Survey of American Fears to find out what ordinary citizens are worried about, and to see which paranormal beliefs are gaining traction. In 2018, 41 per cent of those polled believed that aliens had visited Earth in the ancient past, and 57 per cent believed that Atlantis had existed for real. This was a big rise from 2016, and I find this really concerning. I'll try to explain why.

OK, let's start with Atlantis, the ancient city lost beneath the waves. The famous story comes to us from the ancient Greek philosopher, Plato. In his dialogue texts *Timaeus* and *Critias*, he describes his teacher, Socrates, gathering three men together to discuss the creation of the world and how Athens had previously dealt with foreign rivals. Our two key witnesses are Critias and Timaeus, who describe Atlantis as an advanced island superpower with bonus colonies in Africa and Europe. Critias gives a detailed description of their advanced society, but – long story short – Atlantis had launched an unprovoked war against Athens, only to be defeated by the impressive Greeks. To add a further helping of hubris, they then got wiped out by a natural catastrophe.

And how does Critias know this story? Well, as a boy, he heard it from his grandfather, who heard it from his dad, who heard it from an influential lawmaker called Solon, who heard it from some wise Egyptian priests, who heard it from . . . well, we don't know. This might strike us as somewhat unreliable, but, around the world, oral history has preserved knowledge through the generations, and is an important bedrock of meaning for many Indigenous communities, so I'm not saying we should ignore it. However, Plato's Egyptian priests were adamant this war had taken place 9,000 years beforehand, way back in what we now know to be the Stone Age, when Athens didn't even exist.

You can't see me, but I'm doing my suspicious face.

Ignoring that dodgy detail, a sunken city sounds plausible, right? Well, maybe. A long-standing theory – much investigated, but never convincingly proved – posits that Atlantis represents the Minoan civilisation from the island of Crete. Around 3,500 years ago, this powerful Bronze Age society suddenly declined, not long after a huge volcanic eruption on the island of Thera (now Santorini) had devastated the town of Akrotiri, and sent forth tsunamis to engulf coastal communities. However, Crete didn't vanish beneath the waves. It's still there, and is a lovely holiday destination, if you fancy it? And, to be a boring stick-in-the-mud, archaeologists, scientists, and ancient historians quibble extensively over the hard facts. Thera definitely went 'KABOOM!', but the rest is debatable.

You can see why people love to speculate, but there are obvious holes in the Minoan Atlantis theory. Plato states Atlantis is an absolutely massive island to the west of Gibraltar, happily plonked in the Atlantic Ocean. This has led to all sorts of other Atlantis location theories: perhaps it was the island of Pharos, or Cyprus, or Sardinia, or Malta, or it was off the coast of Turkey, or southern Spain, or it was the Azores, or Cape Verde, or the Canary Islands, or Ireland, or Britain, or Finland, or Denmark, or Sweden, or various Caribbean islands?

During the Renaissance, Plato's forgotten text was reintroduced to European thought by Islamic and Byzantine scholars, which coincided with Christopher Columbus discovering a New World, and Spanish conquistadors encountering the Maya of Mexico; it's no surprise, therefore, that Renaissance thinkers suddenly wondered if the Maya were original Atlanteans. More amazingly, some people have since suggested that Atlantis was based on Antarctica! It's an absurd theory, though I love the idea of an Antarctic superpower ruled by a race of smug, talking penguins who thought, 'Hey, you know who pisses me off? Athenians! Let's sail 8,000 miles and show them who's boss! Wait, what's that sound? Oh no, earthquake!!'

Others have theorised that Plato's Atlantis is instead a folk memory of the biblical Great Flood, the one that sees Noah quickly googling the basics of maritime carpentry. Flood myths are indeed found in multiple ancient cultures, suggesting a shared trauma. I suppose it's possible that a low-lying city was suddenly swallowed by the seas. And, to be fair, eager Atlantis-hunters point to the lost city of Troy, which had always been thought to be pure literary myth, until the amateur German archaeologist Heinrich Schliemann discovered its mighty walls in the 1870s. So, there is precedent for poetry being the handmaiden of archaeological discovery.

But, to me, the discovery of Troy only makes it even more suspicious that Atlantis - supposedly a superpower - gets only a single mention in ancient sources, whereas Troy was extensively depicted in Greek art and culture, to the point that Schliemann knew where to look for it in western Turkey. If mega-punchy Atlantis really had existed, wouldn't we see the Greek victory over the Atlanteans depicted on pots and whatnot? Sorry to spoil the fun, but it didn't pick up extra coverage because Atlantis was never real.

Plato is often described as the 'founder of Western political philosophy'. His book the *Republic* was a landmark text on justice, happiness, and how to run the ideal city-state, focusing intensely on how society should be ruled, and how it should treat its rivals. Viewed in this light, Atlantis is clearly an allegory about what happens when a nation gets too arrogant, avaricious, and aggressive. The story is not historical reportage, it's a fable; an imaginary case study in reverse utopianism, with the destruction of a superpower serving as a karmic warning from history. Some scholars think it's a pointed dig at the rival Persian Empire, and others think it's an attack on Athenian democracy itself,* but the key thing is that the Atlanteans are defeated by the morally superior Athenians – and Plato just happened to be a morally righteous Athenian. Funny coincidence, that.

The fact Atlantis supposedly vanished 9,000 years before Plato lived was a deliberately wild fantasy; it may as well be the opening credits to *Star Wars*, 'a long time ago, in a galaxy far, far away'. In terms of storytelling accuracy, this is basically Plato saying his gorgeous supermodel girlfriend goes to another school, you wouldn't know her . . . Atlantis isn't real.

---

* Plato had strong views on why getting the public to vote for things was a bad idea – a theory later proved by *The X Factor* and Donald Trump.

Plato made it up to prove a philosophical point. And we know this because Plato's student, Aristotle, told us he did.

Despite (or because of) the holes in the story, the Survey of American Fears shows we are increasingly fascinated by Atlantis. It repeatedly pops up in pop culture: there's the DC *Aquaman* franchise; that Disney movie you haven't seen, *Atlantis: The Lost Empire,* and the one you have, *The Little Mermaid.* There's Jules Verne's classic novel *20,000 Leagues Under the Sea,* and the Jules Verne-inspired movie *Journey to the Centre of the Earth.* And there're video games like *Assassin's Creed: Odyssey* and *Tomb Raider.* Plus, there's the TV show *Stargate Atlantis,* and that neatly brings us on to the aliens. Oh boy, the aliens . . .

Hollywood is obsessed with the idea that aliens walk among us, but quite a lot of these stories go further, interpolating their visits into our ancient history. In Ridley Scott's pretty-but-pants movie *Prometheus,* humanity is genetically descended from advanced humanoid life forms who sowed their DNA into the Earth's water supply, then popped back in fairly regularly to see how we were getting on, leaving a star map in Scotland so we could one day drop back in on them.

Meanwhile, the even more terrible *Alien Vs Predator* (part of the same franchise) is set in an ancient Antarctic pyramid built by humans who have, for thousands of years, been worshipping Predators as gods and sacrificing themselves to the alien Xenomorphs to give their overlords something fun to hunt. And in *Transformers: Revenge of the Fallen,* the baddies use the Great Pyramid of Giza as a storage depot for a sun-destroying superweapon, which very much contravenes UNESCO guidelines for best practice.

I have enjoyed loads of these films as fun Hollywood entertainment. However, the moment such alien fantasy then leaks into supposedly factual documentaries and books is the moment I get depressed. YouTube, podcasts, and American TV shows are full of this stuff – particularly the hugely problematic TV series *Ancient Aliens* – all of them giving airtime to science fiction tropes as if they are valid archaeological theories. Does a seventh-century funeral sarcophagus show a Mayan king taking off in a spaceship? No! Were crystal skulls an ancient Mexican link to life on Mars? No, they are nineteenth-century German forgeries! What about Peru's Nazca lines . . .? Nooooo!

This surging tsunami of bullshit all began with Erich von Däniken's blockbuster book *Chariots of the Gods*, published in the 1960s, which has since sold more than 65 million copies. You might assume it's all a bit of fun, no harm done, but I think it's pretty offensive to say these ancient marvels are too advanced to have been built by non-European civilisations, so it must have been Martians. And that brings me back to Atlantis, which has a hidden history more sinister than you might realise.

In the 1880s, the American politician Ignatius L. Donnelly published *Atlantis: The Antediluvian World* which claimed Atlantis was the cradle of civilisation, and also the Garden of Eden, from which all great civilisations emerged. He also thought Atlanteans were later mistaken for heroic gods, inspiring the ancient polytheistic pantheons of Greece, India, Scandinavia, etc. Donnelly's Atlantis had also been wiped out by the famous biblical Flood, save for a few who managed to escape.

Following Donnelly came the occult philosopher Helena Blavatsky. As co-founder of the Theosophical Society she argued that Atlanteans were the originators of the Aryan race in India, whose superior wisdom and technology – plus their ability to communicate telepathically (sorry, *what* ...?!) – inspired the great civilisations. Of course, whenever the phrase 'Aryan supremacy' raises its head, an alarm should be ringing in your brain. Soon came a generation of Germanic writers whose ideas became increasingly esoteric, leading to the birth of the so-called Thule Society which relocated Aryan Atlantis from India to the frozen lands of Scandinavia and the Arctic Circle, otherwise known as the ancestral home of blond, blue-eyed people.

In 1912, *Glacial Cosmogony* arrived on bookshelves. It was written by the Austrian inventor Hanns Hörbiger, who proposed the absolutely bonkers 'World Ice Theory', in which a massive explosion of ice had formed the planets. He claimed Thule–Atlantis had been home to a superior breed of mind-reading, electricity-wielding humans descended from 'divine sperma' who hitched a lift to Earth on a meteor. Their ancient reign had ended when ice moons from outer space had smashed into Earth, drowning Atlantis beneath the surging waters of the biblical Great Flood, but some Aryans had escaped into Tibet, Japan, and India – allegedly founding Buddhism and Shintoism – while another of their descendants was a chap by the name of Jesus Christ. I mean, sure, why not! This, of course, did away with the pesky problem of Jesus having been a Jew.

Hörbiger, who had no astronomy or geology qualifications, said this had come to him in a vision. It's tempting to laugh at this stuff for being so batshit weird, but his pseudoscientific ideas were deeply racist. In his theology, Nordic Aryans were a superior species to Jews, Slavs, and African-descended people, whose evolutionary descent from apes thus made them beastly sub-humans. A keen champion of Hörbiger's warped science was Hitler's right-hand man, Heinrich

Himmler, not least because World Ice Theory denied modern physics, which had been dominated by Jewish intellectuals. A pseudoscientific theory that explained the cosmos without the need for Einstein was always going to be welcomed by an antisemitic regime.

Hörbiger died in 1931, but others took up his mantle. Herman Wirth became the first president of Himmler's ethnocentric taskforce, the Ancestral Heritage Research and Teaching Society, which dispatched archaeologists, linguists, art historians, and musicologists to find proof that Aryan-Atlantean culture had once ruled. This initiative is partially the basis of the Nazi science department known as HYDRA in the Marvel comic book universe, and the baddies in *Raiders of the Lost Ark*. Sadly, in real life, neither Captain America nor Indiana Jones showed up to kick some serious Nazi arse.

Himmler was much more drawn to the occult than Hitler and other Nazis, but the Führer endorsed World Ice Theory, as shown by Eric Kurlander in his fascinating book, *Hitler's Monsters: A Supernatural History of the Third Reich*. Kurlander argues these ideas became widespread in German culture; other historians, like Sir Richard Evans, strongly confine them to the fringes. Either way, the supposed Aryan superiority of alien Atlanteans undoubtedly percolated into the fascist eugenics programme that underpinned the systemic murder of 11 million people during the Holocaust. My great-grandfather being among them.

So, when people claim ancient monuments were built by aliens, they're not only denying the engineering ingenuity of non-European civilisations - stripping these people of their own proud history - but they're also drawing ideas from a poisoned well; one polluted by the toxic ideology of the Third

Reich. And so, as naive as it may be, I really wish people would stop with all the *Ancient Aliens* bollocks, not least because the story of Atlantis was simply Plato trying to win an argument about why democracy is the absolute worst!

CHAPTER 2:

ORIGINS & FIRSTS

5. **When was the first jokebook written and were there any funny ones in it?**
Asked by John

> *Question!* Which is the cleanest leaf among all the leaves in the forest?
> *Answer!* Holly, for nobody dares wipe his arse on it.

This is my favourite medieval joke. It's not brilliant, granted, but I've told it in pubs, and received a volley of mild chuckles as a reward. The premise and punchline are clear. It's nice and short. Oh, and it's about bums - and there's nothing more universally funny than bums.

The gag in question is taken from a short collection of vaguely funny riddles entitled *Demaundes Joyous* (*Joyful Questions*) which was published in English in 1511, during the early reign of Henry VIII. I'll be honest, the joyfulness offered by this text is limited. Most of these humorous riddles don't work for modern audiences, even those who guffaw at the arcane references in Shakespeare plays. The holly joke is undoubtedly the best gag in the book, and here are the next best ones as proof of the decline in quality:

Question! Who killed one quarter of the world?
Answer! Cain, when he killed Abel; for there were only four people in the world.
Question! How can a man perceive a cow in a flock of sheep?
Answer! With his eyes!

In fairness, this second joke does make me laugh because the answer is so stupidly obvious, which is a nice surprise when the riddle format sets us up to expect a clever response. It's the medieval equivalent of: *'What's brown and sticky? A stick!'* Subverting expectation is a huge part of comedy, and many of the best joke-writers are masters of pulling the rug out from under us.

For example, I've noticed recently that people on Twitter are really drawn to a dark interpretation of the famous 'why did the chicken cross the road?' joke, saying it's actually about a suicidal chicken that wants to die (e.g. cross over to the other side). This is a classic example of modern people overthinking stuff, and misunderstanding the point of this deliberate *anti-joke*. You see, it wouldn't have been delivered in isolation, but – as with the previous joke about perceiving a cow in a flock of sheep – would have been designed to follow several other cunning riddles. After numerous challenges that taxed the brain, the expectation is set up that this too is an ingenious work of devilishly delicious wordplay, making the obvious literalism of the punchline, 'to get to the other side', a huge rug-pull that hopefully elicits a grinning, tutting, head-shaking admission of, 'Oh, you bastard! You got me!'

This is the crucial thing about humour. You have to understand the context, and so many jokes operate within cultural frames of reference, which is why most historical jokes don't work for modern readers. Our world has moved on; we don't think the same, we don't fear the same things, we use different slang, the puns don't land any more, the technology changes. Comedy is cultural commentary, but culture never sits still for long.

Jokes can lose all meaning very fast. The historian Dr Bob Nicholson runs a delightful Twitter account called 'Victorian Humour', which tweets jokes from nineteenth-century newspapers and books. You'd think I'd be the perfect audience for these gags: I work in the comedy industry, I write jokes for a living, I'm a historian who is comfortable with nineteenth-century texts ... and yet, I often find these gags utterly baffling, or the punchlines are so clunkily convoluted as to sound as if they've been translated from English into Japanese and back again by a malfunctioning robot. Presumably they were side-splittingly LOLtastic at the time? Or were they meant to be crap on purpose, like the terrible jokes in Christmas crackers?

However, some topics are timeless. The oldest joke in the world is a fart gag dating back 3,900 years to ancient Sumer (modern Iraq) and it goes like this:

> (Here's) something which has never occurred since time immemorial; a young woman didn't fart in her husband's lap.

It's not bad for the Bronze Age, is it? The double negative of 'never happened' and 'didn't fart' makes it tricky to grasp at first, but it's got a lovely visual quality to its premise. We can imagine the scene of the husband's romantic ardour suddenly turning to wrinkle-nosed disgust when his glamorous young wife noisily trumps on his leg, perhaps embarrassing him in front of his friends. There's a real sitcom energy to it. It's a 'show, don't tell' kind of gag where the performance is funnier than the words on the page. Or rather, the symbols impressed into the clay tablet.

But John hasn't asked me *'what's the oldest joke?'*, rather he's demanding to know *'when was the first jokebook written?'*, and that's clearly different. A jokebook is designed to be read. The gags should work on the page, without sitcom actors interpreting them. And there should be many gags. So, how far back can we go with this, then?

The ancient Greeks loved jokes, and the funniest of their playwrights was Aristophanes (446–386 BCE). His wildly inventive surrealism and utterly filthy fart jokes were huge hits in his lifetime, and he's been performed ever since, although much of it sanitised by modern translators. But, even if his plays were an absolute riot of belching and botty-burps, Aristophanes didn't have a collection of brilliant one-liners. If you'd like to know more about ancient comedy, I recommend Professor Mary Beard's book *Laughter in Ancient Rome: On Joking, Tickling, and Cracking Up,* but I'm going to jump past the plays, poems, and pottery, and go straight to the actual jokebooks. And that brings us to 'The Sixty'.

According to the ancient writer Athenaeus – whose *Deipnosophistae* described the witty dinner party chat of a gaggle of expert philosophers – the mighty King of Macedon, Philip II (father to Alexander the Great), was a big comedy nerd who learned that the funniest jokes were to be heard at The Sixty Club, which met regularly at the shrine of Heracles in an outdoor space called Cynosarges, just outside Athens. The Sixty was a boozy philosophical gathering of sixty witty raconteurs whose material was clearly of such quality that even a rival king, several hundred miles away, felt envious to be missing out. Athenaeus tells us Philip sent them a shipment of silver so they would jot down their best gags and post them back to him. It was perhaps the first ever jokebook, written sometime before Philip's murder in 336 BCE.

Alas, The Sixty's raucous banter is lost to history. Nor do we have the jokebooks referenced in the plays of another famous writer, Plautus. But we do have a later jokebook, the *Philogelos* – which translates charmingly as *The Laughter-Lover*. Dating to the fourth or fifth century CE – when the Western Roman Empire was precariously wobbling on the verge of collapse – this book was compiled by Hierocles and Philagrios, of whom we know basically sod all. It's a collection of 265 jokes, but what's interesting about it is the recurrent use of stock characters. There are idiots, doctors, misers, cowards, eunuchs, wits, unhappy people, drunkards, misogynists, horny women, etc. It's very akin to the lazy modern English stereotypes of tight-fisted Scots, stupid Irishmen, and easy Essex Girls.

So, let's see if these jokes make you laugh, shall we? Most of the 265 are utterly terrible, to the point that I don't even understand what they're about. But some make me chuckle. I'm not going to give you the literal translations from the Greek because they're about as funny as anthrax, so instead I've tried to jazz them up with twenty-first-century, down-the-pub, idiomatic phrasing.

Right, here goes!

1. A doctor goes to the house of a grumpy man, examines him, and declares, 'You have a bad fever!' The grump replies, 'If you think you can have a better one, there's the bed. Why don't you have a go?!'

2. An idiot went swimming and nearly drowned. He swore that he wouldn't go back in the water until he'd first learned to swim.

3. PATIENT: Doctor, Doctor! When I wake up, I feel dizzy for half an hour and then I get better.
    DOCTOR: Get up half an hour later, then!

4. A man meeting an idiot said, 'Hey! That slave you sold me died.' The idiot replied, 'I swear to God, he never did that with me!'

5. Two idiots go for dinner. Out of politeness, they both offer to escort the other back to his home. Neither gets any sleep that night.

6. A tired idiot goes to bed without a pillow. Instead, he orders his slave to put a jar under his head. The slave says it'll be too hard, so the idiot says, 'Well, stuff it with feathers then!'

7. An idiot sees a friend and exclaims, 'I heard you were dead!' His buddy replies, 'And yet you can see I'm alive!' The idiot answers, 'Yeah, but the guy who told me is more trustworthy than you.'

8. An idiot is on a ship with his slaves when suddenly a terrible storm threatens to drown them all. The enslaved people start wailing in fear. The idiot turns to them and says, 'Don't worry! If I die, I've freed you all in my will!'

9. An idiot hears that one of the twins he knows has died. He walks up to the surviving brother and asks: 'Did you die, or was it your brother?'

10. An idiot is about to head into town when his friend

shouts, 'Hey, can you buy me two fifteen-year-old slaves?' To which the idiot says, 'Sure, and if I can't get two, I'll get you one thirty-year-old!'

Did any of those provoke a joyful guffaw? The fact slavery features so heavily makes them rather grim by our ethical standards, but I've heard similar versions of these set-ups in my own lifetime. So, there you go, John. The *Philogelos* isn't exactly a ceaseless snortfest, but it seems you can get a couple of giggles from the oldest jokebook in existence.

6. When was the first Monday?
Asked by Thomas

Urgh, Mondays are the worst. The great philosopher Garfield the Cat taught us that, and his wisdom is boundless. Of course, why a jobless feline developed such a specific loathing is puzzling; he's not grumpy about having to go to work, as he has no work to go to, so maybe he's upset that his owner, Jon, has to leave the house to go to his work, having spent all weekend with him. In which case, Garfield's 'I Hate Mondays' motto is actually a plaintive ode to the pangs of separation anxiety. Either that, or Garfield is furious to no longer have a human butler pandering to his lazy, lasagne-loving whims. Hmm, it's probably the latter.

Anyway, Thomas has asked a very good question, and – as with all good questions – its apparent simplicity masks great complexity. The notion that Mondays had to be invented is perhaps not something you've thought much about (unless you're a fan of the brilliant TV show *Russian Doll* and rejoice in the drug-assisted catchphrase of 'Thursday, what a concept!'). Clearly, days of the week are human inventions, much like biscuits, Smurfs, or racism. But when did we invent them? And when did they get their current names? To be totally honest, I'm going to struggle to give you absolute clarity on this one, but we can explore some of the best guesses.

A fun place to start with the history of timekeeping is back in Bronze Age Iraq. The ancient Sumerians were busy building impressive cities some 5,000 years ago and, along with the Egyptians, theirs was an advanced civilisation with a fusion of astrology and astronomy underpinning their understanding of time. More interestingly, they were also fascinated by the purity of the number seven; it crops up quite a lot in their literature. It's been suggested, therefore, that they might have been the first society to decide weeks should be seven days long, perhaps because they saw the Moon going through a noticeable phase of transformation every seven days. This is an oft-quoted 'fact' on the internet, but hard historical evidence is lacking.

Despite the doubts, please allow me another rummage in this mystery box because it's full of really interesting stuff. Bronze Age timekeeping was heavily reliant upon the lunisolar double-act of the Sun and Moon, and we know that by the time the Sumerians had been replaced – first by the Akkadians, and then by the Babylonians in the second millennium BCE – a new month couldn't officially start until the new Moon had been observed, somewhere around day thirty in the lunar cycle. We know from reports recorded in ancient clay tablets that a month might even need to stretch an extra day if it was too cloudy for a priest to stick his head out the window and spot the Moon.

This, I should add, was the religious calendar which governed the performance of sacred rituals. There was also a parallel civic calendar, in daily use by ordinary people, which was much more regular and thus allowed people to figure out repayment plans for taxes and business loans. It had twelve months of thirty days, and the only hidden complexity was this didn't add up to 365 days, so every now and again they had to chuck in a bonus thirteenth month to balance it all out.

In short, Babylonian (and then Neo-Assyrian) sacred time-keeping was based on very smart priests tracking the Sun, Moon, Mars, Mercury, Venus, Jupiter, and Saturn, but they were still figuring out the next bit, which is being able to predict what the planets would do in advance. Rather than being reliable patterns of cosmological order – what we might call the science of astronomy – they thought the movement of the heavenly bodies was the gods trying to tell them stuff about the future; this was astronomy in the service of astrology. However, after centuries of practice, in the 600s BCE predictive astronomy arrived, to be joined by the novel notion of the celestial zodiac, which then was adopted into the ancient Greek world too.

Even though the planets were known to Babylonians at least 3,700 years ago, their famous planetary names – by which I mean *Saturn's day, Sun's day, Moon's day, Mars' day, Mercury's day, Jupiter's day*, and *Venus' day* – weren't attached to the days of the week until the fourth century BCE, when Greek learning intermingled with Egyptian and Persian knowledge, thanks to Alexander the Great's ruthless thirst for conquest. Indeed, these names we use for them aren't Babylonian, Egyptian, Persian, or Greek, they're actually Roman.

However, there's another thing I need to flag up here. Scholars aren't sure when the seven-day week first arrived.

People on the internet seem pretty happy to credit the Bronze Age Babylonians, but I wasn't sure how legit this was. Given that this book is called *Ask a Historian*, I decided to take my own advice and ask a historian! So, I ran this 'fact' past Dr Moudhy Al-Rashid, who is an expert on Assyrian science and medicine, and she was much less confident in this idea. She kindly checked with her colleagues and wrote back saying:

> There is a bit of evidence that seventh days were somewhat important in some periods (i.e. Day 7, 14, 21, and 28 - obviously related to parts of the lunar cycle). Certain activities were prohibited on those days. There is arguably some evidence that in the Old Assyrian period (~2000–1600 BCE), there was a 5-day week.

The evidence for a seven-day week in Ancient Babylonia appears somewhat inconclusive. Other scholars have more convincingly argued for it being an ancient Jewish innovation which borrowed elements of earlier Babylonian tradition, but fixed them into a much more rigid system, built around a recurring holy day (Sabbath). If the Babylonian hypothesis is debatable, then we can only confidently state the seven-day week is *at least* 2,500 years old.

However, don't be fooled into assuming the seven-day week was the only available option. Though that planetary model - fusing Jewish, Babylonian, and Greek traditions - eventually triumphed, thereafter spreading into India and China, there still remained rival timekeeping systems. The ancient Egyptians squeezed a whopping ten days into their week, while in Italy the Etruscans and early Romans anticipated The Beatles by choosing eight days a week, with each day named alphabetically: *A* through to *H*. This clung on for surprisingly long in Roman history, and it was only starting to give way by the time of Julius Caesar, and was only completely abandoned in the 300s CE, when Constantine the Great made the seven-day week official Roman custom.

However, I now want to investigate an even nerdier thing about Mondays, because, strictly speaking, they actually happen on the wrong day of the week. I realise that's a bizarre thing to say, so allow me to untangle it.

Nearly 2,000 years ago, the Roman writer Plutarch wrote an essay entitled 'Why Are the Days Named After the Planets Reckoned in a Different Order from the Actual Order?' Personally, this sounds to me less like a philosophical essay and more like a drunken, 3am Google query. Anyway, you might now be thinking, 'Huh? What does he mean by "different order"?' Well, sadly, his essay got lost down the back of the proverbial sofa, but I think we can guess what he meant by his provocative title.

Plutarch was asking why the order of weekdays didn't mirror how the actual planets themselves were ordered by ancient astronomers. There was some debate among these scholars as to which planets were furthest away, and how best to order them, but sky-watchers mostly started with Saturn, then Jupiter, then Mars, then the Sun, then Venus, Mercury, and finally the Moon. In which case, the week should have started with Saturday, but then gone to Thursday, then Tuesday, then Sunday, then Friday, then Wednesday, and finish on Monday. But it doesn't. So, why doesn't it? Besides Plutarch's lost argument, two theories were put forward in other ancient texts, but the one I prefer was advanced by the Roman writer Cassius Dio. Now, stick with me here because this is a bit fiddly . . .

OK, so, Cassius Dio said every week was split up into 168

hours, and each new day was created after a twenty-four-hour period had elapsed (something we get from the Babylonians who preferred doing their calculations based on multiples of twelve, hence why our hours are sixty minutes long). The first hour of each day was said to be the most important hour, or the *controller*, and this would be dedicated to a god-planet, meaning that day would take the god's name. Put simply, Hour 1 on Day 1 was given to Saturn, the farthest away, thereby creating *Saturday*. The second hour would be given to the next furthest god-planet, Jupiter, and the third hour to Mars, and so on, until the eighth hour returned once again to Saturn because there were only seven planets to choose from.

However, by the time they got to the twenty-fifth hour, that was technically a new day, so whichever god was given that particular sixty-minute slot got to be the controller, and have that new day named after them. Inevitably, that god was different to whichever one had been honoured the day before, because seven doesn't easily divide into twenty-five. In which case – even though ancient astronomers listed the order of the heavenly planets as being Saturn-Jupiter-Mars-Sun-Venus-Mercury-Moon – the days of the week, when arranged by the twenty-four-hour controller system, instead came out as this:

> *Saturn's day, Sun's day, Moon's day, Mars' day, Mercury's day, Jupiter's day, Venus' day.*

Intriguing, right? So, yeah, in the English-speaking world Monday is obviously the Moon's day, and its spelling derives from the Old English word *Mōnandæg*, which itself perhaps came from the Old Norse word for the Moon god, *Máni*. Obviously, the Romans didn't speak Old Norse, and their Latin word for Monday was *Dies Lunae* (as in 'lunar day') and that's where the French word *Lundi* comes from.

In fact, English and French differ a fair bit on naming traditions because the old Germanic gods dominate the Anglophonic days of the week – Tiw gets Tuesday, Woden gets Wednesday, Thor gets Thursday, Freya gets Friday – but the French stick with the Roman tradition of *Lundi* (Lunar), *Mardi* (Mars), *Mercredi* (Mercury), *Jeudi* (Jupiter), *Vendredi* (Venus), and *Samedi* (Saturn). It's only Sunday (*Dimanche*) where they abandon the pagan polytheism and embrace a Christian idea – *Dimanche* comes from *Dies Domenica*, meaning the 'Day of the Lord'. The Spanish, however, instead assign the Sabbath day to Saturday, not Sunday, and so call it *Sábado*.

So, Thomas asked *'how old are Mondays?'* Well, it turns out the seven-day week is possibly older than Mondays themselves, because the ancient Jews didn't name their seven days after the planets, they just numbered them one to seven instead. In which case, it wasn't until maybe 2,400 years ago – when we know the Neo-Assyrian zodiac was definitely up and running in the Greek world – that the Moon formally got a day named after it. I hope that answers your question, Thomas? Although, I'll be honest, there's still a nagging thing I feel I need to share with you.

You see, if Garfield hates Mondays because they're the first day of the work week – meaning his owner Jon leaves him after a nice weekend – then these 2,400-year-old Mondays don't technically match his catty-criteria at all! No, the polytheistic Romans (with their eight-day weeks) actually started their week on a Saturday, and declared Monday to be the third day. Then Christianity arrived, and borrowed the Jewish idea of a Saturday Sabbath, but Christians shunted it to Sunday, which they said was the day that God rested after creating the Earth. This made Sunday both Day 7 in the Creation story *and* the first day of the new week, which is a bit confusing . . .

Monday thus went from being the third day of the week to becoming the second, after Sunday, and this has remained a common cultural tradition in several countries, including America. However, the rise of nineteenth-century industrialisation and the changing rhythms of mass labour helped to bring about the creation of a new temporal concept – the weekend – in the early 1900s. This created a newly secular, more economic meaning for Mondays – one which is now officially upheld by the International Organization for Standardization – and so it is now Mondays, not Sundays, which signal the start of the week.

In which case, Thomas, even if Mondays are at least 2,400 years old, the ones Garfield hates are actually only a century old!

7. What conditions did the Windrush generation meet when they arrived in the UK?
Asked by Marsha

On 21 June 1948, a ship named *Empire Windrush* docked at Tilbury in Essex. Originally a German passenger liner, the British had acquired it as part of Germany's war reparations, and now it was transporting people from the Caribbean and Central America to the UK. At the time, the ship was said to be carrying nearly 500 people, but documents in the UK National Archives suggest it was actually 1,027 passengers, 802 of whom had been residents of Caribbean islands.

Most of these passengers were embarking upon a new life in the 'Mother Country', having been lifelong citizens of the British Empire. They were the first members of the so-called 'Windrush generation', a community of predominantly African-Caribbean immigrants who came to live and work in the UK between 1948 and 1973, and whose numbers steadily swelled to 125,000 by 1958, and kept growing to perhaps half a million thereafter (the statistics are frustratingly vague).

Contrary to popular understanding, the Windrush generation also encompasses people from South Asia, Africa, and other parts of the Commonwealth who came to the UK prior to 1973. However, because the iconic ship is intimately connected to the Caribbean story, and because it's the history I know best, that is where I'll focus my answer.

A second popular misunderstanding is that 1948 was the first time Black people had arrived in the UK in large numbers. In fact, *Empire Windrush* was the third ship to bring 100-plus African-Caribbean immigrants, after the *Ormonde* and *Almonzara* in 1947. And during the Second World War, Britain had played (a mostly) grateful host to 150,000 Black American troops. Even more interesting, perhaps, is that there were already at least 20,000 Black people living in England during the late 1700s, and indeed a Black presence going back to Roman times.*

The people of the Windrush generation chose to emigrate to the UK for various reasons. The pull factors included a sense of British belonging - some had served in the RAF,

---

* For more on these stories, I highly recommend Professor David Olusoga's excellent narrative history *Black and British*, and also the essay collection *Black British History: New Perspectives*, by Professor Hakim Adi.

navy, or army during the war; others felt an emotional connection to the empire in which they'd grown up. For many, they were attracted to the dream of a better life. But this wasn't just wide-eyed romance, it was often hope fuelled by desperation.

Britain's Caribbean colonies were economically underdeveloped. They had barely moved on from the plantation system, even a century after slavery, and the Great Depression exacerbated all the systemic problems. In the 1930s, there were frequent labour strikes, hunger marches, and outbreaks of violence on the islands. People were desperate for a better standard of living.

In 1938, the British government sent out a royal commission to investigate. Its findings – detailed in the so-called *Moyne Report* – were delayed by the eruption of global war, and, even then, the report's 1945 publication disappointed with its watered-down recommendations. Some modest funds were redirected to the Caribbean, but not nearly enough.

Meanwhile, life in the UK wasn't exactly a bed of roses either. After the fight against fascism, the economy was in the toilet and there was a shortage of workers to the tune of a whopping 1.3 million unfilled jobs. Every time African Caribbeans opened a newspaper, they were bombarded with 'help wanted' adverts from across the waves. Why wouldn't jobless, frustrated people in British colonies look at those adverts and think 'London is the place for me!'?

You might assume such people offered a potential source of eager manpower, so presumably the UK's Labour government was delighted to welcome them, right? Not quite. Instead, they sent a delegation from the Ministry of Labour to try to crush the rumours of job opportunities – a rather foolish effort given they were printed in black and white – and to convince the people of Jamaica, Trinidad, Barbados, etc. that Britain didn't need them, didn't want them, and they'd probably all hate the cold winters and get nasty chest infections if they turned up, so it was best not to come.

The scare stories didn't work. The Prime Minister, Clement Attlee, was less than pleased when *Windrush* was allowed to set sail, and he wondered if it might be diverted to Africa instead. When the ship docked in Tilbury, all those aboard had British passports, so there was no legal excuse to turn them away. The official policy now changed; it was decided that these immigrants would be dispersed as far and wide as possible within the UK, in the hope that this would prevent communities being forged and discourage any future boatloads of people.

Marsha has asked about the conditions that met those arriving in the UK. Well, upon disembarking, most of the passengers headed off to jobs and contacts they'd already secured in advance. The remaining 230, or so, were shunted off to a disused bomb shelter under Clapham Common. They descended into the subterranean gloom on a rickety wooden lift, and were issued with thin blankets and bunk beds. Local volunteers served them hot tea and measly rations of bread in dripping. It was quite the shock for those used to tropical sunlight. As one of the new arrivals later recalled: 'We curiously eyed the network of poorly lit, clammy, musty tunnels that had been offered as residence. It was primitive and unwelcoming, like a sparsely furnished rabbit's warren. But in a strange new land there were few alternatives.'

It wasn't much of a warm welcome, and that was no accident. Internally, the Labour government wanted rid, fearing that racial disharmony would only add to Britain's mounting problems, with one MP declaring that mass immigration from the Caribbean: 'is likely to impair the harmony, strength and cohesion of our people and social life and cause discord and unhappiness amongst all concerned'. The Colonial Secretary, Arthur Creech Jones, reassured his anxious colleagues by predicting the bitter British winter would do the job for them. However, it soon became clear these hard-working immigrants were very much wanted by British employers, and they weren't going anywhere.

The journalist Peter Fryer – later to write the landmark book *Staying Power: The History of Black People in Britain* – met many of the passengers as they disembarked at Tilbury, and he then contacted them again three weeks later to see how they were getting on. He reported that: '76 have gone to work in foundries, 15 on railways, 15 as labourers, 15 as farm workers, and 10 as electricians. The others have gone into a wide variety of jobs, including clerical work in the Post Office, coach-building and plumbing.' At this early stage, the Windrush generation comprised mostly men. And yes, contrary to Arthur Creech Jones' prediction, the men endured their first British winter and were still hard at work when the daffodils sprang into spring bloom.

Initially, African-Caribbean immigration was very limited. Another 180 people arrived in Liverpool aboard the *Orbita* in October 1948, but then it was just a few hundred people for the next couple of years. With Winston Churchill now back in power, 1951 saw a rise to 1,000 immigrants per year, reaching 3,000 by 1953. At this early stage, it was mostly men making the journey. It was too expensive for whole families to go, so those left behind had to scrape together the ticket money and join their loved ones when they could. However, 1954 brought a big jump up to 10,000 immigrants. Why the sudden surge?

Most likely, living conditions in the Caribbean were still dire, despite the *Moyne Report*'s findings. With no hint that Britain would grant these colonies their political independence, and with no benefits offered to the many unemployed, their only hope was to leave their families behind and get on a ship. 1955 saw 42,000 people make the trip, a rate which then held steady as major employers, such as the National Health Service, hotels, and London Transport, began recruiting African-Caribbeans to work in hospitals, hospitality, and on the buses.

Life in the UK promised so much to those raised in a colonial education system that taught how the Mother Country was a place of prosperity, sophistication, and decency. The streets were meant to be paved with gold! In reality, the UK was a battered nation, still rationing its food until 1954, and the jobs on offer were often low-skilled. Peter Fryer found that more than half of the Caribbean immigrants in 1950s London were overqualified for their new roles. They were working night shifts, doing manual labour, cleaning the streets, or working in service jobs that white people didn't much fancy. And yes, to top it all off, the weather *was* crap.

In general, many of the Windrush generation felt a similar emotion. In his book, the historian Professor David Olusoga notes that the most-used word in memoirs was 'disappointed'. People who thought of themselves as British felt disrespected by the menial jobs on offer. Above all, the necessity of finding places to live proved frustratingly hard. Many immigrants were refused lodgings by landlords, sometimes with overt hatred in their voices, but more commonly with faux commiseration that the room was inexplicably no longer available. Such exhausting discrimination helped drum up business for ruthless slumlords who pretended to be supportive to the

Black community but then revealed themselves to be exploitative bastards; the most notorious was Peter Rachman.

There was also increasing tension as more Black faces were seen in British streets. The historian Dr Amanda Bidnall has shown that UK media representation of the Windrush generation had initially been positive. From the 1940s until mid-1950s, the newsreels and newspapers had warmly described people from the colonies as being proud patriots doing their bit for Blighty. But once annual immigration hit 42,000, the mood rapidly changed. Casual bigotry was rife. African-Caribbean people were commonly believed to be backwards, illiterate, diseased, sexually aggressive, and sometimes even cannibals. Interracial friendships or romances with white people were seen by many as disgusting and dangerous.

Resentment and racism now bred violence. A young Jamaican named Wallace Collins had a fairly standard experience when, on his first weekend in London, he was called the N-word and had a knife pulled on him. In Nottingham, in 1958, the St Ann's riots brought horrific attacks, as a small group of Black people were targeted by a huge gang of blade-wielding thugs. It allegedly broke out in a pub when a Black man was seen chatting to a local blonde-haired, white woman. By the time the police arrived, 1,000 people were involved, and many horrific knife wounds needed stitching up.

The following week, the infamous Notting Hill riots erupted in west London. Once again, it began with a hostile crowd gathering around an interracial pair, a Black man and his Swedish wife. She was assaulted the next day, for supposed crimes against her race, and then a group of 400 white men – many drawn from other parts of London – began chanting racist slogans, attacking African-Caribbean people in their homes, and firebombing Black businesses.

Many of the victims recalled getting little sympathy from the police, even when the violent perpetrators were caught and charged. Senior officers tried to write the whole thing off as the fault of ruffians, not racists, despite extensive testimony from victims and on-duty police officers. There was a concerted effort to suppress the shameful truth that Britain was home to such open bigotry.

For the victims, this added up to more than just disappointment and disillusionment. It was a betrayal – the rhetoric of the 'Mother Country', and of inclusive Britishness, had proved a mirage. An immigrant named Baron Baker later recalled in an interview: 'Before the riots I was British – I was born under the Union Jack. But the race riots made me realise who I am. They turned me into a staunch Jamaican. To think any other way would not have been kidding anyone else more than myself.'

The shocking violence of the Notting Hill riots was widely decried, but the media and some politicians were still happy to stoke anti-immigrant division. Even great statesmen were thinking it; three years earlier, in 1955, Harold Macmillan had noted in his diary that Winston Churchill had privately mused about 'keep England white!' as 'a good campaign slogan!'. More infamously, Enoch Powell's 1968 'Rivers of Blood' speech – in which he opposed mass immigration – saw him sacked from his shadow cabinet post, but it made him a popular politician among core Conservative voters.

This was Britain's story half a century ago. But, sadly, modern politicians have continued to fail the Windrush generation. Marsha asked about the conditions they faced on arrival, but it's much more recent history which has proved an even greater betrayal – and it's not just African-Caribbean immigrants who have been let down. In 2018, the Windrush scandal broke when the *Guardian* newspaper revealed the UK Home Office was denying rights to, and even deporting, vulnerable people who'd come here from the Commonwealth and colonies before 1973, even though they were rightful, long-standing citizens. Theresa May's anti-immigration policy of creating a 'hostile environment' made their lives miserable with thoughtless, cruel, and - as it turned out - unlawful harassment. At least eleven people were deported from their homes, and died in exile, while still fighting for an appeal.

So, Marsha, I'm ashamed to say the Windrush generation came to my country to offer their help in rebuilding it, only to be failed twice by those who were meant to protect them.

8. When did birthdays start being a thing people celebrated or even remembered?
Asked by Anna

I don't know about you, Anna, but I've never been one for birthdays. Or, at least, not for my own. I'm a tremendous advocate of cake, and everyone likes getting gifts, but - in all my thirty-eight years on the planet - I've filed very few birthday memories in my memory banks, apart from two rather emotional ones: my twenty-first, when I awoke to discover a lump on my testicle (and immediately decided I was dying), and my thirtieth, which was a genuinely uplifting day of celebration with friends and family after I'd survived a long period of suicidal depression.

Birthdays are a celebration of life, but somehow - in my stupid brain - they symbolise the inevitability of death. And this isn't me just being a miserable, misanthropic git who's terrified of the ageing process (OK, it's partially that . . .), but also it seems I'm continuing an ancient tradition that stretches back at least as far as early Jewish custom. According to the Talmud (the key law-giving text in Judaism), the great prophet Moses died on his 120th birthday. This idea of a pre-programmed deathday – in which a person completed their allotted time and then immediately conked out, like a piece of software reaching the end of its product licence – was continued in early Christian theology too. Jesus Christ is said to have died on the anniversary of his miraculous conception, 25 March, which was also the anniversary of God apparently saying 'let there be light' to kickstart the planet.

And just as a bit of unrelated mortuary trivia, we can add William Shakespeare, Ingrid Bergman, the Caesar-stabbing Roman conspirator, Cassius, and Raphael (the Renaissance artist, not the Ninja Turtle) to the list of people whose birthdays took a terminally downbeat turn. Cassius lost a major battle and killed himself using the same dagger he'd plunged into Caesar's body, whereas Raphael's death was blamed on having too much sex with his girlfriend. I think we can agree which is the better way to go.

But let's get back to the first person to remember their birthday. We don't know when Moses walked the Earth – assuming he was even a real historical figure? – but various scholars have suggested he was born in the 1300s BCE, and lived into the 1200s BCE. This probably makes 120-year-old Moses the oldest person on record to have known when their birthday was, in both senses of 'oldest', though we don't know if he did anything to celebrate it. Chances are, he was just too knackered from being ridiculously ancient. Imagine the arthritis in those knees after that lifetime of desert-wandering and mountain climbing!

For knowable birthday commemorations, we might have to look instead at Moses' famous adversary. According to the Book of Exodus, an almighty Egyptian Pharaoh cruelly enslaved the Jews and made them build his cities and monuments. But which specific Pharaoh are we talking about here? Well, modern scholarship tends to poke the accusatory finger at the most famous of them all, Ramesses the Great, who was indeed very fond of building whacking great cities filled with whacking great statues of himself.

We're not sure whether Ramesses marked the day of his actual birth, or the day of his *divine* birth – i.e. the day he became a ruling Pharaoh – but he seems to have commemorated at least one of them, which I'm chalking up as a technical birthday. However, the story that often gets told to tourists is that Ramesses celebrated both of these days, and even had the architects of his great temple at Abu Simbel carefully place its orientation so that sunlight illuminated his statue on those two days of the year, one in February and the other in October. The sunlight is true, the statues really do light up beautifully on those two days, but there's zero evidence for any birthday link.

Of course, prophets and Pharaohs were rather fancy sorts, and it's hard to know whether your average Joes and Janes were also popping on their party hats and making a wish as they blew out the candles. If we want evidence of birthday celebrations among the general population, then the ancient Greek historian Herodotus tells us that, 2,500 years ago, the Persians – whose massive Achaemenid Empire spread throughout the Middle East and Western Asia – went big on their birthdays, regardless of their social rank. He wrote: 'The day which every man values most is his own birthday. On this day, he thinks it right to serve a more abundant meal than on other days: oxen or horses or camels or asses, roasted whole in ovens, are set before the rich; the poorer serve the lesser kinds of cattle. Their courses are few, the dainties that follow many, and not all served together.' Sounds tasty.

And it's worth noting that the Romans were especially keen on celebrating not only their own birthdays, but also those of their friends, patrons, bosses, and emperors. Indeed, it was important to make sure others knew you were thinking of them, particularly if they had some influence over your family or career. Some of the surviving Roman birthday messages seem rather po-faced, over-sentimental, and wordy; I'm not sure Romans would've enjoyed those cheekily rude birthday-banter cards that you can buy in WHSmith's that call the recipient fat, past it, or ugly.

Saying that, there's an unintentionally funny message from Emperor Marcus Aurelius saying: 'on birthdays, friends undertake vows for the one whose birthday it is; but because I love you just as I love my own self, on this birthday of yours I want to offer prayers on my own behalf'. Gee, thanks, Marcus! Have you bought yourself a present too? What a cheeky sod! Given this aspect of his personality, Marcus Aurelius presumably got to enjoy multiple birthdays: his own actual day of birth (*dies natalis*), those of his various friends and family members, the occasional birthday commemorations of past emperors, and a commemoration of the day he became emperor (*dies imperii*). With all those special days in the calendar, he must have been absolutely swimming in book tokens and wrapping paper, most of which he presumably gave to himself.

So, Romans were avid birthday fans, but how did they celebrate them? Well, we know they hosted parties because archaeologists excavating the military fort at Hadrian's Wall

- the northern defensive screen designed to keep the Picts out of Britannia – have found the so-called Vindolanda tablets, which are messages between soldiers, their families, and their contacts. One of these messages is an invitation to a birthday party, sent by a woman named Claudia to her pal Sulpicia. As for what went on at such parties, we believe they likely involved gift-giving, wearing a special white tunic, the ritual burning of incense, the munching of little cakes, a potential animal sacrifice, and the chucking of special wine onto a hissing fire. Sounds fun, though Roman birthdays were more sacred rite of passage than a cheerful day of partying.

And, before I wrap up, here's a final surprising thought on the history of birthdays – Anna, I presume your birthday is on the same day every year? Well, in the past, some people's birthdays had to move; George Washington spent the first two decades of his life celebrating on 11 February, but for the rest of his life it was on February 22nd. This wasn't just a strange personal whim, but rather a consequence of Britain (he was still a proud Brit in 1752) moving from the old Julian calendar to the new Gregorian one, which meant eleven days vanished to make room for the new system, with 2 September being followed by 14 September.

This meant Washington's twenty-first birthday had to be relocated to 365 days from his last one, taking into consideration those eleven missing days. A full calendar year from 11 Feb was – weirdly enough – 22 Feb. It meant, technically, he got a week and a half younger on the day that he got a year older!

CHAPTER 3:

HEALTH & MEDICINE

9. How did women manage their periods before the twentieth century?
Asked by Ally

Aha, the old faithful! When I toured my first book, which was about the history of daily life, this was the most common query whenever I did public events. And yes, I do have an answer for you, Ally, but I always like to couch it in hand-waving caveats because there have been roughly 54 billion women since the dawn of our species, and a sweeping answer risks overgeneralising so many different individual experiences, particularly when not every woman will have experienced menstruation. But, then again, this book would be thunderously boring if I met each question with an arse-covering excuse. So, let's have a crack at it, with the proviso that I'll limit my answer to the areas I know best – Europe and America.

Let me begin by saying that for many women, 'dealing with their periods' wouldn't just have been a monthly routine of bleeding and discomfort, but also a worrying question of fluctuating health. In the pre-Antibiotic Age, when food could be scarce and diseases were endemic, many people suffered from vitamin deficiency, illness, stress, or sheer exhaustion. The historian of ancient medicine, Dr Kristi Upson-Saia, once told me on a podcast that Romans experienced bad health as the norm, and good health as an enjoyable rarity. Indeed, Dr Alexandra Lord has shown that impoverished women in eighteenth-century Edinburgh were well used to missing their periods in the winter months, when nutritious food was hard to find. In 1671, the midwife Jane Sharp had noted that periods: 'sometimes flow too soon, sometimes too late, they are too many or too few, or are quite stopt that they flow not at all . . .'

Back in the ancient and medieval world, such hormonal imbalances weren't well understood. Influential thinkers, such as the illustrious Greek physicians Hippocrates and Galen, comprehended the body as a system of four *humours*: black bile, yellow bile, phlegm, and blood. These not only determined someone's personality or 'temperament' - we get the emotional adjectives *melancholic, sanguine, phlegmatic,* and *choleric* from these ideas - but a humoral imbalance would cause disease. In general, the internal organs were thought to get too hot, too cold, too moist, or too dry. The usual cure was changes in diet, or therapeutic bloodletting, to bring the body back into its natural balance.

Hippocratic tradition (which was later influenced by Aristotle) argued that men ran hot and dry - making them more inclined towards violence - but it also made their bodies more efficient at excreting unwanted impurities through uri-nation, defecation, sweating, nosebleeds, beard growth, and by having big, blue, chunky veins. Women were said to run cool and moist, and were thus incapable of having nosebleeds, didn't grow beards, had small veins, and didn't digest food as well as men. Therefore, the only way to purge the bad stuff from their bodies was through the womb. But if the body was purging it, then it wasn't good for the body, and if it wasn't good for the body, then it was clearly dangerous, right?!

Such thinking seems to have influenced religious doctrine too. In the Hebrew Bible, Chapter 15 of the Book of Leviticus describes bodily emissions as impure and unclean, while Orthodox Judaism's traditional Halakha laws prohibit a menstruating woman from sexual activity until she has slept on white sheets for a week, and then bathed in the sacred mikvah bath. Similar rules apply in certain traditions of Islam and Hinduism. Menstrual blood hasn't just been seen as a bit icky, it was widely understood as a pollutant. The most outlandish articulation of this menstrual terror can be found in the outré opinions of Pliny the Elder, the big-brained Roman naturalist who died recklessly racing towards the eruption of Mt Vesuvius in 79 CE when everyone else was running away. He described period blood as if it were toxic spillage oozing from a chemical dump, saying it: 'turns new wine sour, crops touched by it become barren, grafts die, seed in gardens dry up, the fruit falls off trees, steel edges blunt and the gleam of ivory is dulled, bees die in their hives, even bronze and iron are at once seized by rust, and a horrible smell fills the air; to taste it drives dogs mad and infects their bites with an incurable poison'. Obviously, if a bloke sat next to you on a train and started whispering that bee colonies are collapsing because his sister is on her period, you'd definitely change seats.

These Greco-Roman ideas clung on through the centuries like limpets, giving rise to the popular medieval belief that men could be cursed with just a glance from a hormonal woman, and that a drop of menstrual blood might burn the sensitive flesh of the penis, as if it weren't just the lining of her womb but the acid coursing through the veins of the

terrifying xenomorphs in *Alien*. If a medieval fella were brave
enough, or horny enough, to impregnate a woman during
her period, then it was claimed she would gain strength from
his heat, but he would be gravely weakened from her cool
moistness, and the resulting baby would be meek, deformed,
and ginger (sorry, redheads . . .). What's more, the risk didn't
dampen with age: peri-menopausal women were believed to
have stored up a dangerous excess of menstrual blood during
their lifetime, meaning the poison vapours might escape
through their eyes and nose, and contaminate – or even kill –
nearby babies and animals.

Of course, many women in the past would've suffered
painful period cramps. The medieval abbess Hildegard of
Bingen explained these as Eve's punishment for convincing
Adam to munch Eden's forbidden fruit. I mention this because
some medieval nuns managed to completely suppress their
menstrual cycle through extreme fasting and bloodletting,
and this was interpreted as God rewarding their impressive
holiness with a reprieve (. . . a *repriEVE?*) from hereditary
punishment. We now know that this was simply the result
of extreme anaemia, or so-called 'holy anorexia', which did
to their bodies what winter malnourishment did to those
eighteenth-century Edinburgh women I mentioned earlier.

Despite all these scare tactics, ancient medical writers
argued that a regular menstrual cycle was vital to female
health, so, for many women, getting their unreliable reproductive systems back into gear was the priority. Medical
manuals often advised married women with menstrual issues
to simply have regular sex and eat healthily, which sounds
like good advice to me. If that didn't work, gentler remedies
included potions of herbs and wine, or vaginal pessaries made
from mashed fruits and vegetables – we're wandering into

Gwyneth Paltrow Goop territory here, but it's still not too bad considering where this answer will soon end up.

The barber's knife was, mercifully, the absolute last resort for irregular periods, though Hippocrates had no qualms in bleeding a young woman from the veins - all blood was the same to him - and, if that didn't work, the next best thing was to irritate the womb into action. Yes, here comes the promised weird stuff. Hippocratic advice suggested cramming beetle carcasses into the vagina, specifically *cantharides* (blister beetles) which excrete a toxic chemical that causes swelling and increased blood flow. Also known as Spanish fly, *cantharides* has the rare honour of being one of history's most infamous poisons and/or aphrodisiacs, depending on the dosage. The fact it does both strikes me as a risky bedtime gamble, but I've never been much of a thrill-seeker.

Filling the vagina with toxic beetle bodies sounds more like an extreme dare on some unethical Japanese TV game show, but ancient physicians believed it necessary, otherwise the womb would allegedly dry out and then start wandering aimlessly around the body looking for a moist organ to attach itself to. Indeed, a Greek physician named Aretaeus thought the womb was akin to an independent animal living within a human. Luckily, he thought it was sensitive to strong aromas, so could apparently be forced back into position by the patient drinking foul-smelling concoctions, or it could be lured back into place with sweet-smelling vaginal pessaries, much like a dog can be retrieved from a squirrel hunt with some tactical sausages. I guess that's what the pessaries of mashed-up fruit were for? Please don't tell Gwyneth, OK?

These treatments were designed to return women to full reproductive health. After all, producing children was an important religious and social duty. Of course, physicians also feared that any woman left untreated might suffer a build-up of maddening, menstrual blood around the heart, and this could tip her towards fevers, fits, depression, and - *shock, horror!* - overtly masculine behaviour, including swearing, anger, and voicing loud opinions. By the 1600s this was known as *hysteric affection*, later to be renamed *hysteria* (from *hystera*, the Greek word for 'womb'), although its history is rather confusing because it began as a supposed womb disorder, but, in the 1600s, was understood to be a neurological disorder affecting men too.*

So, that's what pre-modern European women were advised to do if their periods were irregular. Let's now turn to questions of menstrual hygiene when women were in good health. If you believe the internet (always a reckless thing to do), Hippocrates supposedly mentioned that small wooden sticks, wrapped with soft lint, might have been used as a primitive tampon. Sounds plausible, right? Alas, this particular claim is probably the result of a modern misunderstanding and has been debunked by the historian of ancient reproductive medicine, Professor Helen King. If tampons *were* a thing in the ancient world, we don't actually have any evidence to back it up.

But we do have decent evidence for menstrual pads being used by Roman women 2,000 years ago, and such practices

---

* These competing ideas of physiological versus emotional causation also tussled it out during the nineteenth and early twentieth centuries. Sigmund Freud flip-flopped a lot, but he decided men could be hysterics too. However, despite this, popular usage of *hysterical* is still highly gendered, and is often used against women when they're judged to display heightened emotion. But, oddly, it's also a complimentary adjective for someone who is hilarious. There's a lot of mixed messages in this linguistic mystery box.

were likely much older. After all, the technology isn't exactly complicated: recycled or low-quality cloth was held between the legs to absorb the flow, and then it was washed and reused. Throughout the ages these had various names, but the Bible calls them 'menstruous rags', while the medical historian Dr Sara Read has found that in Shakespeare's day they were also known in England as 'clouts'.

You might understandably assume the 'clouts' were stuffed into the gusset of a woman's underpants, but - perhaps surprisingly - underpants are very modern; prior to the 1800s, most European women went commando, like Lindsay Lohan in the early 2000s (but minus the horde of hostile paparazzi). So, the obvious question is: 'how did the clouts not fall down, then?' Well, we know that Queen Elizabeth I of England owned three black silk girdles which she wore around the waist to cradle her linen sanitary towels, or '*vallopes of Holland cloth*', and this sort of thing would have been easily worn by lots of different classes of women, even if silk was much too fancy for their budgets.

The other common habit was to forego such rags, and to simply 'free-bleed' into one's clothes, or onto the floor. The reason you probably don't know many people who do this now is due to the 'germ theory' revolution, in the late nineteenth century, which introduced the terrifying concepts of bacteria and viruses, and led to a great stiffening in personal hygiene. In came luxury soap brands, early deodorants, and a new genre of nagging, negging marketing designed to destroy people's self-esteem so they rushed out to the nearest shop to buy the overpriced miracle products that promised to make them happy again. Sound familiar?

In which case, an elegant Edwardian lady in the 1900s–1910s might have worn a 'menstrual apron' under her skirts - this was a washable linen nappy, held in place by a girdle/belt and joined at the rear by a protective rubber skirt to prevent the embarrassment of visible staining. To ensure undercarriage warmth and reputational decency, ankle-length, crotchless knickers were also worn beneath the apparatus. But gradually these cumbersome undergarments were phased out as a new twist on an ancient technology began to emerge – hygienic, single-use pads or tampons.

During the First World War a company called Cellucotton discovered its wood-fibre field bandages, intended for soldiers in the trenches, were also being grabbed by field nurses and stuffed down their pants. It turns out that Cellucotton had created a highly absorbent, hygienic sequel to the clout. The company got wind of this and, rather than chastising the nurses, decided to market the pads as a new commercial brand, Kotex, using advertising campaigns that highlighted the comfort and relief afforded by their reliable product. It was a wise move.

As for tampons, these were invented by the American osteopath Dr Earle Haas. His 'applicated tampon', developed in the 1920s, allowed the user to insert the absorbent diaphragm without having to touch her own genitals. It was a great idea, but he struggled to market it, so in 1933 Haas sold the patent to an industrious German immigrant called Gertrude Tendrich. She started making tampons by hand, with little more than a sewing machine and an air compressor to help her. But you know what they say about German efficiency. Before long, the one-woman factory had grown into a company called Tampax, which now claims half of all tampon sales worldwide. Presumably, Earl Haas' descendants must curse their bad luck at not having retained the stock options.

10. Has hay fever always been an allergy, or do we only suffer from it now that we live in cities?
Asked by Anonymous

I'm a chronic asthmatic with a wide panoply of exciting allergies; I wheeze in the winter, I gasp like an old man in the presence of kittens, I sneeze near horses, my eyes become waterfalls when dogs wander past, I can't eat shellfish without rapidly inflating like an airbag. Just the smell of nuts is enough to make my throat tingle, while eating them dramatically ruins my afternoon. Even methylated spirit, that purple stuff you chuck on disappointingly tepid BBQs, turns my eyes into watery traitors. My hair-trigger immune system goes off like a faulty car alarm several times per month. But, weirdly, I've never had hay fever. Chuck me in a bucket of pollen and I remain oddly unsnuffled.

Hay fever is a tricky one for historians, because it's only really been called that for the past 200 years, and diagnosing ailments from afar is never easy. We can certainly see the ghost of summer allergies in medical writings from ancient China, Egypt, and Greece, in which the authors pondered if environmental factors caused shortness of breath or irritated noses, but these were perhaps asthma and colds. In truth, our earliest evidence for historical hay fever comes from the brilliant Persian scholar, Abu Bakr Muhammad ibn-Zakariya al-Razi – also known as Rhazes – who made a convincing argument in the late ninth century that noses might get snotty in the springtime when rosebushes gave off their powerful scent. Ding, ding! Ten points to him.

But what about modern hay fever? Well, our hero in this story is the Liverpudlian physician John Bostock who wrote a medical paper in 1819 describing all the tell-tale sinus symptoms plaguing a single patient. That patient was actually Bostock himself. Since boyhood, he'd suffered with 'periodical affection of the eyes and chest', particularly in June, and he'd tried to treat it with a wide array of dramatic remedies, including bloodletting, cold baths, and opium consumption. When Bostock wrote a follow-up in 1828 – having identified twenty-eight other sufferers – he was now calling it 'summer catarrh' (as opposed to *catarrhal deafness*, which in the 1800s was understood to be a contagious disease caused by parasites in the nose and Eustachian tubes of the ears).

By this point, however, others had already read his first paper and given the condition a catchier name, 'hay fever', despite Bostock's insistence that hay was blameless, and the true cause was excessive summertime heat. Various medical investigations followed, but the most significant researcher was Charles Harrison Blackley who, in the 1870s, zeroed in on pollen as the culprit, thanks to an impressive series of experiments. He measured pollen counts in the air, the distance it could travel on a windy day, and its allergic effect even when diluted in liquid solutions. Before long, he had correctly concluded that pollen was the primary cause of hay fever. Case solved, hooray!

Actually, let's hold off on the celebrations . . .

Blackley was rightly bemused to discover that farmworkers – who spent their days being bombarded with pollen – didn't suffer with hay fever at all, whereas the spluttering, sniffling patients at his GP surgery, who lived in nice houses and read highbrow books about art theory, were peculiarly afflicted. From this, he deduced two potential reasons: either prolonged exposure to pollen made countryfolk immune, or hay fever was a disease only affecting highly cultured specimens of humanity. Obviously, he was a damn-sight closer with the first theory; unfortunately, it was the latter which caught on.

The late nineteenth century was an era of heightened anxiety for the privileged classes of Britain and America. There were novel threats to the accepted order – women were wearing bloomers, scooting around on bicycles, and demanding the vote; gay and bisexual people were being dragged through the courts for their supposed-crimes of degeneracy; and the imagined superiority of the Anglo-Saxon race was being challenged by defeats on the battlefield in Africa. New, high-speed communication technologies also seemed to be making life more stressfully frenetic. From this maelstrom of anxieties emerged an imaginary new nervous 'disease', *neurasthenia* (or *Americanitis* in popular lingo), believed to only hit well-educated people with superior intellect and breeding. Curiously, hay fever was co-opted into this same logic.

As the medical historian Professor Mark Jackson shows in his fascinating book *Allergy: The History of a Modern Malady*, having the sniffles now became a marker of racial, class, and gender division. We see this in Sir Andrew Clark's lecture of 1887, in which he claimed that hay fever: 'exhibits still further the closeness of its relationship to the nervous system by choosing the man before the woman, the educated before the ignorant ... it prefers the temperate to the torrid zone, it seeks the city before the country, and out of every climate which it visits it chooses for its subjects the Anglo-Saxon, or at least English-speaking, race'.

The American doctor William Dunbar followed up in 1903 with the racist logic of the confident eugenicist: 'the fact of exemption from hay fever of savages, and practically of the labouring classes in civilised countries ... suggest[s] that we must look upon hay fever as one of the consequences of higher civilisation'. This nasty argument built on the writings of a throat doctor called Sir Morell Mackenzie whose book, *Hay Fever and the Paroxysmal Sneezing*, argued: 'sufferers from hay fever may, however, gather some crumbs of comfort from the fact that the disease is almost exclusively confined to persons of cultivation . . . we may, perhaps, infer that the higher we rise in the intellectual scale, the more is the tendency developed. Hence, as already hinted, our national proclivity to hay fever may be taken as proof of our superiority to other races.'

You and I might sensibly theorise that those who hired servants to do all the dusting and dirty work might simply have failed to develop allergen immunity through exposure. But to the sufferers of hay fever – now thought to be a rich man's ailment – there emerged a bizarre sense of misplaced pride in acquiring such a miserable condition. Indeed, it became a point of national rivalry when the American physician William Hard boasted in 1911 that hay fever had become 'an American speciality . . . the English compete with us no longer', as if proof that American society had eclipsed its old colonial masters to become a leading civilisation worthy of relentless sneezing.

Of course, doctors had a vested interest in marketing hay fever this way. A wealthy clientele might have their ego flattered by the diagnosis of: 'you're just too intellectually sophisticated for your own good!', with the good news being that expensive wellness clinics offered a remedy. Yes, the great thing about a rich man's disease is you can charge a premium for the cure, and, by bringing sniffling clientele to the same place for treatment, therapists not only promised the alleviation of symptoms, but also created hay fever hubs for like-minded people, turning these sniffle exclusion zones into welcome opportunities for high-status social networking. Going to a hay fever retreat was not so different to summering in the Hamptons.

Those who made the most of their diagnosis, advertising their running noses as a mark of quality, were commonly mocked as 'hayfeverites' in the press, but they didn't seem to mind. Instead, in America, they rejoiced in joining the United States Hay Fever Association, founded in 1874, which had its annual get-together first in the White Mountains of New Hampshire and then at the Lake Placid Club situated in the beautiful Adirondack Mountains of New York State. The latter was, apparently, a safe haven from pollen, though ticketing certainly wasn't cheap. And nor was it a welcome facility to Black people or Jews, with the logic being that they didn't need it because they weren't deemed as racially advanced as the sneezing WASPs . . .

By 1906, there was also a new scientific terminology to chuck around - 'allergy' - coined by Clemens von Pirquet. Such a condition was a mark of distinction, but gradually hay fever rates began to climb throughout British and American society, and then elsewhere around the world, perhaps as a consequence of mass industrialisation and increased rural migration to cities, or simply because homes and humans became increasingly hygienic - with ever more soaps and disinfectants available to buy - causing immune systems to become overly enthusiastic in fighting off fake threats.

By the 1930s, 5 per cent of Americans had become inveterate summertime sneezers, and newspapers were now printing pollen counts in their weather forecasts. For the US, ragweed was the primary culprit, but in Britain it was grass pollen; in France it was cypress trees, and in Japan it was cedar trees. Hay fever rates have climbed ever since, meaning the eugenicist argument of human exceptionalism has long since evaporated. Apparently, I'm a particularly rare case because asthmatics are usually the first to succumb. It's not often I get to pat my stupid immune system on the head, but, on this occasion, I'll make an exception. Hooray for me!

11. Did European people really eat ground-up mummies?
Asked by Katie

When I was a kid, I probably devoured a few too many tales of imperialist adventure, because I recall spending quite a lot of time wondering how best to escape from quicksand or from being lowered into a massive cooking pot by chanting tribal warriors. In truth, the perils of quicksand were vastly oversold to me - I can't say leafy Surrey is particularly afflicted with such treacherous ground conditions - and my engagement with cannibalism is very much limited to watching *The Silence of the Lambs*. Regardless, there remains a long-standing, colonialist trope that cannibalism was something that only ever happened in faraway jungles. Well, if that idea sounds about right, I have two words for you: *corpse medicine*. Yes, Katie, European people really did eat ground-up mummies.

Since ancient days, and around the world, some humans have eaten each other not just because they're hungry, but in order to heal themselves by absorbing another's life-force. The Romans were certainly keen; they treated epilepsy by drinking dead gladiator blood (they believed blood from someone who had died young, and suddenly, was especially powerful), and they thought eating the liver also gave other medical benefits – Hannibal Lecter's accompanying glass of Chianti was purely optional, I presume. The same logic also applied in the 1500s, when poor people hovered near the chopping block in the hope of catching a cupful of blood from a beheaded criminal. Whether they drank it is hard to know, but there was presumably some potent reason to collect it. Other writers of the time suggested recipes for heating blood into a sticky 'marmalade', which would be a decent plot if Hollywood ever made a terrifying mashup of *Sweeney Todd* and *Paddington*.

If blood wasn't available, the Greco-Roman physician Galen, writing in the late second century CE, also recommended a broth of ground-up bones, but wisely advised that patients shouldn't be told what they were gulping down, in case it made them feel queasy. In the seventeenth century, the Irish natural philosopher and chemist Robert Boyle – one of the big names in the early years of the Royal Society – was happy to recommend the moss that grows in human skulls as a cure for nosebleeds, while skull scrapings allegedly prevented epileptic fits. His contemporary Thomas Willis preferred to mix skull fragments with chocolate; I guess that's the plot of our terrifying 'Sweeney Todd-meets-Willy-Wonka' reboot?

Meanwhile, battlefield corpses might be processed for human fat which was another common ingredient in medicines. Indeed, as Dr Richard Suggs describes in his fascinating book *Mummies, Cannibals and Vampires: The History of Corpse Medicine from the Renaissance to the Victorians*, pretty much every part of the body could be considered medicinal at various stages in European history, including a person's: 'hair, brain, heart, liver, urine, menstrual blood, placenta, earwax, saliva and faeces'.

But Katie's question is very specifically about mummies, so let's focus on that. Personally, I think of a classic mummy being an ancient Egyptian body wrapped in bandages, or a bandage-wrapped janitor trying to spook the gang in *Scooby-Doo*. I'm also willing to accept a mummified cat, so long as bandages are involved. But, actually, the word *mummy* derives from the Persian/Arabic word *mumiya*, which roughly translates as that sticky, oily pitch we call now bitumen (the stuff used in road surfacing) which was used to coat the bodies of high-status Egyptians. So, technically, it's this, rather than the bandages, which really matters.

We know that ancient Egyptian mummies were consumed as medicine from the Late Medieval period onwards, but their importation into Europe caused a shortage. Inevitably, the law of supply and demand kicked in, so various dodgy entrepreneurs decided to manufacture new mummies by oven-drying recent corpses sourced from the local Egyptian population, or shipped in from Arabia and the Canary Islands. We have warnings of these dodgy knock-offs from seventeenth-century writers, but presumably enough people carried on being duped for the practice to continue. Once purchased, the grease from the preserved mummy flesh would be added to medicinal concoctions, sometimes known as the undeservedly delightful 'mummy treacle', which could be used to treat coughs, bone fractures, open wounds, painful ulcers, gout, fatigue, the reversal of poisoning or paralysis, and whatever else ailed you.

And how does one create such a treacle, you may ask? Well, in 1651, John French wrote in his *Art of Distillation*: 'Take of Mummy (viz. of mans flesh hardened) cut small four ounces, spirit of wine terebinthinated [infused with turpentine] ten ounces, put them into a glazed vessell, (three parts of four being empty) which set in horse dung to digest for the space of a month, then take it out and express it, let the expression be circulated a month, then let it run through Manica Hippo-cratis [a cloth bag for filtering out impurities in wine], then evaporate the spirit till that which remains in the bottome be like an oyl, which is the true Elixir of Mummy. This Elixir is a wonderful preservative against all infections . . .'

John French certainly wasn't the first to offer such recipes. Mummy had been recommended in the medical treatises of the great polymath of the medieval Islamic world, Ibn Sina, who suggested blending it with marjoram, thyme, elder, barley, roses, lentils, jujubes, cumin seed, caraway, saffron, cassia, parsley, oxymel, wine, milk, butter, castor, and syrup of mulberries. I don't know about you, but that sounds sur-prisingly tasty – dare I say, it might have made for a veritable yummy mummy. I'm not saying I'm on board with eating dead people, per se, but, if I absolutely *had to*, a nice concoction of mulberry mummy would be my preference.

Equally delicious/disgusting (delete as applicable) was the somewhat legendary custom of *mellified men* in medieval Arabia. According to the later Chinese writer Li Shizhen, these were old men who sacrificed their final month on Earth for the good of others. They ate only honey, and bathed only in honey, until they were literally pissing and pooing it out like some sort of a human bee. Obviously, they then died, presumably of acute onset diabetes, and were buried for a hundred years before being dug up and eaten as medicine.

Let's return to Europe, where references to medicinal mummy-munching appeared in the English Renaissance literary classics of Shakespeare, John Donne, and Edmund Spenser. It was also commonly favoured by monarchs looking to preserve their good health. In the early 1500s, King Francis I of France was said to have carried a pouch containing crushed mummy mixed in with rhubarb, in case he got any bumps and bruises while out hunting.

However, when Francis died, his son King Henri II took the throne, and hired a new royal doctor who was not keen on the mummy craze at all. Ambroise Paré was one of the giants of sixteenth-century medicine, and an early advocate of discovering treatment efficacy through experimentation. He said he'd run a hundred tests and found that mummy was actually a very wicked cure which produced unintended side-effects of heartburn, sickness, and 'stinke of the mouth'. Charming! Alas, his bad review must have got lost in translation because, a century later on, King Charles II of England, Scotland, and Ireland was still cheerfully partaking in mummy powder and spirit-of-skull to supercharge his immune system.

We might understandably gag at the grossness of chowing down on ancient (or not-so-ancient) corpses. But Christianity had already embraced holy cannibalism in its theology; it was there in the Catholic Eucharist, where transubstantiation was believed to turn the communion wine and wafer into the actual flesh and blood of the Messiah. So, perhaps it wasn't any stranger to gulp down dried-up bits of some 3,000-year-old Egyptian? And such logic might explain why a dying Pope Innocent VIII was alleged to have drunk the blood of three Jewish boys in 1492, in what was potentially the first attempt at a blood transfusion. In truth, this story sounds suspiciously like antipapal and antisemitic propaganda, and is probably total nonsense, but I'm including it because I adore the gothic image of a vampire Pope.

Corpse medicine started to die out in the early nineteenth century, when the fascination with mummies switched from their medicinal potency to their historical significance, leading to famous mummy-unwrapping displays by Thomas 'Mummy' Pettigrew, whose book on the history of mummies is one of our key sources for the history of corpse medicine. Oh, and that's S-O-U-R-C-E, not S-A-U-C-E, just in case all that talk of blood marmalade has addled your brain. Hmmm, I'm craving mulberry marmalade now . . . is that weird? It's weird, isn't it?

12. What is the strangest (and on the surface most incredulous) medical procedure that turned out to be medically sound?
Asked by Paul

Humans have walked the Earth for quite a while now, and, in that time, we've experimented with all sorts of cures for our many ailments. Some cures worked, some were harmlessly ineffective, and some were actually dangerous (stay tuned for more on that later!). But Paul has asked a fun question about historical medical treatments which, on the face of it, appear absolutely bonkers and yet have since been scientifically proven to be effective. Well, Paul, I'm delighted to report there are quite a few to enjoy.

Let's start with the leeches. For me, the first thing to come to mind is the classic BBC sitcom *Blackadder*, in which sixteenth-century Edmund visits the quack doctor only to discover the cure for absolutely everything is blood-sucking parasites:

BLACKADDER: I've never had anything you doctors didn't try to cure with leeches. A leech on my ear for earache, a leech on my bottom for constipation . . .

In truth, such enthusiasm for therapeutic bloodletting certainly wouldn't pass muster today, but for much of history, until the 1800s, the ancient idea of the four humours (see p. 53) was held up as established medical science, meaning patients with a fever, or a head wound, or a chest infection, or just those who seemed rather poorly, might receive the standard treatment of purging excess blood. About twenty leeches would drain a pint of the red stuff.

The extensive use of pond-dwelling vampire worms might strike us as ridiculously medieval and horrifically gothic, but actually it wasn't medieval at all – leeches were only recruited in the 1500s, and medieval blood-draining was done with trusty blades. Truth be told, plenty of historical patients probably died after being drained of 40-50 per cent of their blood, including George Washington who died of a throat infection compounded by overzealous doctors (indeed, his friend Dr Thornton arrived too late, but offered to reanimate Washington's cold corpse with a blood transfusion from a lamb*). However, let's not blame the leeches for what the medical men got wrong.

Indeed, leeches have made an unlikely comeback in modern surgery – though for rather different medical reasons to their prior usage – and serve as ugly sidekicks to plastic surgeons. Their helpfulness comes from their emitting anti-clotting chemicals into the patient's bloodstream, which makes them brilliant accomplices in micro-precise reconstructive surgeries to reattach severed body parts. Repaired blood vessels often swell too much, but leeches drain that excess away, plus

---

* The prospect of a zombie George Washington would make for a bold twist on the *Resident Evil* videogame franchise – they could call it *President Evil*.

they deliver their own natural anaesthetic while they feast, so the patient doesn't feel a thing. How thoughtful!

Someone who seems to have benefited from leeching was Napoleon Bonaparte. On the eve of the Battle of Waterloo in 1815, the French emperor had a nasty case of anal piles, caused by sitting in the damp, cold saddle for too long. With an era-defining battle awaiting him in the morning, Napoleon called for his surgeon, Baron Larrey, who we suspect attached leeches to deflate the haemorrhoids and get the battlefield wizard back in the game. It wouldn't have been the first time; Napoleon had also used leeches to apparently treat his constipation.

Sticking with engorged French arses – yes, that *is* a reference to Napoleon's ego – another successful surgery that sounds barbaric, but was the basis of a procedure used today, is the lancing of an anal abscess. In the 1300s, the pioneering English surgeon John of Arderne was the go-to guy for bum-gland and fistula problems, not least because he was living through the Hundred Years' War in which armoured knights were constantly chafing their buttocks in the saddle. He wrote:

> An abscess breeding near the anus should not be left to burst by itself . . . be it boldly opened with a very sharp lancet so that the pus and the corrupt blood may go out. Or else . . . the rectum that leads to the anus will burst within the anus . . . if it bursts both within and without, then it can never be cured except by a surgeon full expert in his craft. For then may it from the first day be called a fistula.

That neatly brings us on to France's illustrious ruler, King Louis XIV. When he developed an anal fistula in the late 1600s,

John of Arderne's techniques seem to have been forgotten, and doctors could suggest no cure, so his surgeon - a brave chap by the name of Charles-François Félix - spent months conducting numerous slicey, pokey experiments on peasants in a charity hospital. I'm not sure quite how keen they were to volunteer, and it's likely some of them probably died of infection, but Félix remained determined not to make a fist of his fistula research. Eventually, he'd learned enough to construct his own fistula-bursting implement with which he took a run at the royal rump. Miraculously, the operation was a success. However, because everything King Louis did became fashionable, his courtiers then demanded the treatment themselves. A perplexed Félix sensibly declined to puncture any more anal glands than was strictly necessary.

Paul, you'll have to forgive me for the bottom fixation - I blame my working on *Horrible Histories* for this childish bent - but I have yet more bum history to share with you. Back in the first century CE, Pedanius Dioscorides was a Greek doctor employed by the Roman army. As well as being a noted pharmacologist who wrote an influential text on the use of healing plants, Pedanius also suggested using a type of electric ray, called a torpedo fish, to treat patients with a prolapsed anus. This might strike us as, at best, foolish and, at worst, utterly deranged.

And yet, a 2017 article in *The Journal of Anatomy* described how anorectal electro-stimulation 'has been reported to have a positive effect on the functionality of treated patients' and that their results showed that it 'had not only a positive effect on the structure (morphology) of all tissues associated with the rectum and anus but, more importantly, on the structural gain of the muscles . . . reinforcing the applicability of A.R.E.S as a non-invasive treatment for anal incontinence'. Bizarrely,

this means Pedanius' electric-fish bum therapy was a genuinely good idea, even if his patients understandably took
some serious convincing.

Oh, and my sincerest apologies, but I really can't move on
without briefly mentioning another anal electrocution story
that makes me cry with laughter. Fascinated by electricity,
the brilliant German scientist and explorer, Alexander von
Humboldt, conducted an experiment on himself in the 1790s;
he popped a zinc-tipped electrode into his mouth and in-
serted a silver electrode 'approximately four inches' into his
rectum. He then switched on the live current. The outcome
was hilariously unpleasant:

> The introduction of a charge into the armatures pro-
> duced nauseating cramps and discomforting stomach
> contractions, then abdominal pain of a severe magnitude
> . . . followed by involuntary evacuation of the bladder . . .

However, my fave bit is the next line . . .

> What struck me more . . . is that by inserting the silver
> more deeply into the rectum, a bright light appears
> before both eyes.

It's the 'more deeply' that gets me every time. What a maso-
chist! I suppose Humboldt was lucky he didn't get himself
killed; imagine his family giving the tearful funeral eulogy:
'Alexander died doing what he loved: auto-rectal electrocution. He will be sadly missed.'

I actually mention him here because, between 1799 and
1804, Humboldt also explored the flora and fauna of South
America. The dangers were sizeable, but had he been sliced

open by a pouncing panther, Humboldt could have relied upon Mother Nature for surgical stitches to shut the wound. This part of the world boasts a species of ant called *Eciton burchellii* which is renowned for its wide, sharp jaws. The Aztecs, and various other peoples of the Central and South Americas, used these ant jaws as primitive surgical stitches. The trick was to let them bite the skin then snap their heads off, leaving just the mandibles in place as strong staples to clamp the wound shut.

DIY needlework with decapitated ant skulls is pretty gnarly, but, if you want truly hardcore skull surgery, let's now explore the late Stone Age, when people drilled holes into each other's heads. These drillings were done to living people, but they weren't the victims of some terrifying Driller Killer psychopath; more than half of the skulls show signs of prolonged healing over several years, meaning most people survived. Why risk it, though? Presumably the hole-poking was intended to cure headaches, epilepsy, traumatic brain injuries, or mental illness. And people kept doing it. It's known as *trepanning* or *trephining*, and it's been practised across the globe, with evidence found from historical sites in Europe, China, South America, and Africa.

When the Stone Age evidence was first identified by the French medical anthropologist Paul Broca, back in the 1860s, his fellow surgeons were puzzled; their experience of trepanning - which had continued to be practised throughout history - was accompanied by high mortality rates in their patients. And yet prehistoric people living in caves were surviving the procedure. How come? What Victorian surgeons didn't know was their dirty scalpels and unwashed hands, made all the worse by treating several patients in a day, were causing dangerous post-operative infections, whereas people in the Stone Age presumably weren't queuing up their patients in such a scheduled way.

However, once germ theory was understood, and surgical antiseptics came into use, trepanning became a useful emergency procedure for head trauma patients with brain swelling. Remarkably, that means Stone Age people were possibly doing the same sort of lifesaving cranial surgery that might be undertaken today on a car-crash victim. And many were living to tell the tale.

I mentioned antiseptic there, and that's where I want to finish. In 2015, a microbiology study caused global headlines when it announced that a 1,200-year-old medical remedy could kill the hospital superbug MRSA. To the astonishment of the researchers, the combination of onion, garlic, leeks, wine, and cow's stomach bile – steeped in a bronze pot for nine days – somehow knocked out an antibiotic-resistant bacteria which kills over 10,000 people in the USA every year.[*] The original remedy, found in a ninth-century Old English text called *Bald's Leechbook*, was recommended for curing an infected eyelash follicle, but when modern researchers set about reconstructing it from the medieval recipes, they were amazed to see it rivalled the bug-killing potency of the most powerful antibiotics.

So, Paul, what we can take from this wide array of miraculous, but weird, cures is that sometimes humans got the answers right the first time around; and perhaps there are more marvellous medicines awaiting us in other long-forgotten

---

[*] Freya Harrison, Aled E. L. Roberts, Rebecca Gabrilska, Kendra P. Rumbaugh, Christina Lee, and Stephen P. Diggle, 'A 1,000-Year-Old Antimicrobial Remedy with Antistaphylococcal Activity', in *MBio Journal*.

texts? But, saying that, I refuse to put an electric eel up my jacksie. A man needs to draw the line somewhere.

13. Apart from the modern age, in which period in history would we have been best able to deal with a zombie-causing virus?
Asked by Alex

Hi Alex, I'm writing this having spent the past nine months living through a global pandemic, and let's just say the experience has somewhat coloured my opinion of governmental incompetence. In short, if a devastating zombie plague were to suddenly tear through our lives, I fear the official response would be to close the pubs an hour early and ask the public to wear bite-proof chainmail armour. Yes, there might be hordes of ravenous, flesh-eating zombies lurching through the high streets, but that's no reason to shut down the economy. Of course, it would then turn out that the contract for chainmail distribution had been given to the brother of the Minister for Transport, even though he was eaten by a zombie back in February. Cynical, me? Surely not!

Hollywood has already terrified us by showing that a zombie apocalypse would be extremely difficult to contain because infected patients quickly become threats; they don't need hospitalisation, they need decapitating, but it would surely be very emotionally traumatic to have to kill a family member, even if they were smeared in blood and bellowing, 'Braaaaaiiiiinnnns!' This widespread grief would surely mean loads of people agonising a few seconds too long, only to be fatally bitten by their loved ones, and then themselves becoming part of the problem. Zombie numbers would therefore surge, and the army would have to cull the infected population in a brutal, flame-throwery sort of way. Horribly messy.

As with the Covid-19 pandemic, urban population density would prove particularly problematic. A zombie outbreak is less of a headache in the Lake District than London. The crucial factor is the time-honoured movie fan debate about whether our zombies would be shambling lurchers who move at the pace of a wobbly toddler, or if they'd sprint at us like feral, rabid athletes. If the latter applied, a team of statistical modellers at Cornell University showed in 2015 that a capital city with a population of many millions might become an apocalyptic hellhole in a mere twenty-four hours, as the infection rate, or 'R value', skyrocketed. However, rural areas would have a lot more time to respond and adapt.

That brings me on to Alex's hypothesis: which historical society would be best equipped to handle a zombie outbreak? Firstly, let's be clear, this is a what-if question – and later in the book I'll explain my problem with those – but I'll let you off, Alex, because it's a great idea for a movie, and maybe a producer will read this and offer me a million quid for the rights. I've given this a lot of thought, and I could make cases for lots of different historical societies being the most zombie-repellent, but I'm just going to give you my least controversial answer, based on some useful criteria I've drawn up.

OK, here's the list of variables I pondered. Any historical society wanting to fight off a zombie apocalypse would probably have needed to tick all of these boxes:

- Population distribution much more rural than urban

- Widespread availability of sharp-bladed weapons for maximum head-lopping potential
- Widespread military training and functional fitness among the population
- Easy access to large bodies of water and plenty of boats (I'm assuming zombies can't swim!)
- A good supply of bite-proof protective clothing
- An ability to understand that zombie bites are how the disease spreads
- Pre-existing myths/literature that speak of the undead, so people aren't too freaked out by the concept
- Good communication networks to warn others

So, what's my answer? Well, perhaps it's because I was once a medievalist, but my mind immediately conjured up an image of zombies getting their arses kicked in the picturesque fjords of Scandinavia. Yes, if you want to cancel the zombie apocalypse, I think you're safest with the Vikings. Here's why.

Overwhelmingly, Viking society was rural and agrarian. Population estimates by archaeologists tell us that Early Medieval Scandinavian towns were often home to only a few hundred people, and even major cities – such as Bergen – welcomed only a few thousand. Indeed, some scholars have estimated over 90 per cent of people in Viking era Norway and Denmark lived outside of the urban centres. This scattering into small communities would have given the zombies a big commuting problem once they'd ravaged the central business district. They'd either have run out of people to chomp, or the townspeople would have managed to send for help before things got too scary.

Viking society wasn't as psychopathically violent as the usual pop culture portrayal; they spent much more of their

time trading, farming, reciting poetry, and fishing than running around with axes. Saying that, they weren't exactly shy
when it came to a scrap. A decent chunk of society would've
had access to bladed weapons – not just battle equipment
like swords, axes, and daggers, but also farming utensils (you
can do some nasty damage with a garden hoe if your life
depends on it!). Warriors with regular military experience
might also have had a coat of chainmail handy, with which
to protect themselves from the gnawing and gnashing of the
brain-munchers.

As well as warriors, there would have been plenty of strong
and physically fit farmers, sailors, blacksmiths, woodworkers,
and fishermen who could handle themselves in a fight. Plus,
Viking society had an underclass of enslaved people, known
as *thralls*, who would have been well used to hard physical
labour. I realise this is a long list of blokes, but it's not just
Viking men we'd have been relying on, either. In the event
of a hypothetical zombie attack, boys could have joined the
fray too, as they were likely raised with some basic martial
training, and may have been comfortable with swordplay,
spear work, javelin-hurling, archery, and axe technique by
the time they were twelve, even if manhood began properly
at sixteen.

As for Viking women, the Norse sagas tell fabulous stories
of trouser-wearing warrior women, known as shield-maidens,
who rampaged around, traversed the seas, fought in battles,
and generally had a rollicking good time. Historians of Viking
gender, like Professors Judith Jesch and Jóhanna Katrín
Friðriksdóttir, caution that these characters are more akin to
our superheroes, and don't seem representative of ordinary
women's experiences. They stress that Viking women were
empowered in other, less violent ways.

That said, there is a lot more investigative work being done on women warriors in the Viking world, and an exciting archaeological discovery recently tantalised the world's media. I say recently, it was actually first found in 1878. It's a warrior burial from Birka in Sweden, and until the 1970s it had been presumed to be a male skeleton because it was buried with multiple weapons and gaming pieces, and was found next to a military camp. However, a recent chromosomal analysis proved it to be biologically female. Oh, how the internet rejoiced; Viking lasses were as hardcore as the lads!

But then voices of caution arrived. Several experts noted the bones show no signs of battle injury, or the muscular development associated with regular physical training. Rather than a kick-ass warrior, they asked whether this woman was buried with weapons and gaming pieces because she was a political heavyweight, and they were status symbols of leadership rather than warrior ability. Or maybe she never got injured because she was just really good, or was new to combat? Intriguingly, the lead author of the study, Professor Neil Price - the author of the best book I've ever read about the Vikings, *The Children of Ash and Elm* - accepts that this likely was a female warrior, and that archaeologists will probably discover yet more case studies. But he is commendably cautious in stressing that we should consider multiple possibilities, including that - regardless of the XX chromosomes - perhaps this person lived and identified as male.

Professor Friðriksdóttir concurs, noting in her book *Valkyrie: The Women of the Viking World* that Icelandic sagas treated warrior status as masculine by default, meaning that while most literary shield-maidens were described as asskicking warrior women, some acquired male names and pronouns when they took up their weapons. Was that just a literary device, or is it a clue to how gender could be expressed in Norse society?

We can ask all sorts of questions, but we don't have clear answers. The chromosomal make-up of the Birka human remains is scientific fact, but how we interpret them is up for debate. Sadly, we cannot ask this person to speak for themselves. Nevertheless, given the archaeological and literary evidence, I see no reason to exclude either possibility: that perhaps some Vikings were transgender or gender non-conforming, and that maybe women fought as warriors.

We can definitely surmise that many Viking women were hardy, resourceful, and were often left to get on with things when the men in their lives went off to raid or trade for a few weeks. Not only did they have more legal and political influence, compared to the Anglo-Normans in England, they possibly had to deal with the occasional onslaughts of raiding parties, poachers, criminals, runaway animals, and drunken brawls. If they could handle a lairy stag party, smashed on home-brewed mead, I'm pretty sure they could have handled zombies.

Of course, fighting might not have been necessary. The other great Viking advantage was their being master seafarers with a wide array of naval longships, trading vessels, and fishing boats to hop into – indeed, they had a variety of vessels for different waters, so really could adapt to any situation. They were skilled at navigating the fjords, choppy rivers, and even the fearsome Atlantic, with the famous explorer Leif Erikson getting as far as Newfoundland in North America. With so many Norse settlements having been coastal, or established on major waterways, the simple truth is that any zombie invasion might easily have been dodged by everyone leaping into the longboats and then peppering the zombies from a safe distance with a volley of flaming arrows.

The final thing that gives me confidence in the zombie-proof resilience of Viking society is that Icelandic Vikings – who were a little different to their Norwegian, Danish, and Swedish counterparts – actually had a sort of zombie monster in their mythology. According to the *Grettis Saga,* these bloated, rotting, undead corpses were called *draugr*, and they mostly guarded their funerary treasure, but sometimes burst forth from their tombs to attack people and animals. Unlike the low-energy lurch of the classic Hollywood zombie – as if they've awoken from a night of hard boozing to discover they've slept on the toilet, and then tried to waddle forward with their trousers around their ankles – *draugr* had super-human strength and good intelligence. However, they didn't retain their human identity or memories; they were sense-less, foul-smelling bodies reanimated through dark magic, allowing them the power to shapeshift, bring darkness in the daytime, curse people, spread disease through a village, and invade people's dreams.

And how did the Norse hero, Grettir, deal with such a threat? He chopped off the head and put the skull between the *draugr*'s knees. Simple! This *draugr* idea also chimes with the medieval English tales of *revenants* – a cross between vam-pires and zombies – who were thought to be sinners whose pestilential bodies returned at night to harass their commu-nities. We know of their supposed rampages thanks to the twelfth-century chronicler William of Newburgh; allegedly, the cure was decapitation, or shoving a brick in the skull's mouth, so they couldn't bite. Such cultural fears seemingly extended beyond myth into real practice, and archaeologists have excavated medieval graves where bricks were crammed into jaws, or where heads were missing, or placed between the knees.

What this tells me is medieval people were already up to speed with how to stop a zombie apocalypse, so I've hopefully done justice to Alex's question. The much bigger question is whether any wealthy movie producers want to option my idea? Call my agent, yeah? Cheers.

CHAPTER 4:

FOOD

14. Who was the first vegetarian?
Asked by Lev

Well, Lev, I'm not a man of religious faith, but there are many people for whom the answer to this question is blindingly obvious. The first vegetarians were the first humans - Adam and Eve, the original cast of Planet Earth according to the Abrahamic faiths. The Book of Genesis tells us God plonked his new romantic couple into Eden, but left a note on the proverbial fridge saying that the plants and the fruit were the only things available to eat (apart from the fruit from the Tree of Knowledge). The animals sharing this earthly paradise weren't for chewing and weren't allowed to chow down on each other, either. Eden's lions and tigers were presumably just really into mango smoothies and kale crisps.

Of course, things went disastrously wrong, and Adam and Eve were banished. With the gift of knowledge, humans turned out to be utter bastards, and a regretful God hit the 'massive flood' reset button and wiped everything out, save for Noah and his maritime menagerie. After that catastrophe, God relaxed the rules of dining etiquette and declared meat-eating was fine, which presumably led to an awkward conversation between Noah and the delicious animals he'd

just rescued, who suddenly went from being vegan boat buddies to lunchtime prey in the space of a sentence.

In short, we can track utopian ideas of vegetarianism back
to the oldest of the Abrahamic faiths, Judaism. Scholars disagree on how old these ideas actually are; the all-important
Torah (the first five books of the Hebrew Bible, known to
Christians as the Pentateuch) was probably only written
down in the sixth century BCE, but there are definitely some
elements dating back to the time of Kings David and Solomon,
some 3,000 years ago. I suppose the key question is whether
such vegetarianism was more than just a creation myth, and
whether it was also part of daily life for ancient Jews? Given
that most meat is kosher in the ancient dietary laws, I'm
guessing it probably wasn't.

Beyond Adam and Eve, where else can we look? We know
that the majority of ancient Eurasian societies – including the
ancient Egyptians – didn't eat much meat, simply because
it was too expensive or difficult to mass-produce. Call me a
cynic, however, but I'm not sure it counts as vegetarianism if
the only reason you don't devour a fillet steak is because you
can't afford one. However, it's often stated in popular history
books that ancient Egyptian religious priests were vegetarians, for strict religious reasons of bodily purity. Is that true?
Well, it might depend on which era we're looking at . . .

We know from various tomb inscriptions that during the
Bronze Age – roughly 4,500 to 3,000 years ago – priests were
in charge of performing animal sacrifices in the sacred tem-
ples, and one of the priestly perks was being allowed to share
leftovers with their loved ones. Indeed, in 2010, a research
team from Manchester University investigated the mummified bodies of several Egyptian priests and, contrary to the
claims in some history books, they hadn't been anything like

clean-living hipsters at all. No, these dudes were basically feasting on goose-meat burgers like Vegas-era Elvis, and this fatty, fast-food diet clogged their arteries and stopped several of their hearts before they could even see fifty.

In which case, where does the popular idea of veggie Egyptian priests come from? I suspect it's from the much later period of Egyptian history, handily called the Late Period, when we know quite a lot about Egyptian culture thanks to the gossipy reports of the ancient Greek traveller and historian Herodotus, who lived until 425 BCE. At this point, Egypt had been conquered by Persia, and this coincided with the rise of spiritual vegetarianism appearing almost simultaneously in Greece, India, Persia, and China.

So, who can we identify as the big influencers in this sudden surge towards tofu appreciation? Perhaps the earliest of the vegetarian philosophers was Zoroaster (also known as Zarathustra, of Richard Strauss' classical fame), a Persian priest perhaps born in the seventh century BCE who claimed to have received a vision from the high god Ahura Mazda which told him to reform religion and society along monotheistic lines. Zoroaster abstained from eating meat and brought in restrictions on animal sacrifices, and there are still many Zoroastrians who follow suit in modern Iran.

I'm not confident enough to assert that Zoroaster was the first vegetarian in history, as that's setting myself up for a fall, but it's possible that his ideas percolated into Persian-controlled Egypt, and thus influenced the practices of those supposedly veggie priests. If so, they in turn then had their own major influence on one of the ancient world's most famous vegetarians, the Greek philosopher and maths boffin Pythagoras, who is somewhat unreliably claimed to have arrived in Egypt in 535 BCE, initially to study, before being taken hostage by the Persians and sent to Babylon. According to at least one ancient source, Pythagoras even studied directly with Zoroaster himself, though we should take that with a pinch of salt.

You might assume Pythagoras was just a boring triangle nerd, obsessed with squaring the hypotenuse, but, in addition to his fascinating work on the mathematics of musical harmony, he also became one of the weirdest cult leaders, founding his own mystical religion with over 2,000 converts. The rules were apparently pretty extreme, if we're to take the ancient sources at face value. New recruits took a five-year-long vow of silence and weren't allowed to see Pythagoras' face until they'd completed it. They also gave up eating meat – apparently because it prevented the mind from receiving prophetic dreams – plus they weren't allowed to wear animal products as clothes, or eat beans in case those beans contained the reincarnated souls of his dead friends!

Yes, fava (broad) beans were excluded from their vegetarian diet because it was basically considered a sort of strange cannibalism. In fact, one ancient story tells that Pythagoras allegedly chose to be murdered by an angry mob rather than run to safety through a bean field, because he didn't want to trample all his old, reincarnated buddies – say what you like about him, that takes real commitment to a lifestyle choice if it means dying for it. Pythagoras was so renowned for his meat aversion that veggies were commonly referred to as 'Pythagoreans' in Europe and North America well into the early twentieth century.

While Pythagoras was setting up his mystical cult in the sixth century BCE, religious vegetarianism was also growing in India, thanks to the parallel rise of Jainism, impelled by the teachings of by Nataputta Mahavira, and then Buddhism, founded by Siddhartha Gautama. Buddhism was spread across South Asia by the almighty conqueror Ashoka the Great, who renounced brutal warfare in favour of an intensely relaxed outlook. Oh, and while Buddhism was spreading through India, China was welcoming the foundation of Daoism (also known as Taoism) and Confucianism, both of which later were associated with some aspects of vegetarianism, but not as a strict rule. Indeed, we are told in one text that Confucius was so moved by a piece of music that he stopped eating meat for three months, though he returned to consuming it in small amounts.

So, we'll probably never know who the first vegetarian was, as there may have been millions of them whose lives weren't recorded for posterity. But we can certainly see that, about two and a half millennia ago, ethical vegetarianism started to spread through some of the largest empires of the ancient world, driven by influential philosophers whose ideas trickled down through wider society. People often assume modern vegetarianism is a twentieth-century thing, but it became quite popular in the UK during the early to mid-1800s, thanks to its links with radical politics, Christian socialism, the temperance movement, and early feminism.

Of course, we've recently seen a great move towards not just vegetarianism, but veganism. The intriguing question is whether this will prove an equally enduring revolution. As an ardent fan of eating baked beans on toast, I'm much more worried about the return of Pythagoreanism, and the devastating impact that would have on my lunch options. Please let me have my beans!

15. How old is curry?
Asked by Anonymous

I can offer two very different answers to this question. You can have very old, or you can have pretty recent. But, as ever, it really depends on your definition. Annoying, I know . . .

Today, curry is global: there are Japanese rice curries, Thai green curries, Jamaican goat curries, Malaysian rendang curries, Maldivian fish curries, South African bread bunny curries, and then, of course, all the celebrated South Asian classics: vindaloo, balti, tikka masala. But are they really South Asian classics? There's an argument made by many food historians that curry is a British invention, and a textbook example of so-called cultural appropriation.

Until quite recently, *curry* didn't mean anything in the many languages spoken on the Indian subcontinent. It's most likely a garbling of the Tamil word *karil* or *kari* (spiced sauce), which came into use a few years after the Portuguese navigator Vasco da Gama sailed around Africa and landed in India in 1498. In Portuguese mouths, *kari* became *caree*, and then gradually *curry*. Curiously, medieval English had a very similar word, *cury*, which meant 'to cook'. In fact, there's an early cookery book held in the British Library, written in the 1390s, called *The Forme of Cury*, which includes recipes using caraway, nutmeg, cardamom, ginger, olive oil, pepper, cloves, and saffron rice - all delicious ingredients for a decent curry - but *cury* and *curry* were totally unrelated, it's just a weird coincidence they look so similar. It's also worth noting these spices were extremely expensive luxuries; nutmeg, for example, was only grown in one place in the world, the Banda Islands of Indonesia, with a shipment arriving in England just once a year, via Arab merchants who then sold it on to Venetians.

Curry is now a British culinary obsession; in 2019 it was estimated that curry houses and takeaways were worth £5 billion to the UK economy, although at least a billion of that was me ordering too many garlic naans (it's just so delicious!). The roots of this British love affair date back to the early 1600s, when the smooth-talking agents of the newly created East India Company managed to dislodge the Portuguese from the good graces of the Mughal emperor Jahangir, who ruled much of Southeast Asia. These English merchants were increasingly given greater access to India's ports and resources, until by the mid-1700s the East India Company had bulked out into a mercantile beefcake, throwing its weight around and even assembling its own army to protect its interests and add to its landgrab. Given such extractive control over a lucrative foreign territory, many young Brits sailed off to become Company men, hoping to get rich quick.

There, many of them developed a taste for South Asian flavours. Some of these extend a long way into the past, with archaeologists having recently found the residue of turmeric, aubergine, garlic, and ginger on the surfaces of 4,500-year-old bowls excavated from Bronze Age sites of the Harappan civilisation in India and Pakistan. Those flavours sound very tasty, but what's missing, of course, was the famous heat. Indian food has always incorporated a range of spices; and although not everything grew native in those lands, there was extensive ancient trade between Asia, Africa, Europe, and the Middle East, meaning fenugreek, onions, coriander, cumin, cinnamon, fennel, and tamarind were all imported through the Silk Roads, while black pepper was sent back the other way by Indian exporters. We know, for example, that wealthy

Romans in the 300s enjoyed Parthian chicken which was heavily seasoned this way.

However, the biggest culinary transformation arrived in the decades after 1492, when Christopher Columbus went looking for a new spice route to the Indies, but blundered into the New World instead. There he found chilli peppers, which he confused for actual pepper (hence why we call them chilli peppers). Several other foods were soon encountered by Europeans - including tomatoes and potatoes - and these novel ingredients were introduced into European and South Asian cooking in the 1500s by seafaring merchants, with fiery chillies first arriving in Goa before spreading through the Indian subcontinent.

OK, so here's the big question: did curry exist before American chillies showed up? Personally, I'd fudge it and say: 'Yes, so long as we don't actually call them curries!' I'm very much a mild to medium spicy kinda guy, and coconut masala is my bag, so I'm undoubtedly a terrible judge of 'what is curry, and should it melt your face off?'. But, actually, there are plenty of mild dishes in authentic South Asian cuisine, so volcanic heat isn't essential. Rather, I'd assume it's more about the flavours, and that opens things up a bit. After all, it's not as if ancient Harappan recipes were blander than a Coldplay grime rap album; they landed their punch with a potent blend of pepper and mustard to tickle the taste buds. But can we call that curry? I feel unqualified to judge!

In which case, let's see what the experts say. According to several food historians, including Madhur Jaffrey - whose cookery books introduced Indian cuisine to many Western-ers in the 1970s - *curry*, as we understand it, doesn't predate Columbus because it was a colonial British invention that lumped together South Asian culinary diversity into one homogenous thing. Before the Brits showed up, a medieval Chinese writer had observed: 'The Indian people are very dainty in their diet – they have a hundred ways of cooking their food, varying it every day.'

But, for the British colonials, this wide array of sensory delights could be lazily summed up in a lone recipe. As the food historian Dr Lizzie Collingham describes it:

> Curry became not just a term that the British used to describe an unfamiliar set of Indian stews and ragouts, but a dish in its own right, created for the British in India. One surgeon described curry as 'a most heterogeneous compound of ginger, nutmeg, cinnamon, cloves, cardamoms, coriander, Cayenne pepper, onions, garlic, and turmeric, ground to a powder by a pestle and mortar, made into a paste by ghee . . . and added to a stewed kid or fowl.'

Not only did this sweep an entire continent's culinary traditions into one large bucket, labelled with an erroneous name that Indians didn't even use, it also asserted the dubious idea of a definitive, singular curry taste; what became known – and then was cunningly marketed – as 'curry powder'. When the East India Company men and their families returned home to Blighty and their disappointing Sunday dinners of boiled beef and soggy veg, they found themselves pining for those old Asian spices. To cater to their demands, curry powder (a pre-mixed blend of classic spices) was imported, leading to the exotic curry beginning its conquest of British tastebuds.

In 1747, one of the first middle-class domestic goddesses, Hannah Glasse, wrote the bestselling cookery book of the century, and it included the first curry recipe in the English language. Soon, curry powder was available as both delicious ingredient and medical cure. An advert from 1784 proudly proclaimed:

> The invaluable rich Ingredient, called CURRY POWDER, brought from the East-Indies by the famous SOLANDER, is NOW to be only had, in its original virtues, at Sorlie's Perfumery Warehouse, No.23, Piccadilly, near Air-street. The celebrated East-India Dishes, and most sumptuous Sauces, are made with this Powder. It is exceeding pleasant and healthful – renders the stomach active in digestion.

The first dining establishment to put curry on the menu was Norrish Street Coffee House in 1773, followed in 1796 by a working-class woman named Sarah Shade who opened a takeaway curry stand to cater to the families who'd returned from India and longed for the taste of cumin and cardamom. Shade had spent time in India, where she'd allegedly survived both a tiger attack and twice being wounded in battle, which seems to me either exceptionally bad luck, or exceptionally good luck, or maybe both?

Britain's first fully committed Indian restaurant was opened by Sake Dean Mahomet in London in 1810. Mahomet was a fascinating chap; born in India, he'd led a well-travelled life before arriving in England, where he built up a variety of high-status contacts by offering shampoo treatments (Indian head massage) to London's well-to-do. The Hindoostane Coffee House was the next step, and he aspired to an authentic Indian experience. The furniture was bamboo, hookahs were available for smoking, and Mahomet offered a variety of Indian dishes to his wealthy clientele. Sadly, the Hindoostane

Coffee House closed after barely two years. Were the overheads too steep? Was its demise linked to the ethnicity of its foreign-born owner? We don't know – but other establishments selling curry, the ones run by white Brits, fared rather better.*

Of course, the twentieth century saw a new influx of South Asian restaurateurs whose curry houses became successful fixtures in our towns and cities, but these business owners knew not to meddle with what Brits craved on a Friday night. In the classic BBC sketch comedy *Goodness Gracious Me*, a group of Asian friends raucously descends upon an English restaurant, and boldly demands, 'What's the blandest thing on the menu?!' This joke is an inversion of Brits seeking out the spiciest curry as a digestive challenge; the hotter the better. Indeed, my first experience of a group curry night was watching friends sweat through a vindaloo, their bodies overpowered by a cavalcade of chillies. I recall my bafflement at their paying good money to endure dinner as if it were a punishment, all the while pretending the oral inferno was no more taxing on the tastebuds than a Petits Filous yogurt.

Did they think the British-Asian staff would mock them if they couldn't handle authentic Indian spices? Maybe. The truth, however, is that vindaloos, tikka masalas, madrases, kormas, and the rest, aren't authentic Indian dishes at all. The famed balti, fried quickly in a steel wok, was perhaps invented in Birmingham in the 1970s, and the vindaloo – what used

---

* Luckily, Sake Dean Mahomet found his happily-ever-after when he relocated to fashionable Brighton and established himself as 'shampooing surgeon' to high-status clients, including the king himself! Indeed, such was his influence, we can likely thank him for the modern popularity of the word *shampoo*.

to be the pinnacle of face-melting heat when I had an Indian with my mates* - is a garbled mispronunciation of the medieval Portuguese meal *carne de vinha d'alhos*, which was meat marinated in garlic and vinegar. When the Portuguese landed in Goa, they had the local cooks make this vinegary Portuguese dish, but the local cooks added bonus spices. Chillies, from the Americas, joined the ingredients in the 1600s, and this Goan fusion was then reinterpreted and repackaged in the modern era for heat-seeking Brits, who ramped up the spiciness to eye-watering levels.

In short, as I promised at the start, *'how old is curry?'* is a difficult question to answer; the core elements easily date back an impressive 4,500 years. And yet, curry itself is a modern European desire imposed upon South Asia; one which has forced modern cooks of Asian heritage to please their customers by using ingredients from the other side of the world, and repeating recipes invented for eighteenth-century Brits, and using a nonsense word - *curry* - which Madhur Jaffrey called 'as degrading to India's great cuisine as the term chop suey was to China's'.

And yet, even as Jaffrey tried to move people's ideas of Indian food closer to its authentic myriad subtleties, she was still forced to title one of her bestselling books *The Ultimate Curry Bible*. So, in some ways, curry is properly ancient, and in others it's the product of colonialism. And yet for the modern cooks trying to reverse the old myths, the story is perhaps only just getting started. But given its popularity in the UK, I don't think curry - whatever we mean by that - is going away any time soon. In fact, I reckon chicken tikka masala might qualify as our national dish.

---

* Phaal is now the hottest curry available.

16. How did cooking develop? How did someone work out how to make bread, or cheese, or separate egg whites out and beat them for enough time to make them go stiff. Essentially, who invented meringue and why?
Asked by Alex

Alex, I absolutely love how your question unfolds. You start with the vast totality of all human cookery, but realise that's a bit broad, so you specify just three ingredients, but even that's quite a lot, so then – presumably, while staring longingly through the window of a patisserie shop – suddenly you decide, 'No, sod this, what I *really* want to know is what's the deal with meringues?!?' Alex, I take my hat off to you. Top-drawer question-setting!

Also, I couldn't be happier to be answering this because I adore meringues with the same salivatory enthusiasm puppies display towards slippers. To this day, my parents still commonly reference the time, twenty-five years ago, when we went to a friend's Christmas party and I became the main story. The friend was a wonderful woman named Mary and she'd baked an enormous stack of meringues drizzled with pineapple chunks, and I systematically ate thirteen in a row. The other guests watched in bemused fascination as I commuted back and forth between my seat and the dessert table, with only one meringue on my plate per journey (I didn't want to seem rude by piling them up). By my estimate, I devoured 2,000 calories, 150g of pure sugar, and an entire pineapple. I'm unsure how I swerved diabetes, but I had one hell of a sugar crash that evening.

Anyway, Alex has asked me three, or possibly four,

questions here, and I'll tackle the bread query in the next answer. As for cheese, it's a similar story; these days archaeological science moves quicker than a whippet on a moped, so this answer might already be out of date when you read it, but a team at Bristol University analysed dairy residues on a cheese-making sieve found in Poland and discovered it was 5,000 years old. There's also evidence of dairy residue on pots from northern Turkey dating back 6,500 years. This shouldn't surprise us. Cheesemaking is pretty simple; normally, you add citric acid to milk, and the resulting curdling process then separate the curds from the unwanted whey.

It's quite likely the prehistoric technique didn't involve a squeeze of lemon juice, but rather the stomachs of cows and sheep, which contain an enzyme called rennet that does much the same thing to milk. Why they thought to dip a cow-tummy in a glass of milk is anyone's guess; perhaps they punched holes in it and used it as a handy sieve, or stretched the gut into a milk storage vessel? Regardless, the curdling process meant cheese was likely edible for the high percentage of Neolithic people with lactose intolerance, meaning they got to enjoy a nutritious nibble of brie without the resulting farting and belly cramps.

As for general cookery, well, that's a MASSIVE subject, but allow me to direct you towards a recent collaboration between Assyriologists, food chemists, and culinary historians from Harvard and Yale; together they reconstructed Bronze Age recipes from Babylonian clay tablets written in cuneiform (the oldest known type of writing). These dishes, which included a type of lamb stew still eaten in Iraq today, are over 4,000 years old, and weren't just random ingredients bunged in a pot; these were the work of cooks experimenting with flavours and textures, and the tablets even include recipes from foreign cultures. Yes, even the Bronze Age seemingly had trendy food writers evangelising the simple pleasures of exotic cuisine: 'Darling, you haven't tried Elamite broth? Oh you must, it's so simple, but so scrumptious, you know?'

But enough of that, we all know what we really came for: unleash the meringues!

Let's begin with sugar. First consumed in the islands of the Pacific, ancient India is where cane sugar was first refined. You might expect it to have spread quickly - after all, it's so much sweeter than honey - but when Alexander the Great trampled his way into South Asia, planning to conquer absolutely everything, he considered sugar to be a rare medicine rather than a food, so it stayed out of European dessert bowls well until the 1000s. Instead, it was the cultures of the Middle Eastern world that developed sugar, first as a medicine and then as a delicacy for the rich. We have the nice phrase 'sugar and spice' which separates them, but they thought sugar *was* a spice. These cooks crystallised it, blended it with almonds to make marzipan paste, and became experts at refining it into a pure, white saccharine jolt to the senses.

Then came the infamous horror show known as the medieval Crusades which, amid the slaughter, had the unintended consequence of introducing marauding Europeans to the finer things in Islamic culture, including the joys of sugar. Venice got in on the sugar trade in the 1200s, and, by the 1400s, both the Portuguese and Spanish were planting sugar cane in their respective colonies of Madeira (discovered in 1419) and the Canary Islands (conquered from 1402 to 1496), which served as profitable prototypes for their later colonies in the Americas. Tragically, the surging desire for sugar caused another horror show: the brutal African slave trade, which provided the coerced labour that turned Brazil into a goldmine, soon to be emulated by the British in Barbados, where sugar was called 'white gold'.

This was the geopolitical context which made sugar much more widely available in the 1500s,* so it's no coincidence that this was when meringues began to appear in cookery books. Well, I say *meringues* . . . it's actually rather open to interpretation. The food historian Alan Davidson echoed others when he wrote that the precursor to meringue was a foamy, unstiffened confection of sweet cream and egg whites known as 'snow'; here's a later recipe, translated from French in 1653:

> Boile some milk with a little flower water well allyed, then put it in more than half of one dosen of whites of eggs, and stir well all together, and sugar it. When you are ready to serve, set them on the fire again and glase them, that is, take the rest of your whites of eggs, beat them with a feather, and mix all well together; or else fry well the rest of your whites, and powre them over your other eggs. Pass over it lightly an oven lid, or the fireshovell red hot, and serve them sured with sweet waters.

One technical thing to note, European people didn't have forks in the 1500s – they came into use in the 1600s – so chefs had to whip their egg whites by passing them through a sieve, or by agitating them with a bundle of birch twigs, either rolled between the palms of their hands or just gripped as a sort of hipster whisk.

---

* The brutal efficiency of the slave-powered plantation system allowed for sugar consumption to massively increase in Europe. In 1700, a person might consume 4lb per year, but it had rocketed to 18lb by 1800. By 1750, sugar made up a fifth of all European imports.

We then get to 1604, when a wealthy Englishwoman named Elinor Fettiplace scribbled a recipe book - and it was later annotated by others in her family as it was passed down through the generations - describing what is, to my expertly attuned meringue radar, something rather different to my Christmas party fave:

> Take a pound & a half of sugar, & an handfull of fine white flower, the whites of twelve eggs, beaten verie finelie, and a little annisseed brused, temper all this together, till it bee no thicker than pap, make coffins with paper, and put it into the oven, after the manchet is drawn.

Several food historians have suggested this was an early meringue, because of the whipped eggs and sugar, but it also used flour and the end result was called 'manchet' (a type of bread), so while it might have looked quite . . . er . . . meringuey (is that even a word?), there's an argument for disqualifying it.

However, later in the century we do see the arrival of our first stiffened meringues, commonly called 'sugar puffs' - sounding much like a modern breakfast cereal - but they were also confusingly called 'biscuits'. So, when did the word *meringue* first emerge? The classic story is that a chef called Gasparini invented them in 1720 while working in the Swiss town of Meiringen. Others assert it's derived from the Polish word *marzynka*, and was invented for King Stanislas I Leszczynski, whose daughter introduced it to the French when she married King Louis XV in 1725.

These are both charmingly impossible derivations, because the word *meringue* is proudly present in *Le Cuisinier Royal et Bourgeois*, a cookery book published by François Massialot in 1691, when he was the personal chef to King Louis XIV's brilliantly glamorous brother, Philippe, Duke of Orleans, who was notable for his talent on the battlefield but also for being a gender fluid bisexual who married women, took male lovers, and enjoyed wearing fabulous frocks at the royal court.

So, we don't know exactly who invented meringues, or why they're even called that, but we can say that in the 1700s patisserie chefs were commonly making them as high-peaked, stiff desserts. This was achieved because the whisking process mixes the sugars with the egg proteins, causing the amino acids to form a net of protein-coated air bubbles that support a strong structure. Earlier recipes involving cream had contained fat, which doesn't do this, hence why sixteenth-century 'snow' was a looser, more foamy consistency.

Another way to stiffen meringues even further – thus allowing for fruits, jellies, custards and other things to be delicately plonked on top without the decoration slumping soggily through to the base – was to mix the ingredients in a copper bowl (classily nicknamed *cul de poule*, or the 'chicken's arse', in French). Copper is more chemically reactive than most other materials, so the bonus chemistry was greatly advantageous to the meringue-maker.

By the late 1800s, another cheat had arrived for the anxious chef who feared an embarrassing berry implosion. This was cream of tartar, a powdery, acidic offshoot of wine manufacture which produces carbon dioxide, much as yeast does in bread. The extra gas also stiffens the mix, and when it's used this is known as a Swiss meringue (as opposed to the standard French version, or the Italian type which is cooked over heat). All of these little tricks meant that, by 1935, an Australian hotel chef named Herbert Sachse had mastered the art of the fruity, creamy meringue dessert, and decided to name it in honour of the light, sweet elegance of the celebrated Russian ballerina, Anna Pavlova.

Typically, however, historians have spent the past ninety years quibbling over who first honoured Pavlova with her dessert, as there were apparently several other sweet treats named after her. So, the history of meringues isn't quite as pure and sweet as I'd like, even if the dish itself is to die for. Actually, given the way I can chomp through entire packets of the stuff, maybe all this sugar will indeed be the ending of me. Oh well, there's worse ways to go. Bring on the pineapple!

17. How did early humans discover how to make bread?
Asked by Imelda

This is a question from Imelda, but of course it was also part of Alex's previous meringue enquiry, so I've decided to tackle them as a double-act. Anyway, it's hardly surprising I got numerous questions along these lines. When the terrifying Covid-19 pandemic stopped the world in 2020, panicking Brits raced to their nearest shop to bulk-buy bog roll. Noticing that they couldn't eat it, they then raced back to the shops to clear the shelves of pasta. Once home, they got bored. And then anxious. And then hungry for anything other than pasta. And that's when the Europe-wide flour shortage kicked in.

Yes, among the scary headlines and daily infection statistics, one of the pandemic's most surprising stories was the sudden nationwide impulse for baking. Whether it was a self-soothing activity, or simply a cheap way to make your own food, people went loco for sourdough; Instagram and

Twitter were just visual homages to the joys of yeast. At the time, journalists and commentators were taken by surprise, as were the suppliers of yeast and flour, who struggled to keep pace with demand. But I suppose we shouldn't have been surprised. Popular TV shows, like *The Great British Bake Off*, had primed us to crave utopian visions of doughy goodness baked into delightful shapes, but we'd been too busy holding down careers and family lives to find the time. Suddenly, many people were confined to their homes, with hours to fill. The baking could begin in earnest!

But I also think there was more to it than that. There's something elemental about bread; it is the most basic of staples, eaten in most countries on the planet (though it didn't reach Japan until Portuguese traders introduced it in the 1540s). Bread's nutritious, tummy-filling simplicity has often made it the necessary salvation of the poor, and many historical cultures agreed on its importance.

The ancient Greek poet Homer said humans were 'bread-eaters' compared to the nectar-eating gods; in Arabic-speaking Egypt, the word for bread, *aish*, literally means 'life'; for the Romans, it was so essential to the functioning of society that it was doled out by the state, for free, to 200,000 impoverished citizens. To the Victorians, the colour of your loaf communicated your social status – brown for the humble, white for the well-to-do; and when the poor starved, there were bread riots and even revolutions (just ask Marie Antoinette). Bread is intimately tied up with our historical identity – although there are, of course, many people who dodge carbs and gluten for reasons of digestive health – and we can trace its roots back to the very dawn of civilisation. In fact, we can go beyond even that . . .

When I was a blue-haired archaeology student, way back in the hazy days of the early 2000s, I could confidently tell you that farming was invented right at the end of the Stone Age (the Neolithic era), around 12,000 years ago. This was when people first started to build towns and domesticate animals for food etc., so it made perfect sense that they'd elected to settle in one place now that lunch could be grown outside the back door, instead of having to chase it around the countryside. But there's now tantalising evidence that people had already been experimenting with agriculture 30,000 years ago. That's not Neolithic, that's proper Palaeolithic territory, that.

Firstly, we have multiple sites dated to 28-30,000 years ago, in Central Europe, where there's decent evidence for flour manufacture, from the grinding of vegetables. What does one do with flour? Well, we're not certain, but the clues might lead us somewhere intriguing. Another site on the coast of the Sea of Galilee, in Israel, has been dated to 23,000 years ago. Researchers found the ancient people living there had collected 140 different species of plant, including wild emmer and barley, but also lots of different types of weeds. This was particularly exciting; as any amateur gardener can tell you, weeds are infuriating, unwanted guests that thrust their way out of the soil the moment you plant something pretty. They flourish in cultivated land and delight in bullying out the feeble flowers we actually want to grow. So, the fact that weeds were so present in the soil samples is rather astonishing, because it suggests humans weren't just eating wild crops, but were perhaps planting their own. This, of course, was a whopping eleven millennia before we apparently invented farming.

That's not all. The archaeologists also found evidence of a grinding slab for processing cereal grains, and sickle blades for harvesting. Are all of these sites, from 23-30,000 years ago, proof that prehistoric people were making a simple porridge to fuel them through their morning hunt? Or might this have been the earliest efforts at home baking, long before people invented the concept of the home? As much as I love the idea of a Stone Age showstopper being judged by a proto-Paul Hollywood, I'm not sure we can fully commit to a bread theory at this stage of prehistory, though it's perhaps plausible.

Let's instead jump to 14,500 years ago, and shuffle over from Israel to a site in modern Jordan, where the Natufian people were living a semi-permanent existence of hunting and gathering, but with experimental agriculture chucked in for good measure. And this time we have actual proof of primitive bread production. Dr Amaia Arranz-Otaegui, the lead archaeologist on the excavation, described finding evidence of unleavened flatbreads in the ashes of a hearth. This was likely the product of extensive grinding with pestle and mortar, or a quernstone. She depicted the probable process as: 'grinding cereals and club-rush tubers to obtain fine flour, mixing of flour with water to produce dough, and baking the dough in the hot ashes of a fireplace or in a hot flat-stone'.

And why all that grinding? Why not just chew the plants like a chimp? Well, as Dr Arranz-Otaegui puts it: 'The modi-fication processes that are involved in bread preparation (i.e. cereal dehusking, milling, drying, cooking, and baking) reduce noxious and indigestible components such as cellulose-rich chaff, improve starch accessibility and protein digestion, and produce a particular taste.' Ah yes, who wants a chaffy croissant? Not me! So, the manufacture of bread may have been the safest, most appetising way to digest those necessary calories.

However, we don't think they were binging on bread rolls on any given Tuesday. No, the quantities produced seem to have been very small, and it would have been a very labour-intensive process. It's possible bread was more of a very rare treat, or associated with some religious event. If agriculture wasn't well-established, then the ingredients might've been thin on the ground too. But clearly these Natufian people had thousands of years in which to get the recipe right, and, once crops were more reliably grown, mass-produced bread became the staple food that powered the expansion of the Bronze Age civilisations of Egypt, Sumer (in Mesopotamia), and the Indus Valley Harappans (in Pakistan and India).

Although these large city-states built big bakeries with domed bread ovens, which are vital to baking a nice raised loaf, they were initially enjoying flatbreads. The leavening process - in which yeast puffs up the dough with a blast of carbon dioxide - was perhaps only discovered by accident, when some careless beer brewer, drunk on their own supply, splashed their yeasty concoction over a tray of uncooked dough. Indeed, beer is basically liquid bread, and some archaeologists have argued beer was equally, if not more, important than bread as a calorific supply in these early societies. When this miraculous yeast process first became understood is unknown; it's possible it happened very early on, and was adopted by Bronze Age Egypt and Mesopotamia 5,000 years ago, but some scholars seem cautious in dating it to only 3,000 years ago.

So, if our question was *'how did early humans discover how to make bread?'*, then the answer is probably through repeated trial and error, the occasional accident, no small amount of effort, and maybe someone spilling their pint! But it may well have been an experiment that began much earlier than we thought, meaning the history of bread is helping archaeologists to redefine how we think about the basic fundamentals of humanity's epic story.

CHAPTER 5:

HISTORIOGRAPHY

18. I'm a zoologist and we like dinosaurs A LOT. But these are 'prehistoric'. So, when did 'history' begin?
Asked by Chris

OH NO! Chris, you've asked the cursed question and summoned the ghosts of squabbling historians past! Now my room is filling up with howling spectres yelling at each other about the flaws in their prescriptivist definitions of what is, and what isn't, history (and should it be spelled *History*, with a capital H?). Please call the Ghostbusters and tell them that E. H. Carr has G. R. Elton in an ethereal headlock!

You might be surprised that this is a tricky question, Chris, because surely historians know what they study? To this obvious conclusion I respond with the important fact that the collective noun for us is 'an argumentation' of historians, so that gives you a clue as to our general temperament. Perhaps I can put it in zoology terms for you. I'm no dino-connoisseur; however, I understand your field recently had its own bust-up about the dinosaur family tree?

As I recall, all dinosaurs used to be categorised as either lizard-hipped or bird-hipped, but there's now a whole third category called Ornithoscelida to consider and quite a lot of feisty debate to be had. Well, historians are much the same in

our ongoing disagreements, and we get caught up in seman-
tics, philosophical arguments, and we also have to deal with
new types of evidence changing how we think about the past.
Ultimately, 'History' has multiple meanings, so finding consensus on when it began is going to be tricky. But I'm a glutton
for punishment, so onwards into the murky waters we go . . .

Let's start with the obvious problems of common language. *History* is an annoyingly vague word, deployed in
all manner of situations. Most obviously, it gets used as an
interchangeable synonym for 'the past' – there are loads of
anniversary-based podcasts, books, and internet articles
called things like *On This Day in History*. Moreover, when we
visit our doctor or dentist, they read through our 'patient
history' before treating us; and when we can't find a funny
thing we saw on YouTube, we scour our 'internet history' for
the hyperlink. If two people are looking awkward at a party,
trying not to make eye contact, our friend might lean over and
salaciously whisper, 'Oooh, I bet they've got *history*!' When an
athlete wins a trophy, or a government passes a law, they are
'making history'. Indeed, many people will cheerfully accept a
definition of history as anything that happened yesterday, or
just now (like you reading this. And this. And this also).

History is anything that is past, whereas *historic* is anything
important that might be remembered in the future. There's
nothing wrong with such everyday usage, but, when I put my
professional historian trousers on, I try to adopt more precise
language, if only for clarity of comprehension. To be a tedious
nerd about it, History – with a capital H – isn't a time or a
place in the past, it's an intellectual attempt at reconstructing
what we think happened in the past. Historians *do* History in
much the same way that Detective Poirot does country-house
sleuthing; it's a process of inquiry, based on the available

evidence. Annoyingly, we don't have the luxury of gathering the suspects in the drawing room for our big announcement, and only some of us can deliver our big reveal with an outlandish Belgian accent.

I'm not an Agatha Christie aficionado, so I might be overstating things, but it seems every time I watch an adaptation of Poirot or Miss Marple, the accused killer immediately confesses their wicked deed in front of everyone, and Poirot/ Marple gets to be smug about their powers of deduction. Alas, historians very rarely elicit a confession from the dead, and will mostly spend their careers drawing incomplete conclusions. In fact, sometimes I describe my job as being like a portrait artist who has to paint a subject they've never met, and all we have to go on are the subject's wallet, their work diary, a meal receipt from a restaurant, and an item of their clothing – you can learn quite a lot about a person from these things, and yet you can still accidentally end up painting someone totally unrecognisable from reality.

Now for the vital bit – the *past* is unchangeable. The only way to alter it is to jump in a DeLorean and drive at 88mph while your white-haired scientist friend gets attacked by terrorists. By contrast, *History* is constantly changing; it's the endless churn of argument and interpretation as each generation rewrites what they think happened in the past. This is the essence of History as a pursuit, and it always makes me either laugh or despair – depending on my mood – when outraged newspaper columnists decry, 'Historians are rewriting history!' whenever someone points out a statue of an iconic national hero also happens to depict a slave owner. 'Yes, obviously!' I want to shout. 'We rewrite History every day! Hence all the new History books in your local branch of Waterstones, you absolute numpty . . .'

Let's get back to Chris and his question of *'when did "history" begin?'* The pioneer of History as an intellectual practice is usually said to be the ancient Greek writer Herodotus of Halicarnassus, whose magisterial study of the Greco-Persian Wars, *The Histories* – which he composed around the year 430 BCE – was the first major text in which a scholar travelled around, gathered a massive bunch of evidence, and then explained how he'd come to his judgements.

In fact, our word *history* derives from the Greek *historia* which translates as 'inquiry' or 'research' - it's for this reason that Herodotus is commonly referred to as 'The Father of History', although those who think he made up his journeys prefer to dub him 'The Father of Lies'. I should just add that the ancient Greeks also talked about an earlier generation of historians, including Xanthos of Lydia and Charon of Lampsacus, but modern scholars can't decide if they lived earlier, later, or if they were Herodotus' contemporaries. Basically, Herodotus gets to keep his trophy for now, while the stewards hold their inquiry . . . or should I say their *historia*?

So, can we declare the idea of doing History started roughly 2,500 years ago? Maybe! But it's not as if Herodotus was the first person to notice there'd been stuff before him, and thought, 'Hey, I'd better write this down!' If we're willing to tweak our criteria and shuffle away from the analytical source criticism of Herodotus and his pals, we can find much earlier historical narratives. In the Jewish tradition, the Book of Judges belongs to the so-called Deuteronomic texts in the Hebrew Bible and these were perhaps written down a good century before Herodotus had even grown his first beard hair.

These sacred texts don't have the inquiring Herodotus commentary running through them; they're just conventional storytelling highlighting key characters, notable events,

causes, and consequences, helping to explain how the Israelites kept falling in and out of Yahweh's good books. The texts
perhaps don't feel like 'works of History' because we can't
hear the voice of the critical historian in them, but they are –
in a much grander way – the history of a people, and of how
the Israelites came to end up in Babylonian exile. This, then,
becomes a major sticking point: do we want to demand that
History be an intellectual activity focusing on examination
and explanation, or do we want to loosen our belts and allow
for it to be any account of prior events?

If we're happy to accept the latter, we can find lots of
historical annals in ancient Egyptian or Babylonian writings.
We have such knowledge thanks to the invention of writing,
which arrived about 5,400 years ago, first with the Sumerians
developing cuneiform – a system of triangular marks made
with a reed stylus, impressed into clay tablets – followed very
soon after by the Egyptians conjuring up hieroglyphs, and
then the Chinese coming along a few hundred years later
with their own early script. These technologies were radical
innovations that changed the course of humanity, and the
invention of writing is conventionally the point at which 'recorded History' is said to have begun.

Anything before this point automatically moves into the
inbox of archaeologists, and becomes eligible for the clunky
title of *prehistoric*, a label first used in 1851 by Daniel Wilson.
A subtle thing to note, though I'm not sure if it's an official
thing, is that these days *pre-History* tends to mainly apply to
the Stone Age era of *Homo sapiens* and our early hominin ancestors, but once we get beyond upright tool-wielding apes,
roughly 3 million years ago, we often see a switch to the word
prehistoric for anything involving geology or Chris's beloved
dinosaurs. It seems pre-History is commonly used for humans

and prehistoric isn't. However, to confuse things yet further, we'll often see the study of Mother Nature's bounteous wonders being described as *natural history*, a phrase we find in the title of Pliny the Elder's celebrated book *The Natural History*, written roughly 2,000 years ago.

But I have another rug to pull out from under your feet. If we're willing to say History (with its big H) isn't analytical, but is merely a structured narrative recounting human events, characters, causes, and consequences from the past, then we can burst like Houdini from the shackles of writing alone, and can turn to the Djab Wurrung Aboriginal Australians of central Victoria, or to the Klamath Native American people of Oregon. Remarkably, their oral histories – passed down from generation to generation through precise repetition and recitation – can tell us about the deeds of their ancestors extending as far back as 10,000 years ago.

This is jaw-droppingly astonishing, not least because modern geologists, such as Professor Patrick Nunn, have been able to test the accuracy of these stories, which often tell of volcanic eruptions, floods, and other major natural phenomena, by comparing them to the physical evidence in the landscape. Nunn's book *The Edge of Memory* is a fascinating read, telling of how ancient pre-literate peoples used their histories to bind themselves together as groups, but also as a source of vital intelligence on how best to survive in hostile landscapes where environmental changes brought new challenges.

It's clear, then, that the history of *History* provides ample opportunity for a ruckus over when it all started, but there's a decent shout for saying we've been thinking historically for many millennia, because knowing who we once were helps us interrogate who we are now, and vice versa. Indeed, in 1961, the great scholar E. H. Carr argued in his classic book *What Is History?* that History (with a capital H) is shaped by the here and now, because the world in which a historian grows up will influence the questions they ask, and the meanings they find, in the distant past.

In which case, the very book you're reading right now not only reveals your own twenty-first-century fascinations, through the lens of the questions you all wanted answered, but also betrays my own subtle biases in my responses. When I write about the past, I can't help speaking about the present. That's why everything in this book is ultimately a coded reference to my beloved football team, Tottenham Hotspur, and their ability to be a constant, agony-inducing source of crushing disappointment. You might assume I'm talking about the ancient Greeks, or whatever, but really I'm just processing the heartbreak of Mauricio Pochettino's managerial downfall at Spurs. Oh, Poch, how I love thee . . .

19. Who names historical periods? And what will future historians call us, given that 'Elizabethan' is already taken?
Asked by Alison

I really love this question, Alison, but I'm going to start my answer in a bit of a strange way, so stick with me on this. In 2008, I began working as the historical adviser on a brand-new BBC children's TV show called *Horrible Histories*. It was a silly comedy, but with factual information at its heart, and I was suddenly in charge of explaining all of history ever to our team of writers (so long as it would then be funny for seven-year-olds).

As jobs go, it was joyous and stressful in equal measure, but it also revealed flaws in the way I'd been trained to think about the past. You see, historical periodisation is like the handball rule in football; it's perfectly sensible until you actually try to define it. And then you're in big trouble.

Our TV series was based on Terry Deary's bestselling books, each of which tackles a different historical era: so we had *Terrible Tudors, Awful Egyptians, Smashing Saxons, Gorgeous Georgians, Vile Victorians*, etc. Unlike the books, which stick to one era, we wanted to bounce between different historical eras within the same episode. Realising this might confuse our young audience, we informed them when we were changing eras, using sixteen of Terry Deary's book titles as our signposts between sketches. Before a new sketch, a cartoon person from the new era would pop up and introduce it.

As a helpful guide to our writers, I ordered the sixteen eras chronologically, like this:

- STONE AGE
- EGYPTIANS
- GREEKS
- ROMANS
- SAXONS
- VIKINGS
- MIDDLE AGES
- RENAISSANCE
- AZTECS
- INCA
- TUDORS
- STUARTS
- GEORGIANS
- VICTORIANS

- FIRST WORLD WAR
- SECOND WORLD WAR

I was rather pleased with myself when I jumbled them up and asked the writers to put them in order; I felt like a daytime quiz show host, gently chiding them as they got the Vikings and Tudors in the wrong order. Oh, how smug I felt! However, my smugness backfired. One of our writers then asked me to explain how these eras were defined, and I was embarrassed to realise that my 'correct' timeline was riddled with logic problems.

Most obviously, many categories overlapped. The Romans, Greeks, and Egyptians were all distinct civilisations; but the Romans had conquered the Greeks; and both the Ptolemaic Greeks and Romans had separately ruled over Egypt. So, when we did a sketch about Cleopatra (a descendant of the Macedonian commander Ptolemy who'd fought alongside Alexander the Great), which of Terry Deary's book titles were we supposed to use? Was Cleo Roman, Greek, or Egyptian?

Meanwhile, the Early Medieval English, or *Saxons* in Terry's phrasing, had co-existed with the Vikings, but I'd given them separate eras. And yet, they'd both normally sit under the bigger umbrella of Middle Ages, except I'd limited that to 1066-1485. Of course, the Aztecs and Inca might also have gone in Middle Ages too, but I also made them separate to that, and from each other. What's more, the Renaissance arguably began in the 1300s, in France and Italy, which in England was still the period of the medieval era's Greatest Hits, featuring such classics as the Black Death, Hundred Years' War, and Peasants' Revolt. Conversely, some of the greatest Renaissance artists, such as Michelangelo, lived in the 1500s, which I'd classified as the Tudor era.

Oh, and don't get me started on the Tudors! Though it's a Welsh name, it's a very Anglocentric term for the sixteenth century, and Scottish people justifiably roll their eyes because their royal dynasty at the same time was the Stuarts, but the English only begin the Stuart era in 1603, on the death of Queen Elizabeth I. This meant a *Horrible Histories* sketch about Mary, Queen of Scots - literally a Stuart - fell under our 'Tudor era'. Meanwhile, Shakespeare's life straddled both Tudor and Stuart categories, which was another recurring nuisance because he was a regular character in the show.

The Tudors and Stuarts belong to the wider era known to historians as the Early Modern period, but please don't ask me to define what I mean by Early Modern, as it'll get me into so much trouble with both the medievalists and the Renaissance specialists! After that, we get the Modern period - by which historians confusingly mean anything post-1700(ish) - but which Brits like to refer to as the Georgian era, named after the sequence of four Hanoverian kings in a row who were all called George. But what about King William IV, and the Great Reform Act of 1832? Should he squeeze into the Victorian era, even though Victoria was yet to reign? Should he get his own weird *Williamite Age*? The *Williamian Era*? Urgh, no, that's horrible to say. Ignore that!

Then there's King Edward VII. He only reigned for a decade, and Terry Deary hadn't written an Edwardians book, so when we did him those sketches either had to go in the Victorian era - even though his mum was dead by then - or in the First World War era, even though *he* was dead by then. And then we got to the 1920s and 30s. Were these the consequences of the First World War? Or the causes of the Second World War? The system demanded they fit in one or the other, yet they belonged in neither. Aaaaargh!

This was the tumultuous tempest swirling in my brain at pretty much every writing meeting, and I'm still not over it. But my own personal descent into temporal madness was just a tiny speck in the grand history of periodisation. Historians have been having these debates for centuries. The scholar A. Gangatharan writes that time is a ceaseless continuum, yet the 'historian is forced to create a sense of meaning through the process of gerrymandering'. In short, historians invent arbitrary boundaries to make the massive chunks of human life more manageable. We editorialise the past, deciding key moments were transitional watersheds that can be used to split time apart. But were such events transitional to the people of the time? Sometimes, sure! But nobody woke up on 1 January 1250, turned to their partner, and said, 'I went to bed feeling very High Middle Ages, but suddenly I've come over all Late Middle Ages!'

So, Alison, you have sensibly asked *who names historical periods?* and my very simple answer is: historians do! But we really struggle with it, and it's not a new hobby of ours. Way back in the early 400s CE, the hugely influential Christian theologian Augustine of Hippo divided time into Six Ages of the World, each lasting a thousand years:

1. From the creation of Eden to the Great Flood

2. Great Flood to Abraham

3. Abraham to King David

4. King David to Babylonian captivity

5. Babylonian captivity to the birth of Christ

6. Christ to the Second Coming (Messiah pending . . .)

This sacred timeline was used for the next millennium until the influential Renaissance historian, Leonardo Bruni, pioneered a new way of thinking: he split up the past into three ages, called Ancient, Medieval, and Modern, onto which modern historians now drop much nerdier sub-categories (Late Antiquity, Early Medieval, High Medieval, Late Medieval, Renaissance, Early Modern, Enlightenment, Romantic Era, Long Eighteenth Century, etc.). Oh, and it's not just historians; in the 1860s, archaeologists popped their head in through the window and shouted, 'Morning! We've just invented the concept of the Stone Age, so could you tack that on the front, please?'

Every historian uses periodisation, but we massively disagree over when periods start and finish. I kid you not, as I was midway through writing this answer, a historian named Dawn Saunders ran a Twitter poll asking: 'Which of these defines the Long Eighteenth Century?'

a) 1688–1815
b) 1660–1831
c) 1660–1850
d) 1700–1800

Half of her respondents voted for a), but she received suggestions for nine other possibilities (I cheekily ventured 1688-1832, because I'm annoying like that). You might think this utterly ridiculous, 'How can one era have thirteen possible start and end points??!' But cultural watersheds will differ depending on whether a historian examines literature, religion, architecture, art, language, politics, military technology, scientific development, exploration, empire, etc. Even consensus on the dates of major wars can prove weirdly elusive. We all know that the First World War ran from 1914 to 1918. Except it didn't.

November 1918 brought the Armistice, and the end of the violence, but the Treaty of Versailles wasn't ratified until 1919. In the USA, Congress's emergency wartime powers lingered until March 1921, and were even leveraged to pass the infamous alcohol Prohibition laws. How was this possible? Well, because the US government considered itself still legally at war with Germany until 2 July 1921, when a joint resolution, ending hostilities which had begun in 1917, was signed by President Harding. Some historians, like Professor Robert Gerwarth, have recently gone further, arguing that peace didn't arrive in Europe until 1923, so maybe that's a better date to use as our endpoint for the First World War?

When we name eras, historians also employ anachronistic labels that weren't in use at the time. The Aztecs didn't call themselves Aztecs, they used *Mexica* (hence Mexico); the Vikings didn't call themselves Vikings; the ancient Greeks called themselves *Hellenes*; the ancient Chinese were *Han*; Tudor monarchs were embarrassed to call themselves *Tudor* and Henry Tudor's defeated enemy, Richard III, didn't call himself a Plantagenet. The Byzantines of Constantinople didn't say, 'Hi, we're the Byzantines!', they were *Romans*, but of the eastern part of the empire.

That said, not all historical eras are imposed in hindsight. The concept of a medieval period – in Latin, *Medium Aevum* – was first articulated by the Italian sonnet-scribbler Petrarch, in the 1340s. He was glum about living through what he saw as an age of shadows and gloom, sometimes translated as 'Dark Ages', though that's actually a much later phrase and it's also rather confusing because people now use 'Dark Ages' to mean roughly 500–1000 CE, not the mid-1300s. Also, historians will silently murder you with their eyeballs if you say 'Dark Ages' unironically.* Anyway, Petrarch longed for the glory days of ancient Rome. In looking back with regret, and then looking forward with hope, he casually invented the idea of a cultural resurgence, or rebirth – and true enough, we now call him a Renaissance poet.

As for the word *Renaissance*, we can thank the celebrated sixteenth-century biographer Giorgio Vasari, whose *Lives of the Artists* is our most enjoyable source for all the juicy gossip about Michelangelo, Leonardo, and their paint-splattered predecessors. Vasari also described the idea of a *Rinascita* (Renaissance), but the idea only really caught on in the 1800s, to be applied retroactively by historians. But at least it was an authentic loanword borrowed from someone who used it at the time.

And in the eighteenth century, we got the so-called *Enlightenment* – a philosophical and cultural movement geared towards scientific rationalism, religious scepticism, and the pursuit of knowledge. Though historians have added 'the' at the front, Enlightenment was used by its own protagonists; the influential German philosopher Immanuel Kant even wrote an essay called *Was ist Aufklärung?* (*What Is Enlightenment?*) in which he challenged his reader to stop being lazy and 'Dare to know!', which was very much the 'Wake up,

---

* As well as the notion of a barbaric period in human history, sometimes people use the phrase 'Dark Ages' to mean an era in which the historical evidence dried up, such as the post-Roman sixth century in England. Frankly, both of these usages are wrong, and will make any nearby medievalists absolutely furious, so never say 'Dark Ages' unless also doing massively elaborate air quotes with your fingers, winking constantly, and pulling a grimace like you're chewing a wasp.

sheeple!' of its day, minus the deranged conspiracy theories about chemtrails and all-powerful lizard people.

Speaking of which, that brings us on to our own idiocy-blighted era, and to the second part of Alison's question. The journalist and BBC broadcaster Andrew Marr (who is not an idiot) dubbed us 'Elizabethans' in his 2020 book, following on from the journalist and BBC broadcaster James Naughtie's 2012 book *The New Elizabethans*, and future historians might borrow this monarchical angle, perhaps choosing from *Elizabethans, Elizab2thans, QE2s, New Elizabethans,* or - if they're anything like my Australian buddies - *Lizzos*.

But I'm going to suggest the sheer amount of cultural and technological change since 1952 might exceed the confines of one label. Indeed, I don't think this is just our problem. If you are ever unlucky enough to be stuck in a lift with me, I will eventually launch into my highly controversial pet rant, which is that the Victorian era perhaps wasn't a single era at all. Though it was named by nineteenth-century writers, who referred to themselves as 'Victorians', I think if we compare the astonishing technological differences between 1837 and 1901, and the impact these changes had upon culture and ideas, you'll see the Victorians need slicing up (though not in a grim Jack the Ripper way, I hasten to add). After all, in the twentieth century, periods are allowed to shrink to a mere decade: the Roaring Twenties, the Great Depression, the Swinging Sixties! A Victorian era of sixty-four years seems wildly generous given how much society changed between 1837 and 1901. I'd happily split it into Early and Late Victorian.

Personally, I'd bet my money on our own era being defined more narrowly, with the focus landing on the revolutionary impact of the internet. To me, the fall of the Berlin Wall in 1989, which occurred as more homes started to have personal computers, feels like a potential start-point for what might be dubbed the *Digital Era*, or – if Jeff Bezos continues to dominate the online shopping marketplace – maybe we'll be dubbed *Amazonians* by our grandkids? My friend Henri, who helped me research this book, suggests combining the digital angle with the Trump and Brexit culture wars, giving us the *Binary Age* of both 1s and 0s and oppositional political identities. So, we'll perhaps be . . . um . . . *Binarians*? Hmmm, OK, maybe not *that*.

Maybe future historians will look upon us with anger and despair, having inherited the terrible consequences of our decisions, and will judge our time as one of catastrophic sluggishness in tackling climate change, fossil fuel reliance, the crisis of capitalism, and global overpopulation. Maybe we'll be *The Selfish Generation*, or *The F**k-ups*, or just the accusatory charge of *The Guilty*! In which case, perhaps we should pray for an alien invasion, if only so we can be spared the disapproving scowls of our embittered descendants, and instead lay the blame squarely on the Martians. 'It wasn't us, guv, it was the intergalactic death rays! Honest!'

20. What are some of the greatest 'lost texts' from history that we know existed, but haven't survived?
Asked by Daniel

In 2002, Donald Rumsfeld gave a famous answer at a press conference. Asked about the lack of evidence for Iraq's weapons of mass destruction, Rumsfeld explained his theory of knowledge, noting that there are 'known knowns', 'known unknowns', and 'unknown unknowns'. He was widely mocked for speaking gibberish, not least because everyone hated him for being a warmonger, but I'm convinced it was actually the smartest thing he ever said. I may have loathed the man and his politics, but the wise mantra of *unknown unknowns* informs much of my historical thinking.

When it comes to history's greatest lost texts, obviously we can't deal with the unknown unknowns, because we don't know what they are. However, there are so many known unknowns – the missing masterpieces – which I'll try to include in this response to Daniel's fine question. My brain immediately races to Lord Byron's unpublished memoir, which was burned by his close friend, Thomas Moore. He wasn't a clumsy oaf or a poetical pyromaniac, but rather he was reluctantly acting on the instructions of Byron's closest confidants, who had voted to pre-emptively destroy what might later be used to destroy Byron's posthumous reputation. Clearly, we missed out on some juicy gossip. Another casualty to the roaring fireplace was the first volume of Thomas Carlyle's *History of the French Revolution*, which he sent to his friend J. S. Mill to read, only for Mill's housemaid to mistakenly use it as kindling in the fireplace. Alas, she didn't try to hastily rewrite it herself, in hilarious *Blackadder* tradition, but Carlyle took the disaster on the chin and frantically rewrote the whole thing in a frenzy, arguably producing a better book for it.

We're obviously missing some works by heavyweight celebrity authors who died mid-sentence: Jane Austen's *Sanditon* was never finished, and neither was Charles Dickens' *The Mystery of Edwin Drood*. We also don't have anything of Shakespeare's *History of Cardenio,* and there's an ongoing debate about whether *Love's Labours Won* was his lost comedy sequel, or just an alternative title for *The Taming of the Shrew,* which we do have. Given the number of lazy Hollywood sequels I've endured, I'm not sure we'd need it. If only they'd been chucked into the fire instead of Byron's saucy memoir.

Sticking with comedy, we're sadly without Aristotle's volume of the *Poetics* which handles the rules of comedy, and we have just one complete comedy play by the ancient writer Menander, despite him churning out 100-plus works. You might assume this is a terrible tragedy, but fragments of his work were rediscovered and translated in the twentieth century, causing much excitement among scholars, until it turned out that Menander's missing plays were, for many scholars, actually . . . er . . . a bit crap. Centuries of hype resulted in one of the great letdowns in modern literary history, so maybe it's best if the rest stay lost?

The Roman comic playwright Plautus wrote over 110 works, of which we have only twenty (plus lots of fragments), but I'm more depressed about the fact we only have eleven of Aristophanes' forty comedies. If you'll recall from my earlier answer about ancient jokebooks, he was an absolute hoot with a filthy mind, so we've definitely been deprived of a treasure trove of riotous fart gags. We're also missing Philip of Macedon's famous jokebook mentioned in that answer.

As for ancient poetry, we have only a mere handful of poems and fragments by Sappho, the most celebrated female writer of the ancient world, plus there's a chunk missing from the collected works of the lyrical poet Pindar. Most intriguingly, some scholars think we don't have the original versions of Homer's *Iliad* or *Odyssey*, which – given they're the revered cornerstones of European literature – is quite the provocative hypothesis.

Moving on to the sad stuff, the ancient Greeks produced three master tragedians in Sophocles, Euripides, and Aeschylus. Between them, there are 116 missing plays by Sophocles, eighty-four by Aeschylus, and probably seventy-plus by Euripides, so we're either missing out on an absolute truckload of devastating tearjerkers, or – if we keep Menander in mind – we've been spared an enormous waste of time. My guess is a bit of both.

Turning to Roman non-fiction, we still get to enjoy Julius Caesar's extraordinary account of his conquest of Gaul – Asterix and Obelix not included – but this only makes it all the more disappointing that his other works are lost; Caesar had a real flair for both savage brutality and autobiographical phrasemaking, so they would've been eye-popping reads. Also absent is the autobiography of his successor, Rome's first and greatest emperor, Caesar Augustus, which was presumably a magnificent study in vainglorious ego. Augustus was responsible for the defeat and suicide of the Egyptian Pharaoh Cleopatra, who may have been the author of treatises about medicines and beauty products,* but, alas, we'll never get to enjoy her YouTube makeover tutorial because those are AWOL too.

Another powerful woman who went to the trouble of writing a memoir, only for it to vanish, was the poison-loving Empress Agrippina the Younger, who was sister of Caligula, wife of Claudius, and mother of Nero. Her life was utterly extraordinary, and she had some tales to tell, for sure! When it comes to her astonishing political career, the only tales we have are the ones told about her by snarky, male historians like Suetonius, author of the tasteful classic *The Lives of Famous Whores*, which is missing as well.

---

* There was definitely an ancient person called Cleopatra who wrote about these things, but scholars disagree over whether it was *the* Cleopatra.

Meanwhile, Agrippina's hubby, Claudius - who she allegedly bumped off with a poison mushroom - was a prodigious nerd who wrote twenty volumes of Etruscan history, eight volumes on the story of Carthage, and a whopping forty-three volumes of Roman history. It was such a vast collection that the celebrated Library of Alexandria built an entire new wing named after him, just to cram it all in. Alas, it's all lost, hugely harming our knowledge of those ancient civilisations, and of how a young Rome rose up to destroy its rivals.

As for science and natural history, we're without two works by the ancient Greek genius Archimedes - the fella who yelled 'Eureka!' in the bath - and who himself told us of a missing text by Aristarchus of Samos arguing that the Earth orbited the Sun (however, we do know quite a lot of what was in them, from later summaries or works that borrowed the data and arguments). And we only have a description of the contents of *On the Measurement of the Earth*, in which the ancient Greek mathematician and geographer, Eratosthenes, tried to figure out how big the planet was. We don't have Pytheas' account of his famous journey to Britain and the Arctic Circle, or two works by Thales on equinoxes and solstices, plus we're lacking four books by the Greek giant of geometry, Euclid. What's more, we don't have three histories of how mathematics originated, written by the first historian of science, Eudemus.

And then we get on to ancient philosophers, and - quite frankly - I'm not going to even bother, because I'd be here all week. Let me just say we're missing works by Socrates, Empedocles, Diogenes, Democritus, Heraclitus, Clitomachus, Chrysippus, and yadda yadda, etc. There's also a missing military manual by the Roman General Frontinus, and I'm glum about the loss of five books by Pliny the Elder, not least because I'm so curious as to how he researched his military handbook on how to chuck a javelin while on a horse! What a niche topic for a book; was it just three pages long, or what?!

As you can see, Daniel, this answer could be an entire book in itself. In fact, Stuart Kelly has written a very enjoyable one called *The Book of Lost Books*, while the esteemed historian of print culture, Professor Andrew Pettegree, points out that once we get into the 1500s and beyond, books were always being lost because they were either being officially censored (fairly rare, unless they were religiously or politically provocative), or weren't deemed worthy of saving (much more common): 'They served their purpose ... and then were discarded. Many are known now from only a single copy, often grubby and worn. This applies ... to around 30% of the known corpus of books printed before 1601.'

However, I want to finish with some non-European books which we'd love to find in the back of an attic. For starters, we sadly have only four texts from the ancient Mesoamerican Maya civilisation, because the Spanish conquistadors cruelly burned the rest. There was also wilful burning of the writings of Chinese philosopher Confucius during the reign of the First Emperor, Qin Shi Huangdi. Allegedly, it wasn't just the books that were destroyed, but scholars were buried alive too. Five of Confucius' major texts were recovered, but the fate of his sixth, on music, is debated by scholars: either it was lost forever, had never actually existed, or was incorporated into another, the *Book of Rites* (*Liji*). Either way, we'll never know if he preferred Ariana Grande or Taylor Swift.

And if you think that's bad, in 1900, as a consequence of Western imperial interference, China experienced the infamous Boxer Rebellion which resulted in the loss of one of history's greatest masterworks. The *Yongle Encyclopaedia*, begun in 1402 during the Ming dynasty, was the collaborative project of 2,000-plus scholars, with nearly 23,000 chapters spread across a dizzying 11,095 volumes. Written using an estimated 370 million Chinese characters, it was the compendium of all knowledge in the Chinese canon; a medieval Wikipedia, if you will. Sadly, much of it was lost over the centuries, and then a fire started during the Boxer Rebellion of 1899 claimed even more. European soldiers and officials did save some volumes, and dispersed them around the world's libraries, but only 3 per cent of the *Encyclopaedia* remains in existence today, which is an absolute tragedy.

And I haven't even got on to the religious texts we don't have: the missing books namechecked in the Hebrew Bible and the New Testament, plus the Apocrypha, and the full versions of the Dead Sea Scrolls, or Ibn Ishaq's original biography of the Prophet Muhammad before it was edited by Ibn Hasham. But, the recovery of the Dead Sea Scrolls, found in the 1940s–50s, along with the vast collection of ancient Chinese texts called the *Dunhuang*, found in caves in the early 1900s, gives us hope that not all lost things must remain so.

Very recently, a fascinating sixteenth-century book, compiled by Ferdinand Columbus (son of Christopher), was rediscovered by Professor Guy Lazure in a Danish archive. At a whopping 2,000 pages, it's a chunky tome called the *Libro de los Epítomes* and was intended to be a vast cross-referenced catalogue of all the books available in the 1530s, including a description of their contents. It was basically the sixteenth-century equivalent of the Netflix recommendations page where you scoot through looking for a decent sitcom.

Libro de los Epítomes is a phenomenal find which revealed the vast scale of knowledge in the sixteenth century, cataloguing a library of 20,000 books. Ironically, however, its rediscovery didn't reduce the number of lost books, but instead revealed a massive new list of even more lost works! Whether that excites you or depresses you is a question of personal taste, but I think it's rather wonderful - we'd been living in the realms of the Unknown Unknown, and then along came the *Libro de los Epítomes* to shunt us into the Known Unknown. Historians can now get started hunting down the lost books listed within, and I'm willing to bet they'll find a few . . .

21. What's your favourite historical what-if?
Asked by Dave

Ah, my old nemesis - we meet again! Sorry, not you, Dave, I'm sure you're very nice. No, I mean this question. Yes, hello! My name is Greg Jenner, and I'm pathologically sceptical towards historical what-iffery. Let me clarify - there's nothing wrong with asking, 'What if this hadn't happened?' Indeed, I'd gleefully leap to the defence of such a question, because such thought exercises help counteract the delicious temptation to assume all historical events were inevitable just because we know how they ended. They definitely weren't. Allowing ourselves to explore the chaotic contingency of events is wise, though it does tempt and tantalise our imaginations.

We've all seen *Back to the Future Part II*, and recoiled in horror at the dystopian future where bully-boy Biff Tannen uses a sports almanac from the future to win a fortune and transform his hometown into a sleazy gambler's paradise which he rules with an iron fist. Indeed, such lurid speculation is one of the most enjoyable tropes in modern pop culture, providing jokes for *Rick and Morty*'s surreal adventures, alternate timelines in superhero movies, and setting up a sinister world in which the Nazis and Japanese Empire won the Second World War in *The Man in the High Castle*. 'What-if History' reminds us that the tiniest change in variables might have had the largest of butterfly effects.

That's all great. My grumpiness arrives when we get to the next bit. 'Quick, Batman! To the Harrumphmobile!'

Here is the hill upon which I choose to die: if human events are chaotic and unpredictable, then counterfactual storytelling should also be chaotic and unpredictable. That's not to say that, had Hitler died in the trenches during the First World War, Germany would've ended up being ruled in the 1930s by a sentient lobster, or a goose-stepping cyborg called FührerBot. Chaos need not resemble a Salvador Dalí painting; it can still be a dull deviation of yet more grey-faced men pointing at maps.

But, whenever I see speculative alternative histories being pursued in good faith, I can't help but see the inevitable corralling of all sorts of bewilderingly complex things into an impossibly elegant, neatly ordered narrative. To do this sort of exercise seems to require the application of a screenwriter's logic to the progression of unknowable, unpredictable events; the new possibilities are extrapolated from what *did* happen, and thus operate under the assumption that everyone in the new scenario would behave the same, despite this being a totally new situation. To which I would then shout: 'BUT IF ONE THING CHANGES, EVERYTHING CHANGES!'

After all, the tides of macro- and micro-economics, of scientific innovation, of artistic creativity, of cultural fashions, of linguistic leaps, and so much more, are directed by a billion minuscule nudges that sometimes negate each other, and sometimes coalesce into irresistible, world-changing momentum. If you hypothesise Archduke Franz Ferdinand not dying at the hands of Gavrilo Princip in 1914, not only are you having to guess the new fate of otherwise-doomed empires – Austro-Hungary, Ottoman Turkey, Tsarist Russia – but you're also now having to guess how the absence of the First World War changes jazz music, the art of Picasso, the films of Charlie Chaplin, the emergence of women's football, the price of petrol, the role of women in the workplace, the development of plastic surgery, the evolution of aircraft design, and a bazillion other things.

Even a small tweak causes a domino effect that smashes through all knowledge, until suddenly the world is unrecognisable. Not only do you have to account for the living, and what they get up to, but you also have to theorise lives for those who, in the new timeline, never died in the first place. What if the greatest potential scientist of the 1950s was never actually gunned down at the Somme in 1916? How do we make sense of the impact he would have had, without resorting to wild guesswork? Does Elvis still achieve fame if the First World War never happens? Does someone else, no longer killed in battle, steal his thunder? What if the lack of global conflict in 1918 causes greater price stability in rubber production in British Malaya, stifling the development of the synthetic rubber industry in America, meaning a young Elvis – still a truck driver – tragically dies in a crash because his boss couldn't afford a new set of expensively imported tyres? This stuff is endless!

Maybe you're enjoying these hypotheticals? This is, after all, the premise of the popular movie *Yesterday*, in which The Beatles never existed but a young musician wakes up knowing all of their songs, and thus becomes the greatest songwriter (well, plagiarist) of all time – better even than mild-mannered cuddly warbler, Ed Sheeran (who appears in the film as himself). Cute idea! But a world without The Beatles wouldn't have produced Ed Sheeran, as we understand him. And the much more interesting hypothetical – found in the original draft of the script by Jack Barth, before Richard Curtis rewrote it – is that a nobody with brilliant songs might still fail. Curtis' script argues that Lennon & McCartney's tunes are innate masterpieces, even when divorced from the context of their creation, and so this amateur musician with a head full of perfect tunes becomes a superstar. But Barth's original script, titled *Cover Version*, takes the cynical view; in his version, stardom is contingent on so much more than talent and great pop songs. The musician fails to make it big.

Yesterday is a mildly diverting romcom where one variable switch produces maybe ten noticeable consequences that we get to chuckle at with knowing irony. And yet it's telling that two writers, presented with a single what-if scenario, produced two totally oppositional outcomes. It's proof that two historians examining a single what-if would massively disagree too, bringing into doubt the reliability of their conclusions, not least because neither would be able to account for the complexity of a billion tiny things adding up to so many major deviations beyond the scope of human perception.

So, when people say to me, 'Hey, Greg, what would have happened if . . .?' I find the almost limitless possibilities so horrifically daunting that I want to set fire to my own knees just to stop my brain from thinking about them. That way madness lies. Defenders of this sort of counterfactual History argue that it's a scholarly and serious business that celebrates the significance of the key variable by measuring its loss. Indeed, economic historians are big fans of this approach.

But the moment you're trying to figure out what comes afterwards, well, then you're just writing a very dull sci-fi novel.

But I realise I've just committed the cardinal sin of hectoring you while not answering the question, and Dave really didn't deserve to be yelled at, so – as a gesture of atonement – my favourite what-if is more of a 'Phew! Thank God it wasn't!' In September 1983, at the height of the Cold War, an automated early warning system in a Soviet military base, built near Moscow, detected an incoming missile attack. The computers were 100 per cent certain. The alarm was blaring, the screen flashing with the ominous word 'LAUNCH'. The Americans had finally decided to end the Cold War with a face-melting nuclear inferno.

The duty officer in charge that day was Stanislav Petrov. He didn't have any authority to retaliate; there was no big red button on his desk. His orders were simply to alert his superiors, who – given only a few minutes to act – would prepare for impact and then debate whether to launch a retaliatory strike on the USA. All the men around him were soldiers, trained to follow the same orders. But Petrov had a hunch that something was up. The missiles were being launched one by one, rather than in synchronised unison, and there weren't many of them. That seemed weird. Surely a surprise attack would be launched simultaneously, and in massive numbers, to catch the Soviets off-guard?

Petrov stared at the state-of-the-art bleeping computer, designed by Russia's finest scientists. It was housed in a military bunker specifically built for a day such as this. This situation had been planned for. Every person had been drilled in what to do. It was the height of the Cold War, and US–Soviet relations were at their absolute lowest – three weeks earlier, the

Soviets had shot down a Korean passenger jet, killing everyone on board. A retaliatory strike from the hated USA actually
seemed plausible.

And yet, despite all the noisy, flashing, terrifying evidence
to the contrary, Petrov didn't trust the beeping computer.
Here is where the story is usually rendered terrifyingly dramatic, with Petrov now becoming responsible for the fate
of the world; if he picks up the phone, the Politburo shouts,
'Mother Russia must be avenged!', and all hell breaks loose.
In truth, Petrov wasn't gambling with the fate of his fellow
Russians – if nukes really were racing towards Moscow, then
their doom was already sealed – and nor would his phone call
automatically trigger Armageddon for the Americans, either.
If he'd notified his superiors, they might have decided to wait
for confirmation of Moscow's destruction before issuing
revenge orders.

We don't honestly know what the official Soviet policy
was on nuclear annihilation, but they surely had a plan for
such a situation? Of course, this is me, sitting in my nice, safe
house – many years later on – applying a cool, retrospective
logic to the whole thing. But Petrov was in the eye of the
storm. His worst-case scenario was maybe happening right in
front of him, and he didn't know if the men on the other end
of the phone were rational philosophers with a fondness for
protocol, or if they were hot-headed, Yankee-hating, terrified,
spiteful reactionaries, instinctively ready to think the worst
of the hated enemy. Who's to say even a false alarm wouldn't
provoke one jumpy Soviet general to go all Dr Strangelove,
shoot his comrades in the head, barricade the bunker, and
give the order to retaliate?

The deafening sirens continued to honk in their defiant
certainty. But Petrov chose to wait.

Twenty-three minutes later, Moscow remained intact; the Kremlin still stood. No warheads had pierced the horizon and smashed into busy cities. Petrov had called it correctly. The computer had malfunctioned, confusing sunlight bouncing off some clouds for the mutually assured apocalypse. Petrov got no reward and no punishment for his actions, and, pretty understandably, later had a breakdown from the post-traumatic stress of experiencing the end of the world. To billions of people, it had simply been just another normal day. But to Petrov and the soldiers in that bunker it was the scariest game of Russian roulette imaginable.

So, if you're gonna twist my arm, here's my ultimate what-if: Stanislav Petrov eats some bad soup, gets food poisoning, runs to the toilet, and while he's in there, heaving his guts up, his inexperienced junior colleague sees the flashing lights, picks up the phone, and the guy on the other end freaks out ... Suddenly, Soviet nuclear missiles are being readied, and people are shouting, and then American satellites detect the launchpad activity, and North American Aerospace Defense Command goes into high alert, and Reagan is alerted that the Russians are planning a pre-emptive strike, and now two nuclear arsenals go hot, and two mortal enemies are frenetically trying to figure out if the other is about to attack, and ... well, it's UTTERLY TERRIFYING, isn't it? Yeah, I'll stick to the plot of *Yesterday,* thanks very much.

CHAPTER 6:

ANIMALS & NATURE

22. Why is the Devil a goat?
Asked by Olivia

Well, Olivia, I'm going to assume you don't mean GOAT in internet parlance (the acronym for Greatest Of All Time) because that would make you an enthusiastic Satanist, which seems unlikely. Instead, I reckon you're asking why Satan is sometimes depicted with goat-like features. It's also a question posed in the TV show *Lucifer*, in which the title character is confused to discover he is called 'Goat' by his worshippers, until it transpires that Lucifer's angelic brother started the goat rumour as a hilarious prank.

Anyway, even though the biblical Satan is described in the Book of Revelation as an apocalyptic beast, ancient scripture is sketchy on what that looked like. Moreover, the Devil took an enormous variety of forms in literary and artistic traditions. In his book *Lucifer: The Devil in the Middle Ages*, Professor Jeffrey Burton Russell points out that Satan was understood to appear as an old man, young girl, fisherman, priest, saint, angel, or even as Jesus himself – he was the arch-deceiver, seducing souls by wearing a friendly face. He also had a nice line in animals, including crocodile, deer, snake, monkey, bat, dragon, fox, crow, pig, salamander, rooster, and, yes, sometimes goat.

So, our famous red devil - I'm thinking of *South Park*'s muscle-bound Satan, sadly trapped in an abusive relationship with Saddam Hussein - is not an image drawn from the first thousand years of Christian art, but rather one that only started to show up during the High Medieval and Renaissance eras, presumably as a campaign to scare wayward sinners straight. However, if we ignore art and focus instead on religious writings, then the famous horns do arrive much earlier.

In 447 CE, senior Church fathers met at the Council of Toledo to denounce the heretical theology of the Priscillianists - sadly, nothing to do with glamorous, Aussie drag queens in a tour bus - but, while they were there, they also used their time to describe the Devil as a large, sulphur-stinking, black beast with donkey's ears, shiny eyes, scary teeth, hooves on his limbs, gratuitously massive penis, and horns. Does this sound goaty? Er . . . maybe, a bit? But it also makes him sound quite bullish too. And donkeyish. He's probably more terrifying chimera than woolly ruminant.

There are other goaty clues in Early Medieval art, though rather subtle ones. The stunning sixth-century mosaic in the Basilica of Sant'Apollinare Nuovo, in the ancient Italian city of Ravenna, depicts the Last Judgement. Jesus is looking very fetching in purple robes, flanked by two beardless angels: one in red, who looks a bit like a young Jeremy Paxman, and one in blue, who looks like the prettiest member of a mid-nineties boy band. Next to the red angel are three sheep; and next to the gorgeous blue angel are three goats. The mosaic depicts the section in St Matthew's Gospel in which the saved and the condemned are to be separated by Jesus, as does a shepherd separate his sheep from his goats. The blue angel is Lucifer, and thus the goats were perhaps shorthand for condemned souls? If so, the goats clearly fancy Lucifer because they seem surprisingly cheerful about their eternal doom; they have charming little smiles on their faces. It's totally adorable.

So, is this where the goat thing began? No, I don't think so. The powerful goat-man long predates Christianity, most obviously with the ancient Greek god Pan, who – with his satyr's body of goat legs, human torso, bearded face, and horns – was a wild spirit drawn to the pleasures of music and dance. But archaeologists working on Bronze Age civilisations, like Egypt, Minoan Crete, Mesopotamian Ur, Harappan India, and even late Stone Age Turkey, have found much earlier representations of horned deities. In Egyptian theology, it was Amon; in ancient India, it was Pashupati; in the Gaulish religion of Iron Age France it was Cernunnos.

These figures seem to have been revered as lords of the animal kingdom. But the rise of monotheism, particularly Christianity, resulted in the suppression of these ancient polytheistic figures, and the twisting of the horned iconography into the nastier, more devilish association. If we jump to the 1430s, that monstrous Devil plays a starring role in *The Last Judgement* by the artist Fra Angelico, which shows humans in Hell being tortured by horned demons with green and black skin. Lurking at the bottom of the painting is the Devil himself, a huge black beast with small white horns, who greedily devours the sinners, tearing their limbs and torsos with his massive jaws. Yet, when I look at Fra Angelico's Satan, I don't see a goat; he's more post-watershed Gruffalo, if anything.

Where else can we look? Well, we do get some weird and wonderful goat action during the heightened hysteria of the

European Witch Craze, in the 1540s–1690s, when the accused were alleged to snog the arseholes of goats and cats, in a ritual dubbed the Kiss of Shame! Lurid illustrations by artists, such as Hans Baldung Grien, also depicted sinister Sabbaths where witches ride flying goats instead of broomsticks. This was perhaps a sex thing. Horny goats had long been associated with aggressive virility, and a cuckold betrayed by a cheating wife might be shamed with the famous finger-horns gesture behind his head. In short, ladies straddling gravity-defying goats represented Satan's primal powers of sexual seduction, with the witches literally getting high by riding him all night long.

Alas, I do now have to be annoying and stress that these airborne goats aren't Satan himself; they're demonic familiars working for him, much like the more notorious black cats. So, forgive my presumption, Olivia, but I reckon the demonic goat you're thinking of might not be the Devil at all, but rather the occult Sabbatical goat-man we see on tarot cards, and in the pages of Giles the librarian's dusty old tomes in *Buffy the Vampire Slayer*. This figure, with a pentagram carved into his forehead, isn't actually medieval; it arrived in the mid-nineteenth century, courtesy of the French occultist Éliphas Lévi, who abandoned a career in the Church for a more mystical calling as gnostic wizard. So, where did he get his inspiration? Well, it seems he might have been influenced by a medieval conspiracy theory (yes, they predate the Facebook hellscape of the modern age).

Lévi called his goat-creature Baphomet, this probably being a linguistic fudging of Mahomet (as in Prophet Muhammad). In medieval Crusader literature, Muslims were often denounced as idolatrous worshippers of Mahomet himself, rather than Allah.

That's our first conspiracy, but I'll now shimmy over to a parallel conspiracy: that of the mighty, medieval monastic order, the Knights Templar. You probably recognise the name? They've been the subject of extensive, dubious myth-making over the years, and if you've suffered through *The Da Vinci Code* – either the book or the movie – then you have my sympathy. Much of what's written about the Templars is utter garbage,* but they were indeed real, and became financially powerful until their heresy trial in 1307, instigated by the King of France. As for that promised conspiracy theory, their secret rituals supposedly involved the worship of a magical skull belonging to a bearded man (presumably Mahomet) which they called . . . wait for it . . . Baphomet.

However, the Templars' alleged Baphomet was not goatish, so Éliphas Lévi added that element himself, seemingly drawing on an ancient Egyptian deity called the Goat of Mendes for inspiration. Before Lévi came along, tarot cards depicted the Devil as humanoid with a second face lodged in his belly, eyes on his knees, lion's paws for feet, bat's wings on his back, and deer antlers on his head – it was quite the look. He also sometimes possessed both full breasts and a large penis. In 1850, Lévi transformed this Devil representation into the modern, muscular goat-fella, ditching most of the other body parts, but keeping the breasts and penis, and adding the forehead pentagram and large ram's horns.

The Church of Satan in America (I'm assuming you're not a member, Olivia!) has since adopted Lévi's Baphomet image as their own Satanic representation, and even erected a rather fetching statue of him in Detroit, although they opted

---

* See Dan Jones's recent biography for a great summary of what we do know.

for a less sexualised look to appease the horrified citizens of the city, replacing the sexual organs with depictions of an accompanying boy and a girl to represent Satan's dual genders.

So, Olivia's question of *'why is the Devil a goat?'* is a tricky one, because he traditionally takes so many forms, and it's only when he's being Baphomet that the goat thing really persists. Indeed, if you believe medieval logic, Satan is not going to tempt you as a big horned monster, or as a bleating ram, but may instead come to you disguised as a trusted friend. Not to make you paranoid, or anything . . .

23. When and why did we start keeping hamsters as pets?
Asked by Juliet

In 1802, an English naturalist and churchman named Rev. William Bingley published a popular guide to wildlife entitled *Animal Biography*. It sold so well, he updated it through several editions. Among its most startling paragraphs is this one, dedicated to a ferocious, idiotically brave creature which, with minimal provocation, would charge towards dogs, horses, and humans, and would fight to the death rather than admit defeat:

> . . . it seems to have no other passion than that of rage; which induces him to attack every animal that comes his way, without in the least attending to the strength of the enemy. Ignorant of the art of saving himself by flight, rather than yield he will allow himself to be beaten to

pieces with a stick. If he seizes a man's hand, he must be killed before he will quit his hold . . . He even makes war against his own species. When two . . . meet, they never fail to attack each other and the stronger always devours the weaker.

Sounds like a hellish monstrosity, right? Well, Juliet, you might be surprised to learn the name of this terrifying, war-like beast is one we all know: the hamster.

Yes, it surprised me too. When I was a small kid, we had a classroom hamster at school and, thanks to the generous rota system, each child got to take him home for a week. I can still remember the excitement of bringing him into the lounge, and then the mortifying panic that swamped me when he promptly died, midway through my tenure. Before you call the RSPCA, I'm innocent! It was natural causes, OK?! He was old, or something. I don't know, all I know is we had to bury him in the garden and then buy a replacement hamster from the pet shop. I christened the new one Jazzy – it seemed such a fun name to my seven-year-old self – but my teacher decided to give the back-up rodent his predecessor's name. Much like 'M' and 'Q' in the James Bond movies, being Gizmo the class-room hamster wasn't so much a personal identity as it was a role within the organisation.

So, how did the rampaging beast of Bingley's book end up being the adorable, chubby-cheeked pet in my primary school? The truth is, it didn't. Bingley was describing the black-bellied European hamster, a species of wild animal no child should get near without protective gloves. Indeed, the Victorian naturalist Nathaniel Laurence Austen tried to keep one as a pet, describing it as:

... exceedingly touchy and irascible in temper, and would let no one but myself handle or take him up. When irritated, which was very often, the moment he saw any stranger looking at him, he would grunt with rage like a miniature wild boar, and throwing himself on his back, would gnash his teeth and snap viciously at anything near him.

At one point, Austen tried to scare his hamster by firing a loud pistol near its face. The hamster just glared at him, as if to say, 'Is that all you've got?' It also murdered a kitten when he turned his back briefly. Seriously, do not mess with European hamsters! Fortunately for us, and unfortunately for them, they were extensively hunted for their fur and so are now critically endangered. Chances are, you won't be accosted by one in a dark alleyway.

In which case, the obvious question is: where do the lovely, cute, golden-furred hamsters, which Juliet enquired about, come from? The answer is Syria. The first one to reach Britain was a specimen delivered to George Waterhouse, the curator at the London Zoological Society, in 1839. We also know that a British diplomat, James Henry Skene, brought some Syrian hamsters back to Edinburgh in 1880 and he bred them as gifts for his friends. He died in 1886, but the breeding colony lasted until 1910.

However, to properly understand how hamsters became household pets, we need to scroll forward to 1931, and meet the medical scientist Dr Saul Adler. He needed lab specimens for researching the disease leishmaniasis but his Chinese hamsters stubbornly refused to breed, and importing them from Asia was quite the faff. Based at the Hebrew University of Jerusalem, Adler wondered if the answer to his problems was maybe burrowing away in some nearby desert? He needed a zoologist to track down something appropriate.

So, Adler begged a zoologist colleague, Israel Aharoni, to go fetch him something suitable. Aharoni remembered Syrian hamsters, and in turn begged for help from a Syrian guide called Georgius, who hooked him up with a helpful sheikh, who provided a team of workmen. Together they put in many hours of backbreaking work scouring the landscape for wild hamsters. It was harder than it sounds, but they eventually dug up a nest of twelve hamsters: a mother and her eleven pups. Upon seeing the human predator, the mum immediately decapitated her nearest child. Alarmed, Aharoni had to speedily kill her to save the other kids.

He then gave the baby hamsters to Hein Ben-Menachen, the founder of Hebrew University's Animal Facilities department. Disaster struck as half the pups chewed their way out of the cage and got fatally lost in the lab; if that wasn't bad enough, one of the males then ate a female. Only four hamsters remained, which seemed something of a disaster, given how hard it was to source them. Remarkably, these four survivors sired a breeding colony of 150 hamsters in just a year, and they were split up and shipped off to research labs around the world. It was a big win for science; it meant labs could breed their own supply of experimental guinea pigs . . . but, you know, *not* actual guinea pigs. Of course, it would later prompt serious questions about the ethics of animal testing.

Having barely been known in Europe or North America, hamsters suddenly became rather popular with the public, and, despite the privations of wartime rationing, Britain's official Hamster Club was inaugurated in 1945. Selective breeding made Syrian hamsters even cuter still, with those big, wide faces, which only furthered their appeal. In America, the first big-time breeder was Albert Marsh who, somewhat weirdly, was initially introduced to hamsters when he inherited one as part of a gambling debt – I didn't realise hamsters were acceptable currency in Vegas, but what do I know? Marsh quickly published a guide to keeping hamsters which sold 80,000 copies between 1948 and 1951. A new American pet had arrived.

One of the customers who bought his book, and responded to his adverts in magazines, was a fourteen-year-old boy called Everett Engle, who borrowed money from his dad to set up his own breeding shed in the back garden. Everett was soon supplying the American Midwest, despite still being a school-boy, and by 1961 he'd landed a very notable customer in the form of President John F. Kennedy, who received two ham-sters named Jackie and Billie to amuse his daughter, Caroline. Just as Jackie Kennedy became First Lady, Jackie and Billie became the First Hamsters of America. In time-honoured tradition, they promptly escaped their cage, and were found scurrying around JFK's bathroom. Classic hamster hijinks!

It's a cute story, although the White House kennel keeper, Traphes Bryant, who looked after all the presidential pets, later recalled: 'There was a family of hamsters, like something out of a Greek tragedy. First, one hamster drowned itself in the president's tub. Then the others were eaten by their father. But the final act beat all – the mother hamster killed the father and then died herself, probably of indigestion.' It says a lot about the curse of the Kennedy family that even their pets were doomed to suffer violent deaths.

Although we think of hamsters as cute, such lurid hamster violence isn't uncommon. While I was writing this answer to Juliet, I shared Bingley's hamster observations on Twitter, and was inundated with horrific stories from people about pet hamsters attacking them, or hamsters cannibalising their beloved cage buddies (including a harrowing story of a boy who discovered ten Russian hamster pups devouring their mother, until their faces were soaked in blood!).

So, Juliet, the answer to your question is that hamsters have only been popular pets for three quarters of a century, but their quiet propensity for violence belies their adorable appearance. In actual fact, they're the Macaulay Culkin in *Home Alone* of the animal kingdom; cross them at your peril!

24. How much horse faeces and urine were created per day in London during the reign of Henry VIII, and what was done with it all?
Asked by Donny and Katherine

Look, let's just cut to the chase, shall we? Poo is both funny and interesting. I'm professionally fascinated by the history of sanitation and cleanliness, plus I work on *Horrible Histories*, so the moment I saw this question I knew it was going straight in the book. Unfortunately, it was surprisingly tricky to answer. The specificity of Donny and Katherine's era requirements has somewhat tripped me up, and I'll have to admit that I was unable to find a good source for exactly how many horses there were in London during Henry VIII's reign. So, please forgive me if this answer relies on comparisons rather than direct evidence.

Right then. Horses - they're pretty big, and they defecate quite a lot. An average healthy horse will evacuate its bowels between eight and twelve times per day. As for the weeing schedule, that's even more frequent; you'd likely expect about

10 litres of urine in twenty-four hours, which is basically enough to fill a plastic bucket. When the faeces and urine are combined, the total manure produced by a single horse, in a single day, will typically weigh a whopping 20kg, which is the same as a six-year-old child. Blimey, and I thought my baby daughter pooed a lot!

Needless to say, a major city with lots of horses moving through it was going to get pretty dirty, very fast. Annoyingly, that's about as specific as I can be. In the 1530s, during the middle of Henry VIII's eventful reign, London was home to maybe 60–80,000 people, but accurate equine data has eluded me. That said, if you're imagining a busy city scene with lots of horse-drawn carriages, then please stop immediately! In King Henry's day, horse-drawn carriages were extremely rare in Europe; they were essentially a wooden box plonked on a pair of axles, and their total lack of suspension made them a very bumpy form of transport. If carriages were used at all, their clientele seems to have been restricted to royal women, because powerful men likely rode their own mount or were carried in a litter.

The major change occurred just after Henry VIII had kicked the bucket. In the mid-1500s, during the reigns of his daughters Mary and Elizabeth, newfangled *coaches* began to spread westwards through Europe from Hungary – 'coach' derives from the Hungarian word *kocsi*, which itself comes from the Hungarian village of Kocs, where wheelwrights pioneered the sprung-suspension design. The coach made public transport more comfortable and more popular, and horses were the obvious animal to pull them, but it still remained unaffordable to the vast majority of people for a long while.

Instead, in the early reign of Henry VIII, I'd ask you to

imagine heavy wagons being mostly drawn by oxen, and not so much carrying human cargo but rather goods. There would have been some horses on the roads, sure, but they became much more common in the reign of Elizabeth I. For example, on the route from Enfield to north London, there were a reported 2,250 horses seen in a single day, most of them transporting malt to the big city. Horses also were then being preferred for moving textiles because the cloth could get damp when transported by boat. Besides pulling wagons and carts, or fancy carriages, horses were also ridden by the messengers of the newly founded postal service, established in 1516 by King Henry, and there were even places to hire horses if people couldn't afford to buy them.

Horse ownership increased dramatically in the sixteenth century, and the horse historian Professor Peter Edwards – who is an expert on the social and economic history of horses, rather than an *actual* horse who studies history – has shown that even the small Lincolnshire farming village of Horbling had 60 per cent of its land holdings supporting between one and ten horses, and a further 14 per cent of holdings had considerably more horses than that. There were loads of horses in this small, rural place, and this was no accident.

As well as chronic dissatisfaction with his rotating cast of wives, King Henry VIII was also furious to discover that there was a great horse shortage in his kingdom, most notably of the swift, powerful chargers needed for riding into battle, and also of the strong, hardy draught animals needed to supply his armies. Even though the nature of warfare was changing by the 1530s, and the rise of the gunpowder weapon was ending the era of the armoured knight astride his galloping *destrier*, Henry was still obsessed with acquiring better, bigger, swifter, stronger, and more numerous horses; particularly when he learned in 1540 that four Dutch horses had pulled more weight between them than seven English ones.

Determined to improve this dire situation, Henry reissued his father's law that made it a criminal offence to export horses out of the country, and he increased the regulation of domestic horse sales. His royal parks and hunting lodges were also converted into stud farms, and he used both carrot and stick on his leading nobles and landowners, to cajole and convince them to join his horsey breeding programme. He also traded plenty with continental Europe, exporting a breed called Irish hobbies in return for a variety of draught and riding animals.

If you're really not a horse lover, it's possible you might assume there's only really three breeds available: adorable Shetland ponies, thundering racehorses, and massive shire horses. But there are many more horse breeds than that, and a wealthy landowner would keep all sorts in their stables. For example, a list of horses maintained in the Earl of Northumberland's stables, in 1512, included more than ten different varieties, each with a specific job. As Professor Edwards clarifies, the 'gentell hors' was an expensive thoroughbred; the *palfrey* was a small, nimble-footed, smooth strider ideal for a woman to ride; the *hobbies* and *nags* were small, less powerful warhorses; the 'chariott horse' and 'gret trotting horsys' were muscular cart-pulling horses; the 'trottynge gambaldyn' horse was basically a fancy dressage horse famed for its high knee action, making it perfect for showing off in public; and the 'cloth sek' and 'male hors' were bred to carry luggage and armour across bumpy terrain.

So, although they weren't as commonly seen on the roads as in later periods, Henry VIII's era was a time when the horse became ever more important to his military ambitions and to the wider economy, and their price of sale and number surged accordingly. But now we get back to the hard problem of figuring out how much manure they might have produced. I'll be honest, this is going to take some unreliable guestimation.

I can tell you that in 1795 – some 250 years after Henry's death – the city of Edinburgh (including Leith) produced 40,000 cartloads of horse manure per year, according to a local farmer called George Robertson. At the time, Edinburgh was probably home to the same number of people as lived in Tudor London. It's tempting, therefore, to simply match the number and triumphantly declare Henry VIII's capital city was bestrewn with 40,000 cartloads of crap per year.

But eighteenth-century Edinburgh enjoyed the regular comfort of horse-drawn coaches, and Tudor London did not, so perhaps the ratio and use of horses was very different back in the 1530s. Frankly, I'm just not confident giving you a figure. Sorry to disappoint! But if we remember that the average horse drops 20kg of waste every day, and that there were 2,250 horses using a single road, on a single day, in Elizabeth I's reign, then that would have been one very messy road.

As for Donny and Katherine's question about what happened to the manure, thankfully this is where we know a lot more. Unlike the modern popular notion that medieval people were forever chucking buckets of piss out of their windows, we actually know that such crude behaviour was met with a sizeable fine, as was allowing livestock to defecate on public streets. In Dublin – which fell under English legal jurisdiction, following Henry VIII's assertion between 1541 and 1542 that he was King of Ireland – it was well understood that horses were definitely going to poop all over the place, but a proclamation from 1557 tells us that anyone caught chucking dung into the streets or lanes would be fined, with half going to the treasury and half going to the witness who grassed them up to the cops. The proper thing was instead to cart the waste to special dunghills outside the town walls.

Meanwhile, London under King Henry was a city where paving was starting to come in, and attempts were made to build a sewer system to deal with surface water. Runnels were put in place that moved any foul liquids away from the streets, and into these sewers, streams, and cesspools. But, yeah, let's not kid ourselves; the streets were certainly dirty, and fancy people might have worn chunky pattens on their feet to lift their nice shoes, capes, and skirts up above the filth. But what's interesting is that this sewage wasn't just left to fester.

People in towns and cities were commonly required to sweep and cleanse the streets outside their own homes once a week, usually on a Saturday - presumably ensuring they were clean for the sacred Sunday Sabbath - though in York, in 1550, a rule change demanded streets be 'twysc clensyd and swepyd every weyk'. York's records also tell us that waste collections happened on Tuesdays, Thursdays, and Saturdays. And if the local administrators didn't arrange for regular collections, then around the towns and cities of England, Scotland, Wales, and Ireland, a local businessman or landowner might instead pay the local authorities a retainer for the opportunity to shovel up the poo themselves (or more likely hire a poo-shoveller), and then sell it to local farmers for use as fertiliser.

Indeed, human and animal manure was surprisingly valuable - alarmingly, it was occasionally used in medicines - so rather than people indiscriminately chucking their waste onto the streets and wandering back indoors, many people more likely collected it next to their houses, as a source of income. Local rules often allowed this personal stash to stay for a week, though historians have found it often remained for longer. Frequently, the key rule was that it couldn't block a person's front door or encroach upon a neighbour's property. If the pile got too large, or the homeowner was deemed to be cheekily bending the rules, then they were asked to pay a dungheap tax for the privilege.

So, unlike my twenty-first-century, middle-class custom of paying Surrey County Council a bit extra, on top of my normal council tax, for the bi-monthly collection of my garden waste, which I stash in a large green wheelie bin, medieval and Tudor people were coughing up more for the chance to keep their own refuse (in what was known as a *kennel* or *laystall*), which they could then sell. We all know of the importance of the consumer economy in modern capitalism, but this was an Early Modern economy of literal consumption, digestion, and monetisation that I shall hereby christen *crapitalism* (I refuse to apologise for this).

In the Lancashire town of Prescot, in the 1580s, even the extra fee for piling up a large amount could be dodged by instead building the manure mountain in one's backyard, away from the public streets. In which case, as the Shakespeare scholar Professor Bruce Boehrer notes, we shouldn't think of Early Modern spaces being clogged with discarded waste, but rather they were clogged with *treasured* waste. Horse dung was worth scraping off and keeping, at least for a week or so. To quote Boehrer: 'Even William Shakespeare's father was fined "for making a dungheap (*sterquinarium*) before his house in Henley Street"' in 1552. It's possible this was part of John Shakespeare's job as a glove-maker, seeing as animal faeces could be used to soften leather.

So, when it came to horses pooing all over the roads, there was a system in place to get rid of it and turn a nice profit in the process. However, the more frustrating problem for local authorities was the amount of faeces going into the water supply. In 1556 – a decade after Henry VIII died – court records show that fish sellers working in the area of London called the Strand were fined for allowing their carthorses to poo so much into the 'common water waye' that it became blocked up. As urban London rapidly grew, more and more faeces ended up in the rivers and streams, undoubtedly causing major health and hygiene problems that were only resolved by the construction of Joseph Bazalgette's famous intersecting sewer system in 1865-75.

In which case, the roads were definitely filthy, but it was the water you wanted to avoid!

25. When and where were seeds first sold in packets, and by whom? What did people use before then?
Asked by Charlotte

Through charming coincidence, I'm writing this having spent most of the day at the gorgeous gardens of RHS Wisley, the Royal Horticultural Society's crowning glory in Surrey. I'm lucky to live nearby, so my family make regular trips, and the experience is always heightened by the presence of my dad, a professional gardener, who gleefully waltzes around pointing at rare shrubs and trees while asking me to guess what they are. I'm unfailingly terrible at this game, and have been a horticultural disappointment ever since I was his clumsy lawnmower flunkey in my school holidays. When quizzed, I typically cry, *'Cotoneaster dammeri!'* at any berry-laden shrub; 'Looks like a *Prunus!'* at any tree that isn't an oak; and – when totally baffled – I'll just shout out names of celebrities: 'Hang on, Dad . . . I know this! Is it an alpine Rita Ora?'

But though my dad seems exceptionally knowledgeable to my eyes, he finds RHS Wisley to be a magical mystery tour of delightful surprises. It boasts 12,000 different plants – way more than even he can identify – but that's nothing compared to the number of plant species on the planet: an estimated 391,000! Such abundance truly boggles the mind to contemplate it, and not all of these plants were even known about until recently. But while it's true that the gardens of Wisley are a by-product of eighteenth- and nineteenth-century colonial empire, horticultural science, and modern globalism, don't be fooled into thinking the importation of exotic plants is new. Far from it, in fact.

We know that way back in the Neolithic era, over 12,000 years ago, humans were already experimenting with cereal crops and fruit trees, although the genetic history of flora domestication is proving surprisingly knotty for scientists to untangle. Some species endured for enormous numbers of generations before evolving into a new thing, and some changed much more rapidly.

Take the humble apple, for example; surprisingly, human involvement only seems to stretch back to the Bronze Age, maybe 3–4,000 years ago. The modern apple's ancestor is a delicious species known as *Malus sieversii*, which still grows in modern Kazakhstan. Tweak a letter and you instead get *Malum*, which meant both *apple* and *evil* in Latin, a coincidence that St Jerome exploited in his Latin translation of the Bible to make a memorable pun. It was one pushed further by John Milton in his seventeenth-century epic poem *Paradise Lost,* to flag up Adam and Eve's apple-gobbling error of judgement (it's thanks to Milton that we think it was an apple, when in fact the Bible just says it was a fruit). It's also why Snow White's stepmum gets bonus points for that poisoned Granny Smith - if you're gonna commit a crime, make sure to make the murder weapon a highbrow linguistics joke!

Anyway, humans accidentally invented modern apples by hybridising *M. sieversii* with three other species, and this process seems to have occurred along the Silk Roads trade routes that linked East Asia to Europe and the Middle East (check out Peter Frankopan's brilliant book *The Silk Roads* to learn more). It's possible humans were deliberately exchanging seeds as a form of currency or desirable food technology, but a more likely scenario is that people and animals ate the apples, then walked on for a bit, pooed out the seeds, and thereby spread them unwittingly. So, perhaps apples should be renamed *crapples*? Sorry, is that too much? It's too much, isn't it. My bad.

By the time we get to the Greeks and Romans, agricultural management was a huge deal, written about by some of the most important writers of the ancient world, including Aristotle, Cato the Elder, Virgil, Terentius Varro, and Columella. The Romans in particular were enthusiastic gardeners and serious farmers, so seed-saving was among the most commonly practised habits, in which the best seeds from the strongest plants were stored for the following year, or traded with other landowners to promote healthy biodiversity. Were they sold in little packets? Probably not, but it's not impossible, I suppose.

Of course, Charlotte's question about seed packets conjures up images of local garden centres, with their cheerful cafés and retinue of pottery gnomes. These businesses emerged in the 1960s, as plant nurseries sought to remain open all year round, expanding from wholesale stockists into retail shops serving aspirational suburban homeowners, many of whom acquired gardens for the first time in their lives. Heading to your nearest shop for a packet of seeds, or a pre-grown pot plant, made one's humble patch of scraggly lawn seem like a miniature Eden to be nurtured in one's own divine image. But while the garden centre was a novelty, popping into a shop for a packet of seeds had also been rather common four centuries ago. In fact, it was from a seventeenth-century writer that I've cheekily stolen my Eden analogy.

The brilliant English polymath Francis Bacon – one of the earliest advocates of the scientific method (and reputedly the man who died in 1626 while inventing frozen food, when he caught a chill stuffing a chicken with snow) – wrote an essay called *Of Gardens* in which he said: 'God Almighty first planted a Garden. And indeed it is the purest of human pleasures.' Bacon lived in an England that was increasingly garden-obsessed. Previously, plant seeds were sold by certain tradespeople, but only as a small part of their wider business. By the 1600s, however, specialist seed sellers were sprouting up to deal with a chronic seed shortage. Land use given over to market gardens had shot up, and the fashionable classes were also racing to give themselves domestic gardens designed for pleasure and growing medicinal herbs.

In fact, such was the demand for seeds, a racket opened up for dodgy dealers to travel the kingdom selling old, mouldy, dried-out, or wrongly identified seeds to gullible punters. The churchman Richard Gardiner, who wrote an early how-to manual on growing your own veggies, ranted in 1599 against 'those which bee common sellers of Garden seedes . . .' who he believed deceived many people by selling them old or dead seeds, causing them to waste money on useless products, and then yet more money on the manure and rental of growing land, only for nothing to grow. He finished by saying: 'consider how many thousand poundes are robbed yeerely from the common wealth by those Catterpillers'. I don't know about you, but I think 'caterpillars' is a rather charming insult for enemies of gardeners, given their propensity to destroy plants, though I'd have gone with slugs – the bane of my woeful horticultural efforts (and nightly invaders of my kitchen!).

But by the end of the seventeenth century, England's major cities had specialist seed shops of better repute. In 1677, William Lucas published a catalogue of his wares, on sale in London's the Strand, including: 'Seeds of Roots, Sallad-Seeds, Potherb Seeds, Sweet-herb Seeds, Physical Seeds, Flower-Seeds, Seeds of Ever-green and Flowering Trees, Sorts of Peas, Beans, etc, Seeds to improve Land, Flower Roots, Sorts of choice Trees and Plants', along with gardening tools and various pre-grown plants. In fact, between 1680 and 1780, London's seed dealers grew in number from just three businesses to thirty-five, as more and more species of plant were imported from overseas.

The 1600s saw England's landed gentry go gardening potty, with the diarist John Evelyn and the military commander John Lambert being notably green-fingered. These weren't just places to grow useful medicinal plants, they were also spaces for calm meditation and self-betterment. Garden design also became trendy among royalty when 1688 brought the installation of Dutch Protestant William of Orange as King William III; he and his co-reigning English wife, Queen Mary II, were big fans of large, formal gardens. An imported monarch proved a fitting champion for a floral frenzy because it also led to a much greater variety of imported plants.

The garden historian Malcolm Thick estimated that there had been just 200 species of plant regularly cultivated in the days of Henry VIII. But once the British Empire expanded into the Americas, India, Australia, China, and various other far-flung territories, the range of options became thrillingly vast. By the time an eighteen-year-old Queen Victoria was perched on her throne, in 1837, something like 18,000 plant varieties were being enjoyed in the gardens of Great Britain. As Professor Corinne Fowler has noted in her book *Green Unpleasant Land*, so many of the charming houses and gardens we enjoy popping along to on a bank holiday weekend were the products of empire, and all the violence that could entail.

Meanwhile, in America, seed-saving was widely practised by farmers – including by George Washington, whose crops (grown by the hundreds of people he kept in cruel enslavement) were renowned for their quality. But those looking to purchase seeds commercially went instead to a small religious fringe group called the Shakers. They were an offshoot of English Quakerism and weren't just millenarians, but embraced full gender equality and even proclaimed that that one of their leaders, Mother Ann Lee, was the second coming of Christ in female form. James and Josiah Holmes, from Maine, were the first Shakers to sell their seeds in paper packets, but it became a regular practice throughout the brethren. They didn't go in for fancy fruits and resplendent flowers; flax, onions, and cucumbers were more their speed.

So, we might think ourselves modern in buying the seeds for glamorous perennials from our local garden centres, or in the gift shops at the Chelsea Flower Show, but people were doing the same in London back in the late 1600s, and it was certainly happening commonly in late eighteenth-century America. Of course, when their seeds failed to grow, they blamed the dodgy-dealing 'caterpillars'; but when my seeds fail to grow, I can hear my dad's disappointed sighing on the wind, not least because it's almost certainly my fault. I am, after all, the son who accidentally drove his ride-on lawnmower into a pond.

26. Are there any trees in history that have had a big impact/funny stories?
Asked by Ruby

As J. R. R. Tolkien liked to remind us, trees are wonderful things, standing as ancient mute witnesses to so much of human life. And given their strength, scale, age, beauty, and visibility in the landscape, it's no surprise that people like to gather near them. Trees have played key roles in many major events, or have come to hold symbolic power afterwards, but in terms of Ruby's question, which allows for impactful trees and funny ones, I'll start with the Big Impact and I'll end on the arboreal LOLs.

Of course, I probably have to begin with Sir Isaac Newton's famous apple tree, under which he is said to have formulated his theory of gravity. This story is often embellished in pop culture, but it comes from the horse's mouth. Or rather, it comes from the horse's friend, being described in the *Memoirs of Sir Isaac Newton's Life,* published in 1752 by Newton's eminent friend William Stukeley. He tells it like this:

> After dinner, the weather being warm, we went into the garden and drank tea, under the shade of some apple trees . . . he told me, he was just in the same situation, as when formerly, the notion of gravitation came into his mind. It was occasion'd by the fall of an apple, as he sat in contemplative mood. Why should that apple always descend perpendicularly to the ground, thought he to himself . . .

In the annals of science, Newton's apple tree is a veritable arboreal celebrity. But there are also several trees notable for inspiring other types of realisation; perhaps the most influential in religious terms was the Bodhi Tree, otherwise known as 'the Sacred Fig', found growing in the Indian town of Bodh Gaya. It was beneath its venerable canopy, around 2,500 years ago, that the famous Siddhartha reached spiritual enlightenment, and thus transformed into the Buddha. Cuttings of that tree were taken and propagated, so there are now descendants growing in various sacred places, including at the shrine to Buddha in Bodh Gaya.

Sticking with major religious figures, although moving from philosophical enlightenment to actual light; there is a legend that the German Protestant reformer, Martin Luther, was purportedly the first to mount flaming candles on a Christmas tree, back in the 1500s. This German custom then arrived in Britain thanks to King George III's German wife, Queen Charlotte, who put up a Christmas yew tree at Windsor Castle in 1800. But it wasn't until Queen Victoria and her German consort, Prince Albert, published a famous image of their festive fir, in 1848, that the custom for bringing a tree indoors became popular in Britain.

Of course, some Christmas trees belong outside. Every winter since 1947, London's Trafalgar Square has been beautifully adorned with a lofty Norwegian fir, it being an annual gift of appreciation for when Norway's government and head of state, King Haakon VII, were exiled in London after the Nazi occupation of their country. But for Norwegians, the more emotionally resonant tree was the Royal Birch in Molde, under which Haakon and his son had shielded themselves from a Luftwaffe bombing run in April 1940. A photograph of the two men wearing military uniform, beneath the dignified branches, became a powerful symbol of resistance, and

– though vandals later destroyed the original tree – a replacement birch still grows in the same spot today.

Trees have often been places to bring communities together in defiance or solidarity. We might mention the Liberty Tree in Boston, Massachusetts, under which the 'Sons of Liberty' rallied against the British Stamp Act in 1765, igniting the kindling for what would later become the American War of Independence. Indeed, in 1775, just a few months after fighting broke out, the Brits literally made kindling out of it by chopping it down for firewood.

Two centuries earlier, in 1549, Norfolk in the East of England witnessed a rebellion led by Robert Kett, in opposition to twenty-nine government policies. Kett is supposed to have gathered his council in the shadow of an oak tree, known as Kett's Oak of Reformation, which is long gone. Romantic legend says he then gathered his armies next to a second oak near Wymondham. It still stands today, and is fittingly called Kett's Oak. The rebellion failed and Kett was executed at Norwich Castle, but tradition would have us believe that some of the other ringleaders were hanged from his eponymous tree, under which they had plotted against King Edward VI.

The list of political trees doesn't end there. There's also the Tree of Knowledge, beneath which the Australian Labor Party was founded in 1892. And, in a rather strange story, we have a banyan tree in Pakistan. Generally, banyan trees have long been sacred in South Asia, as they are recognised in Hinduism as places where the spirits of the dead and the divine like to dwell. However, this particular tree had a more bizarre fate, because it was allegedly put under arrest, and shackled with chains, by a drunk British officer in 1898. This was presumably intended as a signal to the locals about what would happen if they defied British colonial rule, although it's obviously way more fun to assume he was absolutely hammered and genuinely confused a stationary tree for a human troublemaker.

And sticking with drunken tree anecdotes, it's perhaps worth mentioning the iconic Tree of Ténéré which, until 1973, was an astonishingly lonesome acacia somehow thriving in the middle of the Sahara Desert. Found in the African nation of Niger, it was widely hailed as the most isolated tree on the planet, being the only one for 250 miles in any direction, and those who saw it up close were amazed by its defiant resilience. Unfortunately, it may have withstood the desert for decades, but it proved no match for a drunk driver who – despite having literally nothing else to hit in a vast, barren wilderness – somehow managed to smash his truck into its trunk. The remains of the murdered tree were moved to the national museum, and today an honorary metal sculpture stands in its stead. Whether it's truck-proof has yet to be tested . . .

Besides Newton's gravitational orchard, the story I immediately thought of when I saw Ruby's question was the iconic tale of a young King Charles II secreted in the foliage of his Royal Oak, in the grounds of Boscobel House in Shropshire, England. This is both an impactful story and a funny one, fulfilling Ruby's double criteria, because the plan to hide him up there was . . . well, let's just say it was a bit of a long shot. This dangerous game of hide-and-seek happened in 1651, in the tumultuous aftermath of the British Civil Wars, and Charles had just been absolutely walloped by the Parliamentarian army at the Battle of Worcester. His father, King Charles I, had already been publicly executed, so the stakes couldn't have been higher for the young Charles. He had to escape capture, or else his fate would be very serious indeed. The problem with escaping, however, was that Charles was *very* distinctive.

You might think that, back in the 1650s, nobody really knew what the King looked like, and it would have been pretty easy to disguise him? But Charles II had a shock of very dark, long, curly hair, a pair of deep brown eyes, plump lips, and he'd seemingly inherited a darker complexion from his Italian grandmother, Marie de Medici. Meanwhile, from his other grandmother, Anne of Denmark, he'd inherited the famed stature of a lofty Viking, meaning he towered over other men. The wanted posters put up around the county described him as 'a tall, black man' - referring to his hair and facial features - and that was him to a tee. Oh, and then there was his accent, which didn't sound very local Shropshire . . .

His supporters did what they could to hide him. The hair was lopped off, his face and hair coloured with plant dyes, and he was given a crash course in chatting like a local, which he apparently managed to learn after some practice. He was also apparently taught how to walk with the notable Worcester gait, which, frankly, leaves me absolutely puzzled - is there such a thing as regional walking styles?! Apparently, there was! Sadly, Charles was rubbish at it. Anyway, I'm getting ahead of myself, because all the disguise malarkey only kicked in once he'd survived the first day of the manhunt. And that was after he'd had his fateful experience in the oak tree.

Having been bested in battle, Charles tried to escape, but his routes were blocked. After lurking uselessly in a hedge, like a giant badger, eventually he ended up scurrying to Boscobel House, owned by William Gifford, in the dead of night. There Charles found one of his loyal army officers already in hiding, the unfortunately named William Careless. With Cromwell's men now searching the area, and with nowhere to hide in the house, both men were instead taken out into the grounds by Gifford's servants, the Penderel brothers, who helped them up into a large oak tree. Here they spent hours hiding, staving off hunger by munching on meagre rations of bread, beer, and cheese which Careless had squirrelled away in his pockets.

At one point, Charles fell asleep with his head in Careless' lap, which is a rather sweet image, but it was actually very dangerous when Careless found his limbs going numb; Cromwell's soldiers were fanning out directly below them, and pins and needles couldn't have struck at a worse time. Luckily, Careless managed to avoid living up to his reckless name, and woke his monarch before the two of them tumbled out of the tree to either snap their necks on impact, or be arrested by those who would happily see them beheaded.

Once safe, Charles then underwent his escape training programme, which in my head was a *Mission: Impossible*-style montage, but with bonus Worcester-walking (whatever that is?!), and eventually he got out of the country after six weeks on the run. Those who had aided him were later rewarded, with William Careless – who had taken such good care of His Majesty – being renamed William Carlos. Meanwhile, once the monarchy had been restored in 1660, Charles II declared his subjects should celebrate Oak Apple Day on 29 May, to commemorate the time he was stuck up a tree like an oversized squirrel. Oddly, that escape had actually occurred in September, but 29 May was preferable because it was both his birthday and the anniversary of his Restoration to the throne.

So, that's perhaps the most famous and mildly funny story involving a tree that I can think of, but, before I tell you my absolute favourite tree story, I posed Ruby's question on Twitter to see if any of my followers had their own suggestions of surprising tree tales from history. They did indeed. Here's a quick selection:

- Nathan Hogg suggested the charming Chapel Oak in Allouville-Bellefosse, France, which is a chunky oak of at least 800 years old. In the late 1600s it was struck by lightning and the resulting fire hollowed out its trunk, so the local abbot decided to build two holy chapels and a staircase inside it. During the French Revolution, when radicals attacked churches, it was very nearly burned again, but a quick-witted local renamed it the Temple of Reason, and that seemed to calm the protests. You can still visit it today.

- Rachel Littlewood pointed out that the Nazis carefully planted 100 yellow larch trees amid a forest of evergreens at Plattenburg, thereby creating a natural swastika pattern (when seen from the air). Obviously, modern efforts have been made to cut down the trees, but unfortunately the swastika keeps growing back.

- Ed Carter suggested Shakespeare's mulberry tree, supposedly planted by the great playwright in the grounds of his New Place home in Stratford-upon-Avon. Mulberries were fashionable at the time because King James VI wanted to start a British silk industry. When the long-dead Shakespeare became a national icon and posthumous celebrity in the mid-1700s, the man who now owned the land, Reverend Francis Gastrell, got annoyed at all the gawking tourists showing up to poke around Shakespeare's garden, and so chopped down the tree. The wood was then used by local craftsmen to make Shakespeare-themed souvenirs, although most were dodgy fakes marketed to gullible Bard nerds who had no idea how much wood one tree actually produces . . .

• Several people suggested the 1,000-year-old Major Oak
in Sherwood Forest, Nottinghamshire, supposedly home
to Robin Hood and his Merry Men, but the historian Dr
Hannah Nicholson suggested another Sherwood Forest tree
called the Greendale Oak, which was absolutely massive. In
1734 Henry Bentinck bet he could drive a carriage and three
horses abreast through the massive trunk. To achieve this,
he had a massive hole cut through it. A later report declared:
'The circumference of the trunk above the arch, 35 ft. 3in.;
height of the arch, 10 ft. 3 in.; width about the middle, 6ft.
3 in.; height to the top branch, 54 ft.' What a whopper!

So, those are some interesting tree facts for you. But my
absolute fave story, which is purely one for the column
marked 'funny', is the fact that the famous Roman politician
Gaius Sallustius Passienus Crispus allegedly enjoyed an erotic
dalliance with a tree. Passienus is a fascinating figure; he was
extremely wealthy, highly intelligent, very well respected, and
was the second husband of Agrippina the Younger (making
him stepdad to the teenage Nero). And yet, despite all this
– or maybe because of it – Pliny the Elder tells us Passienus
became romantically besotted with a sacred tree in a grove
dedicated to the goddess Diana, and as well as offering it wine
(he would lie on his back and pour booze over the roots) he
also fondled and snogged it too. It might have been a very silly
joke, but it made both the tree and the man famous throughout the Roman world.

So, there you have it, Ruby: a veritable forest of historical
tree stories, and judging by my Twitter replies, there's a load
more out there should you want them.

CHAPTER 7:

FASHION & BEAUTY

27. What are some of the strangest qualities ever considered signs of great beauty and why?
Asked by Micah

Ah, Micah, this is a tricky one. And, forgive me, but my first instinct is to wander down a highbrow path for a bit. You see, beauty is a word we often use, but a philosophical question hangs over it like mistletoe at Christmas. Can beauty be defined? Do we know it when we see it? Does it exist as a universal, objective truth - like triangles? - or is it, to paraphrase Shakespeare, a purely subjective experience that's decided 'in the eye of the beholder'? Answers on a postcard, please!

This argument is one of the longest debates in philosophy. The Enlightenment thinkers David Hume and Immanuel Kant were mostly on Team Subjectivity, even if they sometimes tied themselves in knots. Aristotle was on Team Objectivity, as was the influential English philosopher Anthony Ashley Cooper, 3rd Earl of Shaftesbury, who died in 1713. He was convinced that beauty was a cosmic constant and that humans were designed to appreciate harmony and order, hence why we like music and architecture. He also suggested that appreciating beauty was different to finding someone sexy, because then it became about how to personally benefit from the hot, sweaty romping rather than being a cool, rational enjoyment of their aesthetic form. Obviously, he didn't say 'hot, sweaty romping', but I'm sure he would've liked to.

I realise this answer has launched from a weird place, but Micah's perfectly sensible question leads to some conceptual booby-traps we have to avoid. For some of the most significant thinkers in world history (well, so-called 'Western' thinkers, anyway . . .), there was no such thing as the *strangest* signs of beauty, because beauty was considered universal and thus couldn't be alien (*strange* originally meant *foreign*). Even very modern historians, like the controversial Arthur Marwick, continued this argument that beauty is basically a mathematical formula, and that, though fashions changed, the principles of aesthetics didn't.

And yet, others have long argued that beauty was highly dependent on culture. The French philosopher Voltaire said a toad seemed ugly to humans, but beauty to a toad was 'his toad wife with two huge round eyes coming out of her tiny head, large flat mouth, yellow belly and brown back'. He then said something horribly racist about people from Guinea, and then something weird about the Devil only fancying fellow demons with horns and claws. Sadly, Enlightenment philosophers were often disappointingly unenlightened . . .

Despite this racist language, Voltaire's broader point was correct. What you find beautiful, others might find ugly; and vice versa. So, in this answer I'll do my best to offer examples of historical beauty standards that might surprise us, but, really, they're just different to those we hold now. Oh, and another quick warning: beauty isn't always about the physical form. The historian Dr Hannah Greig has written how eighteenth-century female aristocrats of the British *beau monde* were considered physical beauties because of their deportment, clothes, wit, manners, taste, and rank. Privilege made them pretty, regardless of their actual faces (although genuine beauties were, of course, also much admired).

As a historian of celebrity culture, I believe I've seen plenty of evidence for beauty standards changing, even in my own lifetime. When I was a teen, the BBC comedy sketch show *The Fast Show* showcased Arabella Weir's character whose only concern was 'does my bum look big in this?' The answer she craved was 'No!' However, if the sketch were remade today, she'd be hoping for a 'Yes!' The Kardashian–Jenner celebrity axis has been crucial in this turnaround, and plastic surgeons have reported massive increases in the number of young women wanting emulatory bum lifts.

Such rapid change isn't new. In the 1890s, the ideal body shape for a woman had been wide hips and full bust, but with a tiny, corseted waist. That was then supplanted by influential celebrities like Evelyn Nesbit, whose waiflike frame redefined beauty as being girlish and slender. Of course, Marilyn Monroe restored curvaceousness to public esteem in the 1950s, and then the 1990s gave us Kate Moss' heroin chic. Now we're back to Kardashian curves. Trends are apparently cyclical.

But enough on that, let's now look at some specific case studies of historical beauty standards which might strike us as unusual. We'll start with the fact that chunky monobrows were fashionable in the ancient Mediterranean, and Greek women were known to try to unify their eyebrows with paint, or by rubbing on growth hormone, which, in their era, was donkey piss. In short, Frida Kahlo would have had a load of admirers in ancient Athens. As for slightly lower down the face, the eminent scholar Professor Afsāneh Najmābādi has shown that, in nineteenth-century Persia, it was considered beautiful for women – including the Shah's daughter, Esmat al-Dowleh – to have a thin, downy moustache.

By contrast, if we time-travelled to Renaissance Italy, the most surprising beauty trend was one of hair removal, with fashionable women wanting very high foreheads. This was sometimes achieved through shaving the hairline, but various beauty manuals tell us a more common technique was to apply an alkaline hair removal paste. Such a poultice could be made from pig fat, juniper berries, mustard, and boiled swallows, but the most eye-popping ingredient in a 1532 recipe included cat faeces blended with vinegar. In fairness, modern beauty products still include weird stuff like snail slime, but I'm not sure L'Oréal could get away with smearing cat shit on celebs and telling us to do the same, 'because you're worth it'. They'd also struggle to market the moisturiser used by Samuel Pepys' wife in the 1600s: puppy dog urine. Does dog wee smell worse on your cheeks than donkey wee does on your eyebrows? I can't say I'm keen to find out.

Depilation creams were used on the body too; women in Renaissance Italy were thought to be either unwell or overtly masculine if they had dark body hair, so there was pressure to remove it. We also learn in the saucy novel *Portrait of Lozana: The Lusty Andalusian Woman,* published in 1528 and featuring a character who ends up working as a brothel madam, that pubic hair might be removed, either as hygienic choice or because the male clientele preferred it. The flipside of this bush-whacking was the *merkin*, a pubic wig worn by British sex workers in the seventeenth and eighteenth centuries which helped maintain the au naturel look, but allowed the woman to whip it off after sex to help banish genital crabs.

In fact, body hair removal goes back to the Bronze Age, and wasn't just a womanly thing. According to the Greek historian Herodotus - yes, him again - ancient Egyptian priests plucked and tweezed every hair from their bodies, including the eyebrows. Meanwhile, fancy Egyptians shaved their heads, wore elaborate wigs, and - when it came to socialising in polite company, particularly at banquets - seem to have sometimes plonked scented wax cones into their hairpieces. They believed the gods were sweetly fragrant, so this was perhaps a way of aspiring towards divine status.

More permanent alterations to the body were prized by the Maya of Mesoamerica who, as well as tattooing their bodies - very surprising to the Spanish conquistadors, but hardly surprising to us now - also blinged up their smiles by drilling grooves into their teeth and then ornamenting them with coloured jade stones. There is also some suggestion, though not conclusive, that they raised some of their babies to be cross-eyed, by dangling a patch from the forehead to focus the eyes inwards to the bridge of the nose. This may have been in honour of the sun-god, who was depicted as cross-eyed. If true, was this understood to be a sign of beauty, too? Annoyingly, we don't actually know.

Viking warriors also did cosmetic work on their teeth, filing them down into sharpened fangs, but this was presumably to scare the crap out of the enemy rather than to look cute on a first date. But I want to finish with another toothy trend in East Asia, because, until a century ago - when Japan began to bring itself closer in line with Western culture - it was quite common for high-status Japanese women to completely blacken their smiles. This custom of *ohaguro* involved drinking a potent concoction of sake, water, vinegar, spices, and iron to permanently lacquer one's teeth.

The practice possibly dated back to medieval Japan, and presumably was a way for privileged women, including geishas, to heighten the stark contrast of their full face of white makeup, tinted eyebrows, and rouged cheeks. Westerners found it deeply shocking, so it fell out of favour, but was turning teeth unnaturally black really any weirder than the current craze for bleaching teeth until they're whiter than a Bing Crosby Christmas? We might think this was strange, but those Japanese people might have said the same of us.

All in all, I guess Voltaire was right . . . well, apart from the racism, obviously.

28. Why do Greek statues have small penises?
Asked by Anonymous

I'm obsessed with Twitter, and spend hours on there every day, but my excuse is that Twitter is a brilliant hub for historians. There's an entire #Twitterstorians community, made up of thousands of knowledgeable experts, and it means every day produces fun, stimulating conversations that I wouldn't get anywhere else. One of my favourites occurred in 2013 and it was about ancient Roman penises. I don't recall exactly how it started (knowing me, I likely incited this one), but what began as a cheeky giggle turned into something genuinely fascinating, as four eminent classicists joined the conversation to add their insights.

My favourite thing I learned that day was from Professor Llewelyn Morgan, an expert in ancient poetry; he casually mentioned that ancient verse employed multiple poetical rhythms, or rather *metres*, and one of them – the *priapean* – was specifically for bawdy songs about Priapus, a Roman fertility god whose erect penis was so massive it may as well be a third leg. And there was another poetical metre called *ithyphallic* which, in Greek, literally meant 'straight penis'. No subtleties there! In fact, in the 1700s, *ithyphallic* became a catchall term for any rude poem you wouldn't want your mum to read, and to modern doctors an ithyphallic patient is one who's guzzled too much Viagra and can't get rid of his erection.

I was surprised and delighted that amid the highbrow poetry chat, it wasn't me doing the obvious dick jokes about metrical 'length'; in fact, it was the archaeologist Dr Sophie Hay who wryly noted that only a man would be bold enough to claim his cock was a metre! Yes, even academics can be tittering schoolkids. But that's the point, really; expert historians are not prudes and neither were the Romans. They had these sorts of jokes too, and would likely have enjoyed the hilariously puerile sitcom *Plebs*, with its perennially horny protagonists.

Priapus was the son of love goddess Venus/Aphrodite, so you might expect he'd be a smooth romantic, but classical myth said he was cursed to be ugly and lustful, with a downstairs appendage so cartoonishly huge that Roman art sometimes depicted him as having to carry it in his own arms to stop it dragging along the floor. As well as symbolising fertility and wealth, Priapus' job was to be guardian of gardens, preventing intruders and thieves from penetrating the family home through the backdoor by himself aggressively penetrating anyone he caught. Yes, it's pretty weird that the Romans worshipped a god who was part guard dog, part rapist; even more so when we realise he was often treated as a comedic figure in literature and art.

There's a famous fresco of Priapus from Pompeii that shows him wearing a totally inadequate tunic which has utterly failed to cloak his huge, south-westerly facing dong. It's hard not to stare. Indeed, Priapus' prick was often painted red, to make it even more visible – he was the penile equivalent of Rudolph the reindeer. Priapic statues and images were common in the Roman world, but it's obvious why they aren't so commonly displayed in your local art gallery for all the school groups of jeering children to wander past.

Instead, when we pop into a museum, or if we're lucky enough to afford a Mediterranean holiday, we're much more used to encountering a different sort of ancient image: those beautiful, marble statues dedicated to male heroes, with rippling six-packs, powerful thighs, huge arms, muscular bums, broad chests, rounded shoulders, and . . . er . . . well, as our questioner mentions, surprisingly modest gentlemen's parts.

The simplest explanation for this is that ancient aesthetics valued small penises as being more beautiful – priapic whoppers destabilised the elegant symmetry of a statue – but a small package was also a sign of intellectual distinction. Animals, barbarians, and idiots were thought to have big dicks, because they were ruled by their stupid passions and base instincts; but the civilised Greek or Roman was rational, sophisticated, and cultured. His greatness resided in his brain, not in his underpants.

Indeed, to the Greeks, physical beauty was a gift from the gods, but one that also was reflected in the soul; a good-looking chap was also assumed to have a beautiful mind, an idea summed up in the word *kaloskagathos,* meaning beauty and moral goodness acting in harmony. We don't think that way any more, not least because reality TV proves gorgeous people can be awful humans, and not always the sharpest tools in the box. However, the opposite idea remains a common trope in both Shakespeare plays and modern movies, and superhero villains are often ugly or scarred, as if their inner corruption has colonised their faces.

So, in terms of ancient art, a muscular hero with a diminutive dangler was the physiology of cultural snobbery. In Greek thought, sex was about procreation and size mattered in the opposite way we might expect; Aristotle said a smaller penis was better for conceiving because the sperm didn't cool down too much on its journey to the egg. Indeed, the distinguished classicist Sir Kenneth Dover emphatically argued in an influential 1978 book that, for the Greeks, conception was important for maintaining population numbers, but ideal erotic love wasn't between a man and a wife, but between a powerful adult man and a passive teenage boy. This is shocking to us, but it meant that public art in the Greek world reflected the tastes of these older, powerful men who tended to be artistic patrons. And they didn't desire Priapus, with his colossal trouser snake, but rather slim, lithe, hairless youths with small penises.

Saying that, if we return to Rome, there are examples of phalluses scratched into walls, very much the ancient equivalent of boys drawing them on toilet walls, and – please prepare yourself for some very filthy language – there's some boastful graffiti from Pompeii that reads: 'Fortunatus will shag you really deep. Come and see, Anthusa.' This might have been a recommendation from one woman to her friend, or the ancient equivalent of a late-night sext from Fortunatus himself. Another inscription claims: 'Fortunatus, you sweet soul, you mega-shagger. Written by one who knows.'

Again, it sounds like an endorsement, but I can't help laughing at the thought of Fortunatus writing these himself, like Jay, the virginal loser in *The Inbetweeners,* who can't stop graphically lying about his impossible sexual conquests. Funny or not, it's important to note that these brash boasts tell us the penis wasn't just about aesthetic beauty; here are

Romans referencing the phallus as a sexual organ designed to bring pleasure to women. And, despite my earlier point about idealised statues, I think we have to chase this idea further, because size did matter sometimes, and in all the normal ways we might laugh about.

The Romans and Greeks numbered tens of millions of people, all of them with personal passions and sexual predilections, and not everyone desired a modest package. During my 2013 Twitter conversation, the historian Tom Holland quoted a line from the Roman poet Martial, which translates as: 'Flaccus, if you hear applause in the bath-house, it's because Maro & his dick are there.' As Professor Llewelyn Morgan added, Flaccus was a joke name: it meant 'floppy'. This was Martial doubling down on the schlong-shaming of one man by celebrating the praiseworthy penis of another.

There's a similar joke in Petronius' raunchy satire *The Satyricon*, which tells of Encolpius, an ex-gladiator with erectile dysfunction, his companion with a massive wang, Ascyltus, and the teenage boy, Giton, whom they both fancy. At one point, an old tutor is recounting to Encolpius what he'd just seen in the bathhouse, which turns out to have been a nude, heartbroken Ascyltus wailing in despair:

> ... a great crowd gathered around him with applause and the most awestruck admiration. For he had sexual organs of such enormous size that you would think the man was simply an attachment to his penis ... He found assistance right away: a Roman knight rumoured to be infamous wrapped a cloak around the wanderer and took him off home, I believe to enjoy such a great piece of good fortune by himself ...

Moving away from such obvious homoerotic fiction, we also have historical reports of the transgender teenage Emperor Elagabalus, who married five women but preferred having sex with men, wore women's clothes, and who allegedly promised a fortune to any surgeon who could transform Elagabalus's penis into a vagina. According to legend, Elabagalus recruited political appointees by watching men getting naked in the bathhouse and then hiring those with the largest genitals. I presume this must still happen because modern politics is still rife with massive bell-ends.

Assuming Petronius' satire had a touch of truth to its well-endowed character being picked up in the bathhouse, this suggests to us that large penises were sexually arousing to some men, so it wasn't just youthful boys that everyone desired. Indeed, the illustrious legendary warrior Achilles, who was semi-divine and mostly immortal (apart from an annoying patch on his heel), was said to have possessed a lengthy penis worthy of the gods.

Of course, not to state the bloomin' obvious, but half of all Roman and Greek adults were women, and maybe they had something to do with Achilles' legendary reputation. Sadly, we know less about ancient female sexuality – apart from the scandalous stories of Empress Messalina and her twenty-four-hour competitive orgy (look it up!) – but we might assume plenty of ladies enjoyed sex with well-endowed fellas; after all, people's bodies are different, and it takes all sorts.

In which case, the highbrow ideas transmitted by the ancient statues we see in museums weren't necessarily representative of the lusty thoughts enjoyed by millions of ordinary people. The idealised ancient penis might well have been rather different in size, depending on whether you were planning to admire it in the bedroom, or on a marble pedestal.

29. When did high heels come into fashion and why are they found mainly on women's shoes?
Asked by Margaret

Think of a pair of high heels, and what do you see? My brain defaults to two pop culture images: the first is Carrie Bradshaw breathlessly sighing, 'Hello, lover!' while ogling a fluffy pink pair of Christian Louboutins in a boutique window; it's a scene from the zeitgeisty smash *Sex and the City,* a show I enjoyed until the terrible movies poisoned the happy memories. The second image is from *Kinky Boots,* in which a gorgeous Chiwetel Ejiofor plays a drag queen called Lola who needs a reliable supply of amazing leather boots with unsnappable heels. Carrie worships shoes as high art; Lola sees them as signal-sending messengers: 'Look to the heel, young man. The sex is in the heel.' In both screen representations, heels are impractical, expensive, liable to break, and very much reserved for those seeking feminine expression. But the history of high heels is very different. Heels were originally for men; in fact, not just any men, they were for warriors.

We don't know exactly when heels first showed up, but they were being worn by medieval Persian cavalry troops a thousand years ago. The heel safely wedged the soldier's feet in the stirrups while he let go of the reins and drew his bow. According to Dr Elizabeth Semmelhack - who curates the massive collections at the Bata Shoe Museum in Canada - this distinctively Persian footwear arrived into Europe at the very end of the sixteenth century, after Shah Abbas I of Persia had entertained European diplomats while seeking allies against the powerful Ottoman Turks. We're not sure quite how those meetings went, but presumably at some point the European courtiers squawked an admiring 'Oooh!', aimed squarely at the fancy Persian footwear, and a new trend was born. Not long after, we see high heels in numerous European paintings.

Buff, burly, and belligerent young men now strutted around looking macho, using their new heels for both horse-riding and social shindigs. And when the lower classes started to copy them, the privileged retaliated by embracing even bigger heels that were deliberately impractical, knowing full well it would be impossible for commoners to do manual labour while tottering along in such ridiculous footwear. Of course, Europe is notoriously wet and soggy in the winter (and also in the summer, if you're British), so there was a minor problem with these newfangled high heels – they could easily sink into the mud.

The solution was to slide one's riding boots into a pair of flat-soled mules – hey presto, shoes for your shoes! Much like flip-flops, they made a slapping sound during use, and so were dubbed slap-soles. Rich women, in the early 1600s, also began mimicking masculine fashion. But, not needing to ride a horse, their slap-soles were attached permanently; a flat surface glued to the underside of their elevated shoes, creating a triangular gap under the foot arches.

It's worth noting, however, that very tall footwear wasn't a total novelty. The fancy ladies of Renaissance Venice had already been enjoying elevated footwear for a couple of centuries; these were called *chopines* and they were absurdly huge platform shoes, designed to raise the wearer above everyone else in both a figurative and literal sense. Chopines could lift a woman a dizzyingly dangerous 50cm off the ground, forcing her to totter through the streets, or through whichever party she was trying to rock, with servants propping her up on either side. It was a deliberately unwieldy look. The taller the shoes, the more expensive fabric a lady could show off with her long, floor-length dress. In short, chopines were a smug tool for displaying one's wealth by the yard, but, as Dr Semmelhack notes, it may have been a lady's husband or patron who benefited from her being a mobile billboard for his bank balance.

Meanwhile, wealthy men continued to wear their heels into the early eighteenth century. Perhaps the most famed fashionista was France's illustrious Sun King, Louis XIV, whose beautiful shoes of soft leather or fabric were elaborately embroidered, while the heel blocks themselves were painted or dyed in iconic red.

So, if heels were made for men, why don't most fellas wear them now? Well, with the exception of the pint-sized Tom Cruise, who is often claimed to stack his shoes up, the shift away from masculine heels probably wasn't down to any single cause, but we can detect a noticeable attitude shift in the mid-eighteenth century when the rise of rational Enlightenment philosophy, and a snobbish rejection of French styles, saw fashionable British men do away with their prissy, foreign footwear in favour of sensible shoes designed for sensible, rational lives. Heels now became the *sole* (sorry!) preserve of women, who were widely judged by philosophers to be irrational and silly-headed.

But then gradually women also gave up on heels. Around the dawn of the nineteenth century – following in the wake of the violent revolutions in America, Haiti, and France – high-rise shoes tumbled out of high fashion, presumably because those whose hearts swelled with revolutionary radicalism now wanted to wear democratic attire, closer in style to

Roman and Greek traditions, while those who supported the monarchy and despised the great unwashed perhaps noticed the sudden penchant for guillotines and bayonets sweeping the land, and figured footwear associated with the beheaded King and Queen of France probably wasn't the ideal thing to be flaunting, even if it was utterly fabulous, darlings!

And then came the surprise turnaround. Men dug their old heels out from the shoe closet, driven in part by the new fashion for military-style pantaloons. Compared to tight-fitting breeches, these were baggier trousers that had a loop at the end of the legs to hook under the heel of the shoe and hold the trousers in place. And if the men were doing it, then you've probably guessed where this is going next . . . Yes, women's heels were also due for a comeback, and returned with a vengeance in the mid-1800s, assisted by the rise of photography which made it much easier for high fashions to spread quickly through wider society because greater numbers could see what posh people were wearing.

The democratisation of the camera also led to a surge in Victorian pornography, plenty of which featured nude ladies posing in nothing but their heeled boots – it was an erotic trope which still endures today, of course. But this was also the era in which the female gendering of heels now became permanently fixed in wider society. Yet, there were also ardent critics and cartoonists who harrumphed that high heels gave women ugly, forward-leaning, kangaroo-like silhouettes when they walked. Heels might have been *en vogue*, but they weren't without their detractors.

And just as eighteenth-century women had been derided as being largely incapable of rational thought, so too were these nineteenth-century ladies declared undeserving of political suffrage, not least because their desire to wear such silly shoes showed they clearly couldn't be trusted with proper electoral responsibility. Before you send the hate mail, please may I state that these aren't my own personal views. Honest!

But heels weren't going anywhere. In the early twentieth century, the electrifying razzamatazz of Hollywood gave them a further boost in public esteem. But the final major revolution came in the 1950s, and this wasn't just a style revolution but an engineering one. Just as architects were constructing impressive steel skyscrapers across the world's cities, the tensile strength of steel now became crucial in the development of the spiked *stiletto* heel, named after a type of slender-bladed dagger used in Renaissance Italy. With such strength running through its narrow core, the steel heel became extremely narrow and yet robust enough to keep its lofty height. By the 1960s, that metal spike was being wrapped in modern plastics, rather than wood or leather, and shoe designers have continued to tinker with aesthetics ever since.

It's been a long journey since Persian warriors first wore them, but the design and symbolism of high heels keep moving with the times, and they continue to swing in and out of fashion. In fact, I won't be surprised if they become the must-have fashion choice for futuristic fellas, though hopefully not because of their military functionality – call me an idealist, but it would be nice to imagine a future without the need for military conflict. Saying that, if the robots do rise up against us, then what could be more fabulous than the forces of human resistance going to war decked out in 6-inch heels? It's what Louis XIV would've wanted.

30. Which beauty treatment ended up becoming the most dangerous or deadly?
Asked by James

Last week I switched on a BBC TV documentary and watched a smiling young woman receive a dose of lethal neurotoxin. This wasn't a state execution performed on death row, instead she was paying for the privilege and seemed delighted with the results. Botulinum protein, if ingested from a dodgy BBQ sausage, can cause life-threatening botulism, in which muscles are paralysed and breathing becomes difficult. However, that same nasty protein is also a much-desired cosmetic treatment: Botox.

I don't know about you, James, but, as I barrel rapidly towards middle age, I've found myself increasingly thinking about such treatments, and not in a puritanical, judgey way. Sometimes, in my low moments, I wonder if I should get Botox, so I don't end up wrinklier than a bulldog's scrotum. I probably won't. But, truth be told, I had really serious body image issues when I was younger, and, as my youth fades, and the man in the mirror becomes less familiar, I do find the doubts occasionally creeping back in. It means I can sympathise with those willing to spend big money, or even risk their safety, to feel more confident about their looks.

Despite its toxicity, Botox is relatively safe in the hands of a trained professional, and is a key treatment for several medical conditions. However, all cosmetic procedures come with risks, and the lack of UK regulation means there have been numerous cases of nerve damage, scarring, infections, swelling, and - in the worst cases - fatal embolisms. So, without wishing to be a total downer, some safety campaigners might respond to James's question by saying some of the most dangerous beauty treatments aren't historical, but rather are in current usage. However, this book is meant to be fairly cheerful, so let's ignore our own perilous lives and grimace at some historical horror stories instead.

When James asked about dangerous beauty, my brain immediately leapt to the eighteenth-century society beauty Maria Gunning, Countess of Coventry, whose legendary gorgeousness was both her greatest asset and the cause of her early demise. Born in Ireland, she and her stunning sister were the most eligible bachelorettes of the age, and enjoyed a meteoric rise up the social ladder by marrying an earl and a duke. Alas, Maria's use of fashionable white lead makeup, known as *Venetian ceruse*, caused nasty skin breakouts, the only cure for which was to slap on more ceruse to hide the blemishes and protect her beautiful reputation. It was a vicious circle. All the while, the toxic lead seeped into her bloodstream and fatally poisoned her. She died aged just twenty-seven.

Though the pale face aesthetic was a look commonly associated with the 1700s, such white makeup wasn't new. Ancient Greek women had also worn something called *psimythion*, made from powdering and heating corroded lead. And in the 1600s, other equally dangerous options had included makeup composed of powdered white mercury, mixed with lemon juice, eggshells and white wine. Syphilitic men also received mercury injections up the penis with a terrifyingly massive syringe, but that served only to make them more ill.

My own beauty weak spot is the skin around my eyes, which has become alarmingly crepey and baggy. I blame this on a lifetime of chronic insomnia, a terrible habit of violently rubbing my eyes when they get tired, and the recent exhaustion of being a parent to a teething baby. In short, my once laissez-faire attitude to skincare has transformed into an urgent, obsessive hunt for miracle products to decrinkle myself.

Saying that, you couldn't pay me to eat lethal belladonna. This was a nineteenth-century potion eaten or rubbed into the skin which was said to brighten and broaden the pupils. Belladonna is derived from the aptly named deadly nightshade plant, and the side-effects of using belladonna were extensive. Here's a quote from an 1856 medical textbook:

> ... dryness of the mouth and fauces, a feeling of stricture of the throat, difficult deglutition, thirst, dimness of vision sometimes amounting to blindness, dilated pupil ... headache, flushed face, suffused eyes, morbid sounds, irregular muscular contractions, and hallucination or delirium, sometimes followed by a disposition to sleep ... sometimes an eruption on the surface, or irritation of the urinary passages. Occasionally, also, there is some nausea or griping pain with diarrhoea . . .*

Another less dangerous, but arguably more scary, procedure was creating artificial eyelashes by stitching hairs plucked from the head through the eyelids. The best way to alleviate discomfort during this procedure was for the surgeon to rub the eyes with cocaine, bringing a new meaning to the phrase: 'coked up to the eyeballs!'

Getting back to nineteenth-century skincare, it was common for women to use ammonia to freshen their complexion. Beauty journalists gave detailed, matter-of-fact

---

* Dr George Gordon Wood's *Treatise on Therapeutics and Pharmacology or Materia Medica, vol. 1*, published in 1856.

instructions on how to use and store these perilous products, but stressed that it was essential to chow down on a suitable laxative to flush it out of the system, or else it would build up in the body as 'a mass of festering poison'. The ideal solution, recommended by *Harper's Bazaar* in 1870, was French charcoal mixed with honey and your laxative of choice. The name of the helpful article with these useful tips? 'For the Ugly Girls'. Charming!

Arsenic also enjoyed a surge in popularity during the Victorian era. It too was thought to give a glowing complexion, radiant eyes, and plumped-up breasts. Various reports declared it to be popular in an Austrian region of Styria, where the peasants had apparently used it for three centuries. While the women had harnessed it to rosy up their cheeks, men had taken it for digestion and to help them climb alpine peaks. Sounds wholesome, right? Yeah, not so much.

Modern historians, such as Dr James Whorton, have shown that arsenic was used in the manufacture of a wide array of products, most noticeably green wallpaper, meaning people were probably absorbing more than they realised through environmental exposure in the home. There was also a hysterical press reaction from the 1840s onwards to a steady rise in murder cases where wives poisoned their husbands with tasteless, colourless arsenic. And yet, despite all the dangers, people seemed very happy to use arsenic in their beauty regime.

In the wake of its popularity, an article in *Chamber's Journal* from 1857 quoted a cautious Dr Inman who did his best to steer a course down the middle, announcing:

> The human being will bear a certain very small quantity of arsenic without any marked effect; in an adult a tenth of a grain per day is the limit. After this has been

continued about ten days or a fortnight . . . the body is saturated and certain symptoms follow, amongst which are 'swelling of the face and a mild inflammation of the eye' . . . When this appearance is noticed, the careful physician always suspends the use of the drug, knowing that to continue it will be attended with danger.

I suppose Dr Inman realised this still sounded like a positive endorsement, so he added a stark caveat. 'Lastly, let me urge upon all who adopt the Styrian system to make some written memorandum that they have done so, lest, *in case of accident*, some of their friends may be hanged in mistake.' Ah, yes, who among us hasn't picked up a moisturiser from Boots and thought: 'I hope this doesn't lead to my accidental death and a wrongful murder charge against my buddies!' Of course, this was the good doctor simply referring to all those infamous murder cases reported in the press.

As a final thought on James's question, let me offer up the famous wonder drug, radium. And when I say drug, I mean radioactive element discovered by Marie and Pierre Curie in 1898. While *The Simpsons* led me to believe that all radioactive materials glow fluorescent green, radium actually glows blue, and this seems to have helped convince people it held miraculous healing properties. Thus, it became a miracle consumer product.

The Radium Craze was very much one of those 'it seemed like a good idea at the time' moments, whose consequences can be encapsulated by the modern newspaper headline: 'The Radium Water Worked Fine Until His Jaw Came Off'. This startling piece of phrasemaking referred to the 1932 death of a noted industrialist and golfer, Eben Byers, who'd been guzzling a miracle product, Radithor, for five years. Radithor was a solution of distilled water and radium salts, and 400,000 bottles of the stuff were sold to the public before the devastating effects became widely known.

In the case of Byers, cancer ravaged his bones, and surgeons had to remove his jaw. Death followed swiftly after. That put an end to Radithor, which was cheerily nicknamed *Liquid Sunshine*, but strangely not to Thoradia beauty cream, which launched in 1933 and boasted radium bromide in its ingredients. In short, between 1915 and 1935, radium was advertised as the all-powerful tonic to cure all ills. There were also various dodgy devices that could be worn on the body, such as 1915's anti-wrinkle Radior chin strap, which promised to send a 'current of energy into the skin, and before long the wrinkles have disappeared'.

In truth, radium was such a hot topic that many products borrowed its name purely to bedazzle gullible customers. There were radium lipsticks, eye creams, soaps, chocolate, baby powder, condoms, breakfast cereals, silk stockings, and perfumes, few of which probably contained any radium. Such huckstering fraud proved a public health blessing in disguise. In 1925, the first cases of radium necrosis were identified; the victims were the factory girls painting fluorescent radium onto watches and scientific dials. Their oral cancers were horribly obvious to all because, as part of their job, they licked their paintbrushes to moisten them. There were undoubtedly many more victims whose consumption of miraculous, all-healing radium took years off their life, but they were never quite sure why.

So, yeah, in conclusion, we live in an age of expensive and risky cosmetic treatments, but at least we're not guzzling arsenic and smearing ourselves in radioactive material or lead paint. Progress of sorts, right?

CHAPTER 8:

IDEAS & TECHNOLOGY

31. Who invented maths?
Asked by Alex

Oh boy, way to take me out of my comfort zone! This is actually one of the biggest debates in the field of mathematics, and it's not simply a question of which ancient nerd got there first, but rather a fundamental philosophical debate over whether maths was *invented* by humans - like the 'Macarena' - or whether it's a universal law that was *discovered* by humans, like gravity? Is it a human construct imposed upon the natural world, or the underlying structure of the cosmos which we've figured out? Place your bets!

As you can probably guess, I'm not smart enough to have an informed opinion; I unironically enjoy Will Ferrell movies, for goodness sake! Reassuringly, it's also a question that challenges even the most brilliant of mathematical minds. For the sake of balance, Sir Roger Penrose - who worked closely with Stephen Hawking on the brain-melting maths of black holes and the abstract concept of time - is squarely in Team Discovery, following in a long tradition of Realist philosophers going back to the ancient Greek polymath Plato. But there are plenty of other eminent thinkers in the anti-Realist camp who argue that the only way to test such things is with mathematical proofs, designed by humans, and so maths is an invented, human concept.

So, I literally can't answer Alex's question because we don't know the answer. But I don't want anyone to feel short-changed, so instead allow me to briefly gallop through the early history of mathematical thinking. We start, as so often in this book, way back in the Stone Age, because archaeologists have found several prehistoric bones with notches carved into them, some dating to as early as 35,000 years ago, and this might well be proof of tally-sticks, used in counting.

In fact, there's a really intriguing one from 20,000 years ago which was found in 1960, in Ishango (then in the Belgian Congo). This tally-stick features three different columns of notches, but it might have been more than a counting device. Some researchers think it's a lunar calendar, but the more ambitious theory is that it's proof of multiplication. The markings on both Row A and B each add up to 60. More intriguing is that Row A shows 9 + 19 + 21 + 11, all of which are potential evidence for a decimal system based on the importance of 10 (they all equate to 10 + or - 1). Row B contains the descending prime numbers between 10 and 20, being 19 + 17 + 13 + 11. Finally, Row C shows subgroups that suggest deliberate doubling (5, 5, 10), (8, 4), and (6, 3). We don't know who created this, or why, but these were cave-dwelling people potentially doing proper number-crunching.

When our ancestors started to settle into towns, they quickly realised they needed ways to measure and record who owned what, for the purposes of stocktaking, buying, selling, taxing, and - presumably - showing off to their neighbours. Bean-counting is now a clichéd business metaphor, but, in the early days, it was literally how accountancy worked. As for measuring length, this was commonly based on the human body, because that was a widely available measure for an illiterate population. In ancient Egypt, you typically had a *digit* (width of the finger), a *palm* (width of the hand across the middle), a *hand* (length of the hand including fingers) and a *cubit* (the length of elbow to fingertip). There were 4 digits in a palm, 5 digits in a hand, 12 digits in a small span, 14 digits in a large span, 24 digits in a small cubit, and 28 digits in a full cubit.

The Egyptians really seemed to have enjoyed maths. They had a decimal system with hieroglyphs for 10, 100, 1,000, 100,000, and 1,000,000, which came in handy when totting up all the booty they'd nicked from their conquered enemies, or simply when they wanted to count how many enemies they'd slaughtered in battle (the tried and tested tactic was to slice off the penis or hand of the corpses, and pile them up for counting).

Alas, to my knowledge Egyptologists have thus far only recovered a small selection of ancient papyrus texts displaying mathematical ideas, but the Rhind Papyrus, written sometime around 1550 BCE, contains eighty-four maths problems for young scribes to figure out, and one of the puzzles could easily have been in your GCSE exam: 'Seven houses contain seven cats. Each cat kills seven mice. Each mouse had eaten seven ears of grain. Each ear of grain would have produced seven hekats of wheat. What is the total of all of these?' The same document is also the earliest to tackle a variation of what we now call *pi*:

> Example of a round field of diameter 9 khet. What is its area? Take away 1/9 of the diameter, namely 1: the remainder is 8. Multiply 8 times 8: it makes 64. Therefore it contains 64 setat of land.

Pi is also probably represented on a Babylonian disc-shaped tablet from at least 3,600 years ago, and was explored in various other tablets. To keep things simple, the Babylonians rounded Pi down to 3, but we do have evidence that they could also get much closer to the real answer (3.14159) by using a ratio of 25/8 (3.125). There are thousands of ancient Mesopotamian tablets that showcase what we assume to be modern mathematical ideas. The one known as Plimpton 322 is hard to nail down, and scholars disagree on its interpretation, but it seems to showcase Bronze Age trigonometry and what is usually called Pythagorean *triples*.

Clearly, the people of ancient Mesopotamia and Egypt were equally sophisticated, but they didn't agree on everything. Unlike the Egyptians, the Bronze Age Sumerians (living in what is now Iraq), preferred a duodecimal system based around the number 12, which is more versatile than 10 because it's divisible by 1, 2, 3, 4, 6, and 12. When the Sumerian and Akkadian empires fell, around 4,000 years ago, in came the Babylonians. Their cunning invention was the development of an elegant positional counting system that used 60 as the base, but it also incorporated a decimal element too.

I realise that might sound bafflingly unclear, so let me explain. When we write a large number, such as 3,724, we do so using positional columns – the 3 represents thousands, the 7 covers the hundreds, 2 is the tens, and 4 is the single digits. Where they are in the left-to-right columns tells us how to decode this system. The Babylonians did something similar.

Of course, we have to learn 10 symbols – the numbers 1 through to 9, and the always-handy 0 – but the beauty of the Babylonian system was that, when counting up to 60, they only had to remember two numeral shapes: a unit symbolising 1 and a unit symbolising 10. The single unit looked like an upside-down triangle on top of a stick; think of a martini glass without its base. The 10 looked like our capital letter A, but tipped onto its left side. To write the number 34 was easy: three sideways 10 symbols lined up next to each other gave you 30, and then next to that were placed four singles stacked on top of each other. It wasn't so far away from how later Roman numerals worked. With these basics in place, Babylonians could then do complex calculations, and multiply to massive numbers, despite lacking the concept of zero.

In terms of the major developments in big-brained maths, the ancient Greeks usually get much of the credit. Certainly, they had the brilliant Archimedes, the famed triangle-wrangler Pythagoras, the geometry wizard Euclid, the pondering Plato, the paradox king Zeno, and the atomic nerd Democritus, plus the less familiar Hippocrates of Chios, Eudoxus, Theodorus, Theaetetus, and Archytas. Indeed, the Greeks even gave us the word *mathematics*, which broadly translates as 'that which is studied', and I'm particularly grateful to Pythagoras for his mathematical rules of musical harmony, achieved by experimenting with the ratios of string lengths on his lyre. Without him, we'd have no dual-guitar harmonic riffing in Thin Lizzy's 'The Boys Are Back in Town', and that would've been a rock'n'roll travesty.

However, despite Greek cultural pre-eminence, many major developments happened elsewhere. Around 1,500 years ago, India gave the world the concept of zero – a necessary symbol for the absence of something, but also crucial in the positional counting system. Without zero, you go '18, 19, 2 . . . er . . . oh no!' There's some evidence that a prototype zero had been fiddled around with by the Babylonians, and the Maya in Mexico also seemed to have developed it independently, but it's from India that zero spread into common usage.

India also produced the brilliant scholar Brahmagupta, in the 600s CE, who pioneered quadratic equations, algorithms for square roots, and the concept of negative values. He was wrong when he said zero divided by zero = zero (in reality it's mathematically undefined), but at least he was brave enough to give it a try, dammit!

The exporting of expertise from South Asia percolated through the intellectual coffee filter of the Islamic world, which entered its Golden Age in the mid-700s. When Indian numerals finally entered southern Europe in the early 1200s – and were spread by key thinkers, such as the great Italian mathematician Fibonacci – many Europeans assumed these were an Islamic invention. This is why we call them 'Arabic numerals'. Arab scholars were indeed producing fascinating new mathematical ideas themselves. Perhaps the most notable contributor was Al-Khwarizmi, whose Persian name is the origin of our word *algorithm*, and whose hugely influential book, *al-Jabr,* gave us the word *algebra*. It was Al-Khwarizmi who'd translated Brahmagupta's texts, plus several Greek books, into Arabic, and – even though he did actually credit Indian scholars in his texts – we can see how they got forgotten and he accidentally ended up being credited with Indian numerals.

So, the story of mathematics was either one of constant discovery, or constant invention, depending on which side you want to take in that epic philosophical battle. But it's pretty cool that humans have been doing maths since the Stone Age. So, even if it's not as old as the cosmos itself, it is still *pretty* old . . . and that's good enough for me.

32. When were mirrors invented and did people know what they looked like before then?
Asked by Juliet

Chances are, Juliet, you've heard of Narcissus – the self-obsessed youth who's such a stone-cold stunner he can't stop ogling his own gorgeous face in the waters of a natural spring. When most people refer to him, they commonly assume he was a terrible egotist whose self-love was his own fault. In fact, there are various versions of the ancient story, but none blame him directly. In the most famous tale, he's cursed by the goddess Nemesis for having rejected the love of a forest nymph, Echo. She lures him to the quiet pool and curses him to fall in love with himself, until he exhausts all his energies (I guess he starves?) and turns into a narcissus flower.

Other versions say despair sets in, and he kills himself. Or he tumbles in and drowns while trying to get a cheeky snog off himself. But according to a writer called Pausanius, Narcissus was beset by grief at the death of his identical twin sister, and the only way he could remember her face was to stare at his own. That puts a rather more sombre twist on our modern understanding of narcissism. Anyway, the point is that before there were mirrors, the myth of Narcissus tells us there were puddles and ponds, suggesting people have been checking themselves out since the dawn of our species.

And that's not all. We think ancient peoples probably used several other materials as reflective surfaces, besides water. The renowned archaeologist Professor Ian Hodder has spent three decades excavating the Stone Age town of Çatalhöyük in Turkey, built around 9,000 years ago. Among the grave goods discovered by his team have been several polished mirrors of volcanic obsidian glass, with one side made nice and shiny and the other coated in pale plaster. These mirrors date back 8,000 years – perhaps suggesting that urban life brought with it a certain pressure to look good – but it's also worth noting that these mirrors mainly turn up in the graves of women, suggesting they were gendered objects in this late Stone Age society.

Elsewhere, in both ancient Egypt and China, archaeologists have found polished copper mirrors from 5,000 years ago, which is right at the start of the Bronze Age, when humans started using metals. And if we then come forward into the peak of the Bronze Age, some 3,400 years ago, we have a gorgeously decorated mirror case from the tomb of none other than King Tutankhamun. Alas, the mirror was too fancy for its own good, and was nicked by tomb robbers thousands of years before Howard Carter got there.

So, this is all lovely archaeological proof of mirrors existing thousands of years ago, but we also have art historical evidence of how they were used. There's a mirror depicted in a scene from the infamous Erotic Papyrus of Turin – a highly sexualised text created around 3,200 years ago – which depicts a woman holding her mirror while putting on her makeup with a long applicator brush. I won't mention what else is going on in this eye-popping image, in case there are small kids lurking nearby, but – if you're curious – you can google it when the kids have gone to bed. It's very NSFW! You have been warned.

Reflective metal mirrors continued to be used in the ancient Mediterranean world of the Etruscans (Italy) and Mycenaeans (Crete), who were supplanted by the Romans and Greeks, respectively. Such mirrors were often copper, bronze, gold, iron ore, or silver, and tended to be handheld objects of only a few inches in size. Rather than flat surfaces, they seem to have curved, like modern shaving mirrors – either at a convex angle for a more distant, mid-sized image of the face, or the concave angle for a big-faced close-up, allowing for more detail when applying makeup.

Sadly, there's no evidence of those hilarious funhouse mirrors that weirdly exaggerate our bodies, but we do know of one Roman who delighted in mirrors designed to make small things appear unnaturally big. In his book *Natural Questions*, the Roman philosopher Seneca complains about a man called Hostius Quadra whose favourite metal mirror made his fingers look thicker than an arm. And no, this wasn't for funny dinner party pranks; this was a creepy sex thing. Oops, sorry, maybe put the kids to bed again! Yes, Hostius was apparently something of a rampant sex pest, and used his distorting mirrors to both exaggerate the size of his own genitals and to watch himself being pleasured. This appalled both Seneca and Emperor Augustus. So much so, in fact, that when Hostius was murdered by his own slaves for being too much of a lecherous git, Augustus decided he'd deserved it, and so refused to punish the killers.

Polished mirrors were certainly expensive, but they seem to have been relatively common in the ancient world. Indeed, they might also have been used for security purposes. The notoriously paranoid Roman emperor, Domitian, had the walls of his palace lined with a shimmering, reflective mineral called *phengite* so he could see if anybody was sneaking up on him with dagger in hand. I don't know of any occasion where he had to apprehend an assassin, but I like to imagine it would have played out like a toga-clad version of that scene in *The Man with the Golden Gun* in which James

Bond and Scaramanga have a very confusing shootout in a hall of mirrors.

Perhaps I've already answered your question, Juliet, but I presume you're probably wondering when glass showed up? The Latin word *mirari* – which gives us *mirror* – simply meant to 'look at, or admire'. Technically speaking, then, mirrors don't actually have to be made of glass, they just have to let us stare at an image. However, glass is what most of us expect, and there's something profoundly thrilling about the noise and drama of a shattered mirror, and the supposed bad luck it's meant to bring.

In fact, please indulge me in a quick detour to the story of Belgian inventor and musician John Joseph Merlin, the ingenious creator of numerous mechanical automata, clocks, musical instruments, and – most importantly for this tale – roller-skates. He was also something of a charismatic show-man. Sometime in the 1760s or 70s (our source for this story was printed in 1805, so we're not sure of when it happened), Merlin was providing the entertainment at the Carlisle House home of the famous opera singer Theresa Cornelys; these were always enormously lavish affairs with the most illus-trious of guests, and Merlin decided to impress the gathered partygoers by playing the violin while scooting around on his newfangled skates. Unfortunately, he'd neglected to invent the brakes. Needless to say, Merlin lost control and careened into a large, expensive mirror at the back of the hall, smashing it into smithereens, destroying his violin, and doing himself a very nasty mischief in the process.

So, that's what happens when mirrors get smashed, but let's now return to the origins of how glass came to be transformed into a reflective surface. Glass dates back at least 5,400 years, but it wasn't really used in mirrors until the first century CE,

when the famous natural history writer Pliny the Elder described mirror-working glaziers in what is now Lebanon. In
truth, early glass was rough and rather opaque, with a blueish
tinge. For a long time, polished metal was still preferred as the
reflective surface of choice. However, the major leap forward
seems to have come in the 1400s when craftspeople in Europe
learned how to blow flat, uncracked panes of reflective glass
which they silvered with tin-mercury amalgam.

The most celebrated mirrors came from the island of
Murano, in Venice, and the Venetian authorities went to extreme lengths to ensure their industrial secrets weren't stolen
by foreign powers - glassworkers were offered tax breaks,
incentives, the opportunity to marry the daughters of the aristocracy, and a job for life. But if they tried to leave, they and
their families were arrested and tried for treason, or - if they
managed to sneak out - they might allegedly be hunted down
and assassinated.

Saying that, perhaps the most glorious example of mirror
technology is Louis XIV's Palace of Versailles, with its dazzling, 73-metre-long Hall of Mirrors which was constructed
in 1678–84. Though Louis was determined to hire an army of
French artisans, clearly his architect managed to smuggle in
some Venetians to ensure a top-notch finish. And if you've
ever visited Versailles to witness the spectacle for yourself,
you'll appreciate why that was a very wise decision. Thankfully, nobody invited John Joseph Merlin to perform there, or
else it would have been carnage!

33. Who first had the idea of actually going to the Moon or another planet? Did they have any idea how?
Asked by Dan

The Moon has played a game of nightly peekaboo with us since we first evolved, and it performed a key role in the earliest Bronze Age attempts to codify cosmology and time-keeping. The Egyptians, Babylonians, and Chinese were all moon-gazers by night, and sun-squinters by day. But Dan asks a fascinating question which I'll have to nuance somewhat by saying the first person (that we know of . . .) to conceptualise a journey to the Moon did so as an act of satirical literary fantasy, rather than of hard scientific hypothesis.

In the second century CE, the Roman Empire had expanded to include the Greek-speaking world and much of the Middle East. In the lands we now call Turkey, there lived a brilliant writer and orator named Lucian of Samosata who had a delightfully cheeky sense of humour. Lucian was a satirist, and his most notable work took the piss out of the various outlandish travel adventures featured in other classical writings. His most celebrated satire, iron-ically titled *A True Story*, has an absolutely bonkers plot that starts with him on a sea voyage into the Atlantic but ends up with him being accidentally transported to the Moon by a giant whirlwind.

Once there, he discovers the King of the Moon is a human called Endymion, who is locked in the midst of a savage war against the King of the Sun over who gets to control the Morning Star. The Sun King – with his army of giant ants, dog-headed men, and assorted vegetable-wielding weirdos – is eventually victorious, and peace is declared. Lucian then returns to Earth only to be swallowed by a ginormous whale (don't you just hate it when that happens?) inside of which lives a race of belligerent fish-people who Lucian then defeats in battle.

He escapes from the whale, then encounters an island of milk, then one of cheese, and then an island crammed with the ancient heroes of Greek myth and history, some of whom – like Herodotus – are being punished eternally for the sin of lying in their history books. Lucian and his buddies then head off for yet more maritime adventures, before ending the book with a promise of an even more ridiculous sequel filled with even sillier lies.

I realise you might have been somewhat distracted by the island of cheese, or the army of fish-people living inside a giant whale, but let me draw your gaze back to the Moon adventure. Although this is pure fantasy, Lucian goes to some lengths to describe what the Moon is like, and who lives there (bald, bearded humanoids called Selenites who mostly dine on roasted frogs – obviously!). Lucian's absurdist tale is often described as the first science fiction novel, not least for his imaginative description of intergalactic combat which preceded *Star Wars* by 1,800 years. But *A True Story* was anything but intentional Moon theorising. His aim was to mock other writers for their lurid flights of fancy. He didn't *actually* think the Moon was populated by warriors who rode three-headed giant vultures.

In which case, Dan, we probably have to disqualify him from this answer. We might also do the same to the ancient Greek historian Plutarch, whose text *Concerning the Face Which Appears in the Orb of the Moon* presents a lively dialogue on whether life exists on the Moon, and even mentions a hero who visits an island whose occupants claim to know how to get there. However, there's no attention paid to the logistics of an actual lunar mission.

Next we turn to the celebrated astronomer Johannes Kepler – the dude who figured out that Earth's orbit is elliptical – whose fictional story *Somnium*, written in 1608, is a dream narrative of an Icelandic boy and his witch mother discovering that they can travel to the Moon with the help of a daemon, who protects them from the cold of the aether (then understood as lighter-than-air particles in space), and makes them wear sponges on their noses to let them breathe, and who gets them there in a snappy four hours.

Somnium is an eerie ode to space travel that includes fascinating suggestions of how the Earth would look from the surface of the Moon, and what eclipses would look like too. This is still poetry, but it's written by a big-brained astronomer who was influenced by the Copernican understanding of the planets. Kepler even notes that space travel would be extremely dangerous, only lightweight passengers could undertake it, they would have to time their launch to avoid being exposed to the Sun's harmful rays, and that the acceleration to propel people Moonwards would require dosing the astronauts with heavy opiates to get them through the intense physical stresses on their bodies. It's a fascinatingly sophisticated checklist for someone writing four hundred years ago, and Kepler was probably the first to declare a lunar landing could be done.

But, if I'm being a stickler, Kepler's plot point of hitching a lift with a daemon isn't quite the same thing as genuinely wondering how to achieve practical space travel. And the same goes for Francis Godwin, an English bishop whose book *The Man in the Moone* – published in 1638, after his death – tells of a twelve-day journey to the Moon in a sleigh pulled by swans. Having myself studied at the University of York, where hordes of waterfowl roam wild across the campus, I can assure you that swans are much too aggressive for use in human transport.

No, if we're genuinely looking for the first time someone actually wrote a non-fiction paper about Moon tourism, and not a poem infused with myth and monsters, then that brings us to the seventeenth-century natural philosopher John Wilkins.

An Oxford-educated preacher, in 1638 Wilkins published the snappily titled *The discovery of a new world; or, a discourse tending to prove, that ('tis probable) there may be another habitable world in the moon.* Wilkins thought the Moon had land, oceans, and seasons like Earth, and was likely inhabited by Moon-people (like Lucian he also called them Selenites). This idea was potentially verging on heretical blasphemy, so he wrote an amusing caveat about not knowing if the Selenites were descended from Adam and Eve, or how God had created them, but he hoped one day humans would find out in person. Theological crisis deftly sidestepped! Wilkins then pointed out he had no idea how humans would get to the Moon, but that future generations might figure it out and build a Moon colony. Fair enough.

Two years later, Wilkins expanded his ideas. At this point, Isaac Newton hadn't yet figured out gravity, so Wilkins instead relied on the magnetic theory of William Gilbert, whose book *De Magnete*, published in 1600, argued the Earth itself was magnetised and thus would exert restrictive force on any craft trying to leave the ground. Wilkins did some trigonometry and decided the clouds were about 20 miles up, and any craft escaping beyond them would float without resistance. To be fair, modern rockets reach space when they pass the so-called Kármán line, 62 miles up, so Wilkins wasn't a million miles off. In fact, he was just 42 miles away.

He wasn't so good on the next bit, mind, arguing that space itself would be warm because it was closer to the Sun, and that mountains on Earth were cold because they were capped by clouds, which had been created in the Book of Genesis before the Sun was made, and so coldness preceded heat in the act of Creation, but in space it would be toasty. He also thought that the purer air 'breathed by angels' would be excellent to humans. As for the in-flight meal, Wilkins theorised we wouldn't need one as the natural sensation of hunger was just all that pesky magnetism pulling on our stomachs, so anyone in space would feel untroubled by rumbling tummies. Plus, there would be food available on the Moon, what with all those people living there.

In terms of designing the launch vehicle, Wilkins lived in the age of gunpowder. Five years before he wrote his expanded treatise, the Ottoman inventor Lagâri Hasan Çelebi had allegedly loaded himself into a rocket and shot himself into the sky, as part of the birthday celebrations held for the Sultan's daughter. Miraculously, it's said he crash-landed safely in the waters of the Bosphorus. But Wilkins wasn't looking towards explosive fuels to power his astral 'chariot'. Instead, he proposed mechanical gears and clockwork springs attached to giant artificial wings. Failing that, he also suggested a flock of trained swans – I mean, what was it with seventeenth-century writers and waterfowl?

Wilkins clearly wasn't the first to write about a trip to the Moon, but he was thinking about the actual physics of the problem. Perhaps what's surprising to us, given how we often talk of his era as being a time of culture wars between faith and science – most notably with the myth of Galileo being persecuted by the Pope – is that Wilkins saw no such culture clash. He was both a devout Anglican preacher* and a man of experimental reason, as were many others of the age. In fact, Wilkins began the 1660s by chairing the first ever meeting of the celebrated Royal Society, home of Isaac Newton's mathematical genius, but he ended the decade as a bishop. Science and religion went hand in hand. And it was probably for the best, because only a divine miracle would have seen a flock of swans carry Neil Armstrong to the Moon . . .

34. How can you tell that the earliest Stone Age tools are actually tools, and not just rocks?
Asked by Daniel

The nice thing about doing this book is that sometimes people are asking me questions that I myself once posed to others. When I was a young History and Archaeology student, way back in the mists of ancient time (otherwise known as 2001–4), I distinctly remember staring at a small piece of flint and finding myself utterly incapable of deciding whether it was a prehistoric hand axe or just a random lump of rock. Spoiler alert, it was a lump. And I felt like a proper lump for not knowing that.

There will always be debatable examples that split opinion, but archaeologists have spent many years figuring out a useful rubric for judging what is and isn't a Stone Age tool. Saying that, there are caveats I'll flag up at this early juncture

---

* He was also Oliver Cromwell's brother-in-law, having married the Lord Protector's sister, Robina.

- we used to think that only humans used tools, and that's what made us special. Turns out, if you actually watch them closely, loads of animal species do it too, including chimps, apes, birds, and octopuses. Indeed, chimps and apes have been seen to smash nuts by pounding them with large rocks. My baby daughter takes a similar approach to her breakfast, with enjoyably dramatic effect, and it's very probable that our earliest human ancestors also employed the 'smash it with a big rock' approach, meaning Daniel's question - *'how do you tell the difference between tools and rocks?'* - requires us to admit that sometimes you can't, because they were one and the same.

But let's move on to what archaeologists call flintknapping, which is a very specific type of tool manufacture. In 1964, an exciting discovery was made in Tanzania by the married team of Mary and Louis Leakey (their son, Richard Leakey, is also an internationally recognised expert on Stone Age Africa, as is his wife Meave and their daughter Louise - the Leakeys are quite the scientific dynasty). The 1964 discovery was a new species of hominin, from over 2.3 million years ago, dubbed *Homo habilis* (quite literally translated as 'handy-man'), so named because it was buried in the same sedimentary layer as humanly made tools and butchered animal carcasses. More recently, archaeologists have pushed tool usage back to 3.3 million years ago, but there's some debate as to whether these were naturally occurring rocks picked up by enterprising hominins, or if they too were hand-crafted for a specific job.

Stone Age tool technologies began with Oldowan toolkits (named after the Olduvai Gorge in Tanzania) which are rather simple hammerstones for bashing flint cores, and the sharp slicers the bashing produces. By 1.75 million years ago, give or take a few hundred thousand years, early hominins had added Acheulean hand axes to their toolkit; these were either oval or pear-shaped multipurpose tools capable of skinning animals, chopping wood, digging soil, and hammering stuff. I suspect if I showed you one of each, you'd probably be able to see how they were carefully knapped into their distinctive shapes, though I'd absolutely forgive you if you mistook them for any old rock.

Much like Apple iPhones, the evolution of the design continued to get more sophisticated, even if the product remained largely the same. The next leap in technology was the Middle Palaeolithic toolkit, used by early *Homo sapiens* and Neanderthals by 350,000 years ago. These were a lot more faff to prepare, telling us that human brainpower was developing nicely. Instead of just bashing off a useful bit of flint and then sharpening it, the knapper instead took a large cobble - perhaps as big as a rugby ball, or animal skull - and carefully shaped the edges and upper surface with a hammer-stone, creating a hierarchical core. Having judged the angles just right, the hammer stone would then be brought down hard on one end, striking off a big, predictably shaped flake from the upper face. Crucially, it emerged from the core ready for action but was transportable and could be easily resharpened.

You're probably wondering how we know this stuff? Well, before the 1600s those who discovered worked flint lying on the ground thought them to be vaguely supernatural objects, named elf-stones. It's also important to note that the world was then believed to be only 6,000 years old, and it wasn't until the early-1800s - thanks to major discoveries in geology, dinosaur palaeontology, evolutionary theory, and in 1856 discovery of Neanderthal remains - that scholars could even conceive of a prehistoric Stone Age. However, scholarly

research soon began in earnest, and experimental archaeology has a long heritage when it comes to flintknapping.

Indeed, there are some nice videos on YouTube which
reveal the process, if you'd like to have a go yourself. However, please don't use your blade as any kind of offensive
weapon - I don't want to get into trouble with the authorities - and definitely don't drop it in the middle of a field,
because some poor archaeologist will think it's a real one
from the Stone Age, and suddenly the area will be swarming
with eager, trowel-wielding experts. Fake hand axes proved a
major problem in the mid-nineteenth century, when all that
novel excitement from ancient discoveries inspired a forger
called Edward Simpson to spend years manufacturing bogus
antiquities to sell to museums and collectors. Charmingly,
Simpson went by numerous names, including Flint Jack,
Fossil Willy, the Old Antiquarian, Cockney Bill, Bones, and
Shirtless - all superb names for real ales. Less charmingly, it's
likely some of Simpson's forgeries are still on display today.

Alas, this is the problem with dating tools; the stones themselves are geologically ancient, so there's often no easy way
to reveal when the flintknapping happened. Archaeologists
therefore rely heavily on dating stone tools through con-
textual stratigraphy (how far down relatively in the ground
they're buried), or they can sometimes analyse residues of
blood, bone, fur, food, or mineral dyes which might remain
on the sharp edges. There are also rare occasions where
Mother Nature randomly produces flints that look human-
made - for example, when powerful river currents bash flints
together. However, very few of these examples would fool an
expert eye, because truly knapped stones show regular patterns of attack, where a methodical and systematic technique
was patiently employed.

So, just in case you fancy a field walk today, here are a few things to look out for in case you stumble on what looks like a Stone Age tool:

1. The striking platform: this is a zone at the top end of a flake, where the hammer blow has struck it off from the flint core; sometimes there is a tiny circle visible, called the point of percussion.

2. The bulb of percussion: on the inner face of the flake (known as the ventral side), you might see a strange bulge. This will be where the impact of the hammer transferred kinetic energy into the flint, and the fracture caused a sort of visible explosion.

3. Ripples and hackles: the impact can also produce visible ripples which radiate downwards from the striking platform; you might be able to feel them with your fingertips. Hackles are small lines, also on the ventral side, that point backwards to the striking platform.

4. Eraillure scar: next to the bulb of percussion, again on the ventral, you might see what looks like a mini-flake scar where a bit has been knocked off. This is the secondary consequence of the hammer blow; the rebounding shockwave of the force not only produced the bulb of percussion, but also this scarring. It's very convincing proof of a tool being human-made.

5. Serration: if you're looking at a flake, it might have been carefully touched up with tiny chips along an edge to create a serrated effect, like on a steak knife.

6. Flake scars: the outer side of the flake (known as the dorsal side) might have either the original cobble surface, or scars from previous flakes having been struck from the core.

As well as this flaked tool, you might also find a core from which it was created. These are a little less easy to identify, but the presence of multiple flake scars showing the negative versions of the features listed above might be visible. Somewhat confusingly, sometimes ancient people also turned cores into tools, so keep that in mind too.

Anyway, hopefully that answers your question, Daniel, and - just as I once was asking the question, only to now be the one answering it - perhaps you can now write your own archaeology textbook to continue our tradition.

CHAPTER 9:

NATIONS & EMPIRES

35. China is massive. If the emperor died, or a new law was passed, how long did it take for news to reach everyone?
Asked by Anonymous

Ah, now we're talking - enough of all that other stuff, it's time for some properly sexy history: ancient logistics. Phwoar! I'm not being sarcastic; I find this stuff absolutely fascinating, and wrote an entire chapter on the history of communication technology in my debut book. I suppose it's because I live in a world of instant tweets and same-day Amazon Prime deliveries, so I'm privileged to have stuff turn up at my door, or ping into my phone, as soon as I want them. But the story of communication before telegraphy is one of ingenious simplicity, even at massive scale. And you don't get much more massive than China.

Actually, I might need to row that back. It really depends which era of Chinese history we're looking at. The ancient Qin state, which was ruthlessly unified by the First Emperor, Qin Shi Huangdi, between the 230s BCE and 221 BCE, occupied about 900,000 square miles. Obviously, you wouldn't want to have to unicycle across it, but his empire was dwarfed by the Romans - who controlled 1.5 million square miles - and the

Persians, who virtually doubled China's landmass. However, China was still very, very big, so let's look at how it overcame the vast distances.

An early technology which dates back to the Bronze Age was the fire beacon system. We've seen this in *The Lord of the Rings* movies, whereupon a single beacon is lit, becoming visible to the next beacon-keepers, miles away, who ignite their own, and so on, until the message has been delivered to the entire network. It's a cute system. Alas, you have to agree on a message in advance; whether that's 'Send help!' or 'Enemy spotted!' or 'The emperor is dead!' or 'Testing, testing, one, two, one, two'. Beacons are not good for nuanced chatting. They're basically fire alarms made of actual fire. They mean only one thing.

They're also prone to accidents and pranksters. One apocryphal story from eighth-century BCE China tells of King You who lit the emergency invasion beacon and waited for his panicked armies to race towards the palace, ready for war, only for him to announce he'd made up the threat to show off to his girlfriend about the size of his army. Unfortunately, an invading army then *did* show up, but when King You ignited the emergency beacon, his troops did a 'Boy Who Cried Wolf' eye-roll and failed to show up. Classic comeuppance.

Our anonymous questioner, who I shall hereby rechristen Engelbert, asks specifically about the death of a royal, and indeed this was a big deal. Not only would people need to enter into a period of ritual mourning – with the instructions for how this was to be observed, and for how long, being shared across the empire – but rapid and widespread information distribution also helped quell rebellions and coups; if news reached some places more slowly than others, it might allow warlords and regional governors to rise up in rebellion, or launch a power grab, before other factions were able to organise against them.

Saying that, we do have a notable story of a death that was very much hushed up, presumably for similar reasons. The First Emperor, Qin Shi Huangdi, had famously decided he was going to live forever – it's always nice to dream big – but this proved a somewhat awkward boast when he kicked the bucket midway through an imperial tour. To avoid panic and control the succession, his closest advisers decided the tour should continue regardless, because fear of assassination had meant he was never showing his face in public anyway, so there was no need to hire a body double to smile and wave. The emperor's body was left to quietly rot in what was now a trundling hearse. When the smell became a dead giveaway quite literally – the advisers issued an edict declaring that local officials should escort the emperor's carriage with wagons of rotting fish, giving them a weird excuse for the stench of death.

One of the reasons we know Emperor Qin Shi Huangdi planned to live forever is because he sent out executive orders across the empire demanding that local governors hunt down any nearby immortality elixirs for him to guzzle. Several wrote back with disappointing news. How these messages were sent brings us on to the logistics of non-beaconed communication, which was basically using human messengers either on horseback, in wheeled carts, or on foot. Even centuries before Qin Shi Huangdi's time, a postal system had been in place across the rival Chinese states (the ones he forcibly unified), and this process only got more efficient with time.

The trick was to have tons of permanent postal stations dotted at regular intervals, so a messenger could swap horses several times per day, or the tired messengers could themselves be swapped. It's possible the Chinese developed this system independently, but their neighbours, the Persians, had mastered it by the sixth century BCE, so a bit of cheeky Chinese emulation doesn't seem out of the question. Herodotus tells us Persia's relay system, called the *angareion,* could cover 1,700 miles in a mere seven days. By contrast, an ordinary traveller needed three months.

Since the early days of the Qin and Han dynasties, Chinese postal reform had gone hand in hand with road building. By the time of the illustrious Tang dynasty, in the mid-700s CE, there were already 1,639 postal stations dotted around the country. The Song dynasty, which lasted from the 960s until the late 1200s, saw mail stops built every 7 miles and post-houses every 18 miles, to process the incoming and outgoing communications. By the time of the fourteenth-century Yuan dynasty – established after the Mongol conquest – yet more infrastructure had been added, including four arterial roads (*yidao*) which connected up the major cities. These weren't just highways through the wilderness; major settlements popped up along the routes, not least because regular communication fostered efficient trade and civic administration.

I mentioned the Mongols there. Given the vastness of their empire, they too had to become dab hands at postal systems, with the European traveller Marco Polo somewhat dubiously claiming a Mongol could stay in his saddle for ten days without stopping for a meal – oof, imagine the chafing! The mighty Chinggis Khan relied on so-called 'arrow messengers', who were apparently supplied at every 40 miles. According to Polo, 400 horses would be maintained by local families, with 200 happily grazing in the fields and another 200 ready to go once they heard the approaching messengers tooting their horns.

Another European traveller, Friar Odoric of Pordenone, described beacon towers every 3 miles, each of which housed four runners and a postmaster who were provided with: 'a portfolio, bells, a spear with fringes, three feet of oiled silk, a cover in soft silk for the post parcels, a cap and an overcoat for the rain, a secret red stick, and a return ticket'. These runners wore jingling bells on their clothes, so the next messenger could hear them coming and grab the message from their outstretched hand like a baton in a sprint relay. Why so urgent? Well, any runner who was forty-five minutes late was caned twenty times with bamboo. Anyone caught opening sealed documents, or losing them, might receive the ultimate punishment of death.

Polo isn't the most reliable source (scholars are split on the basic question of whether he even went to China?!), but he said Mongol riders could cover 250 miles in a day which, if true, was an incredibly high-speed service. But there were slower, cheaper options. As with our modern postmarks, messages in China would be stamped with the day of their dispatch, the speed at which they'd travel, and the date of their expected arrival. There were perhaps four speeds available: slow, medium, fast, and extremely urgent (this being symbolised with a golden seal). Major delays incurred serious fines for postal bureaucrats - including the docking of a full year's salary! - which is what I might reply the next time I get a text from a courier saying, 'Your estimated delivery time: between 8am and 8pm.' Not helpful, lads!

If the Mongol 'arrow messengers' were incredibly rapid, most medieval horseback messengers were expected to cover a less astonishing 300 *li* per day (almost 100 miles). Terrain obviously varied, and mountains proved tediously trundlesome, but Professor Mark Elvin noted that no city in the empire was

out of contact for more than fourteen days, and indeed sometimes those on the edges of the Chinese state could be reached
in just eight. By the 1700s, road improvements had doubled
that speed, and they even got up to a whopping 800 *li* by 1842.
As for the foot messengers, they likely covered a very healthy
30 miles in a twelve-hour day before seeking rest and shelter,
whereas urgent express documents kept travelling overnight.
It had been a superb system, but years of cutbacks eventually
led to nineteenth-century Europeans dismissing the Chinese
postal service as inadequate compared to their own.

But I'll finish on a celebratory note. In the mid-700s,
Emperor Xuanzong of the Tang dynasty had a legendarily
beautiful consort, Yang Guifei, who adored lychees, but found
herself 750 miles away from where they grew. Xuanzong's big
romantic gesture, which luckily went more Hugh Grant than
Ewww Grant, saw him order a shipment of lychees go by the
swiftest horses, through day and night, meaning it perhaps
arrived in just three days. It was undoubtedly a lot of faff for
a fruit basket, but she was delighted. And at least he hadn't lit
the emergency beacon and summoned the entire army, just
to get Yang Guifei into bed, like King You . . . Honestly, some
men, eh?

36. Did Genghis Khan plant trees wherever he went?
Asked by Katie

Ah, we're sticking with East Asian rulers for a while, though
Katie's question will sound delightfully niche if you didn't see
the widespread news reports in 2011 declaring that Genghis

Khan - or, rather, Chinggis Khan, as he was actually called in his Mongol-Turkic language - was partially responsible for reversing global warming, and was therefore an accidental eco-warrior (with the stress on the *warrior* bit). We might therefore fantasise about a green-fingered warlord who delighted in forestry, ambling around the bloodstained battlefields of Persia and cooing excitedly at green-shooted saplings. Sadly, that wasn't the case. No, Chinggis Khan didn't plant trees; rather the charge against him is that he slaughtered so many people that Mother Nature briefly bounced back, forests regrew, and CO_2 levels dropped.

The headlines that Katie presumably refers to were generated by a 2011 scientific study published in the *Holocene* journal by a team of environmental researchers at Stanford University. The team built a model of global land coverage, and then overlaid climate data from ice core samples from Greenland and the Antarctic, to see whether carbon dioxide levels had changed during four major demographic disasters in global history: the rise of the Mongol Empire in Asia (1200 to 1380), the Black Death in Europe (1347), the Spanish conquest of the Americas (1519 to 1700) and the fall of the Chinese Ming dynasty (early 1600s).

According to the study, which focused on the environmental impact of large-scale agriculture, the most environmentally significant of these four population disasters was the dramatic arrival of Chinggis Khan into China and the Persian world. Even though the Black Death apparently wiped out a third of Europe's population - somewhere between 25 and 50 million people - the Antarctic ice cores basically puffed their cheeks out and shrugged in weary boredom. Yet, according to the Stanford study, Chinggis Khan's Mongolian marauders apparently killed so many people that atmospheric carbon levels dropped by a whopping 700 million tonnes. For those of you who enjoyed the Marvel *Avengers* movies, you'll recognise this as the Thanos approach to conservation.

We do need to be careful, however. As the study fairly acknowledged, other factors might have been at work in producing this surprise result. As a sceptical historian, I'd also add that Chinggis' overall death toll has been wildly exaggerated, and, even if taken at face value, only stretched to a maximum of 40 million people, and ... Hang on, I've just realised that sounds incredibly crass, as if *only* 40 million people were slaughtered – what a centrist moderate he was! My apologies. Let me rephrase. What I mean is that, once we move away from the hyperbolic reports of his enemies, and the exaggerating boasts of his acolytes, Chinggis Khan was probably responsible for fewer deaths than the Black Death pandemic. And yet, according to the study, it was the Mongolian marauder who ended up getting a headline in the *Guardian* that read: 'Why Genghis Khan Was Good for the Planet', because only he was deemed responsible for a fall in carbon dioxide levels.

So, what gives?

In order to explain the odd results, the scientists argued that short-term catastrophes were perhaps less impactful than longer ones. The Black Death was like a brutal hit-and-run; it arrived suddenly, killed mercilessly, and then sped off at high speed. It was devastatingly tragic, and caused major economic consequences, but the environmental effects were perhaps somewhat lessened because forests need a century to fully regrow, and it seems there wasn't time for that to happen.

Because communicable diseases thrive more in dense urban areas, plague tended to hit the cities harder than rural areas, and cities are by definition already largely treeless. And when it did hit farming communities, the vegetation left to rot on abandoned farms still produced CO_2. So, even if millions of medieval farmers perished, their carbon footprint outlasted them. Over time, the population began to recover and farmland was restored, meaning carbon levels remained relatively stable, despite massive human mortality rates.

The study also mentions what happened in the Americas, after the arrival of European conquerors in the early 1500s. Here, the colonial violence was also savage, but the primary cause of depopulation was the terrifying scourge of smallpox, which caused horrific devastation to the Indigenous population (perhaps as much as 90 per cent extinction). Tens of millions of people died. These communities never recovered. This led to long-term regrowth of trees, and therefore increased carbon storage in the Americas which should have produced a drop in CO_2 levels, right? Correct! Except, at the same time, trees were being cut down elsewhere on the planet, and agriculture was intensifying. So, even though there were more trees in South America, there were fewer in other places. CO_2 levels stayed stable because the two effects cancelled each other out.

By contrast, the Mongol expansion under Chinggis Khan wreaked havoc and violence across a vast expanse of territory, and, as we've heard, is claimed to have wiped out 40 million people. Unlike the Black Death, the Mongols then settled down to rule most of Asia for roughly 175 years, bringing about a period of political stability that historians call the *Pax Mongolica* (the Mongolian Peace), during which trade and prosperity flourished. In fairness to Chinggis - actually, I don't know why I'm defending the guy, I'm not his lawyer and he wasn't exactly Greta Thunberg - his supposed death toll of 40 million seems very high given how successful the empire soon after became; its enormous, efficiently collected tax revenues suggest there were still plenty of people taking part in the economy. That makes me a bit suspicious.

And if tens of millions really did die, might there have been other fatal causes contributing alongside Mongol blades and arrows? Perhaps another outbreak of disease or famine? The Stanford scientists, to their credit, acknowledge that there was more to the answer than simply which event killed the most people. They report that CO_2 levels throughout their four transitional periods might have been affected by solar radiation, unusual weather patterns, and unknown volcanic eruptions. Moreover, the Mongolian example was the earliest of the four population collapses, so it's quite possible the reasons the other three events were less environmentally impactful was because they came later, during periods of more intense agriculture, land cultivation, and deforestation around the world.

Maybe Chinggis Khan really did wipe out so many people that he made the forests regrow? But it's important to note that other events might also have done the same, only for other, unrelated factors to interfere with the ice core samples. The boring truth is that it's always exciting when scientific data can be wheeled in to support or challenge our understanding of the past, but we have to be cautious not to give all the credit to just one variable.

Chinggis Khan undoubtedly killed a massive number of people during his conquests. He was absolutely terrifying, and one hyperbolic account from the city of Nishapur says he piled up a pyramid of 1.75 million human skulls, just to teach people a lesson about what happens when you cross the Mongols. Clearly, he wasn't the sort of dude you'd want lurking in your vicinity. But maybe he wasn't the sole antidote to climate change . . . and, even if he was, his method wasn't exactly the nicest way to save the planet.

37. Why is Italy called Italy?
Asked by Anonymous

Lots of modern nations are named after ancient tribes: England takes its name from the Angles; France from the Franks; Russia from the Rus; Belgium from the Belgae; Scotland from the Scotti. And so, you'd expect the land of the ancient Romans to have been named in their honour. After all, they did pretty well for themselves, what with that massive empire. Surely, they'd earned it, no? Oddly, the Romans instead gave their name to Romania – it became part of their empire in the early 100s CE, and the name stuck – whereas the land of pasta, pizza, and Pisa is now called Italy. How come?

Well, it's pretty complicated . . .

Let's start back in the ancient Iron Age. According to legend, Rome was founded by Romulus and Remus in 753 BCE, but it was a modest start-up. Meanwhile, the wider Italian peninsula was divided into lots of different regions and peoples. Perhaps the most famous were the Etruscans, who controlled a large chunk of western and north-western Italy (and who later gave their name to Tuscany), but to their north were the Ligurians, Venetians, and Raetians; to their east were the Umbrians and Picentes; to their south-east were the Sabines and Samnites; to their south were the Latins, who were themselves north of the Bruttii; and there were also the Osci, the Marsi, Pelligni, Lucanians, Calabrians, and Apulians, plus the Sicilians, and lots of other smaller peoples I've chosen not to list because it'll take bloomin' ages!

What's more, many of the major towns in southern Italy were actually Greek colonies founded in the eighth–sixth centuries BCE, such as Naples (then known as Parthenope) and Syracuse, the Sicilian home of the famous *eureka*-bellowing, bathtub-experimenting Archimedes. In fact, the Romans later referred to southern Italy as *Magna Graecia* (Greater Greece). However, we're hunting for the origins of the word *Italy*, and thus far we've drawn a blank. So, what else have we got to play with?

Ancient historians, including the heavy-hitting Aristotle and Thucydides, liked to talk about a king named Italus who'd ruled over a place called Oenotria, which translates as 'the land of the vines'. Oenotria – let's just call it 'wine country' – is seemingly what those aforementioned Greek colonisers called a large swathe of southern Italy, suggesting it was rich and fertile land for viticulture, although I prefer to imagine they called it that because everyone was constantly sloshed on local vino, and thus very easy to conquer. Anyway, Italus was a legendary ruler who, according to Aristotle, gave his name to the very southern chunk of Italy.

However, there's another theory to consider. Modern scholars have proposed that *Italy* instead derives from the Latin word for a young cow, *vitulus*. The land of young cattle would thereby have been known as *vitelia*, which might easily have been shortened to *Itelia*. To add ballast to this theory, archaeologists have recovered many coins from southern Italy – the region supposedly ruled by legendary, wine-guzzling Italus – which are minted with the word *Víteliú* written in the ancient Oscan language. These coins have been found in

several locations, suggesting there was a shared cultural identity across the south.

By the 220s BCE, the Latin-speaking Romans had conquered most of Italy, apart from the south, and it's from
this time that we find evidence to suggest those non-Roman
southerners were being described as *Italics*. One of the best
clues is an inscription found on the Greek island of Delos,
where a public marketplace (*agora*) was dedicated to 'Apollo
and the Italics', which sounds like the name of a fantastic funk
band. Without wishing to completely derail this answer with
anachronistic whimsy, I also like to imagine they were called
the Italics because they walked around looking a bit *slanted*,
like the italic font, probably because they came from wine
country and were permanently tipsy. I have zero evidence to
back this up, but it's my book, so who's going to stop me?

Anyway, back to the actual facts. When the Delian agora was
dedicated, Italics were still not considered Romans. Though
Rome was the dominant power across the peninsula, it treated
the other peoples as foreign allies (known as *socii*) rather than
legitimate Roman citizens. After extensive demands to be let
into the club, and plenty of stubborn door-slamming from the
huffy Romans, the *socii* launched a devastating four-year war
against Rome in 91 BCE; it was known as the Social War, but
there was nothing friendly about it. Around 100,000 people
are said to have died. Rome proved victorious, but knew it
couldn't afford to fight off another uprising, so caved in to the
demands of the Italics, Etruscans, Samnites, etc.

Suddenly, everyone was a Roman.

It seems the next half-century also brought another big
change: the word *Italics* stopped applying to just southerners,
and now extended to the lands touching the River Rubicon,
in the north-east, which bordered enemy Gaul. Once the

all-conquering Julius Caesar had smashed through them, the realms of *Italia* then extended up to the Alps. Indeed, when Rome got its first emperor in 27 BCE – the exceptionally confident Augustus Caesar – he split the Italian peninsula into eleven provinces: Latium and Campania, Calabria and Apulia, Lucania and Bruttium, Samnium, Picenum, Umbria, Etruria, Aemilia, Liguria, Venetia, and Transpadane Gaul. But as a collective noun, Augustus referred to them as *Tota Italia* ('all of Italy'). The Roman Empire would grow yet further, but many of its citizens were now classified as *Italians*.

End of story? If only! This is where things get really complicated. *Italy* now became a useful political term, but it proved a slippery concept. When the Western Roman Empire fell to the Goths in the 470s CE, the new top bosses – including Odoacer and Theodoric the Ostrogoth – dubbed themselves 'Kings of Italy'. But when the Frankish emperor Charlemagne added Italy to his Holy Roman Empire in 773 CE, he preferred to call himself Emperor of Rome, with the Kingdom of Italy being treated as a subsidiary part of a wider empire.

Now things get too complicated for me to summarise in this simple answer. Italy's medieval history is a whole thing, and I don't have the time or willpower to explain it. If you'd like to dive into the story, try David Abulafia's edited book *Italy in the Central Middle Ages* for a thematic guide to life at the time, or for a swifter, more straightforward chronology you can go to Vincent Cronin's *Italy: A History.* All you need to know right now is that it split across the middle; the southern half became the Kingdom of Naples in the 1280s, while the north fractured into rival city-states – Florence, Milan, Venice, etc. – which claimed independence, but still had to deal with meddling from the Holy Roman Empire.

In 1494, all of Italy was turned into the boxing ring for a brutal dynastic punch-up, called the Italian Wars, between the superpowers of France and the Holy Roman Empire. This grudge match lasted for decades and caused untold carnage, not least because from 1519 onwards the Holy Roman Emperor, Charles V, was also ruler of the mighty Spanish Empire too, meaning he could pour extra troops and resources into the Italian campaign. Remarkably, it didn't derail the cultural flourishing we now call the Renaissance; in fact, arguably it fuelled it. And one of the interesting curios was that, despite all the factional politicking, both Popes and poets still embraced the word *Italy*, suggesting there was still some semblance of a shared identity amid the cannon fire.

Jump forward to the 1790s, however, and the Holy Roman Empire now came up against the mighty military maestro, Napoleon Bonaparte, who – seeking to protect the French revolutionary republic from Austrian invasion, by sticking a friendly Italian buffer in the way – decisively booted the Holy Roman Empire out of the peninsula, established a series of small northern republics, and then figured he'd rather collate them into the Kingdom of *Italy*.

Of course, in ancient days, Italy had once been the name for just the southern part of the peninsula; but Napoleon's Italian kingdom was only in the north. The southern chunk of the peninsula was still called the Kingdom of Naples, and he gave it to his brother to rule, and then to his general, Joachim Murat. However, Napoleon then met his Waterloo at the Battle of Waterloo in 1815, and, in the following year, Italy was restored to its factory settings. In came the ex-Holy Roman Emperor to reclaim his prize, having rebranded himself as Emperor of Austria.

But some of the big republican ideas instilled by the

Napoleonic era started to bubble away among the people, and it soon frothed up into the *Risorgimento* (Resurgence), a literary and revolutionary movement led by Giuseppe Mazzini, which was pushed forward by the famous military heroics of Giuseppe Garibaldi. In 1859, Garibaldi's Piedmontese forces defeated the Austrians and united most of Italy. In 1866 they took Venice, and in 1870 they marched into Rome. At long last, the peninsula was a unified country once more, and its name was shouted aloud by its new citizens: *Italy!* But this new nation had 1,500 years of history to unpick; and so many languages and regional traditions to fold into one identity. Indeed, Massimo d'Azeglio summed it up when he famously uttered the words, 'We made Italy. Now we need to make Italians.' Given the north–south divide in the modern Italian economy, and the frequent drama of Italian politics, there's arguably a long way still to go.

38. How did the modern boundaries of African nations come to be?
Asked by Donald

Cripes! OK ... there are big questions, and then there are BIG questions, and Donald's is the latter. Africa is the planet's second largest continent and the second most populous. It is home to 1.25 billion people, and is geographically divided up into fifty-four sovereign states, two contested states, and ten foreign-administered territories. Meanwhile, this book is a cheerful collection of brief answers ranging from 1,300 to 2,500 words in length. In short, if I were foolhardy enough to accept Donald's challenge, and provide a potted history of each African nation, I'd be working with a mere forty-six words per country, and ... dammit, I forgot to include this introduction! Make that forty-three words.

Instead of that miserly approach, I'm going to tackle the most famous story of how modern Africa's borders were created. And then I'll explain why it's too simplistic. Sorry! Here's the story ...

In 1884, the political heavyweights of Europe (and the USA) gathered in Berlin to carve up Africa, as if it were a tasty birthday cake. They'd spent the past two decades jostling in the 'Scramble for Africa', which was an attempt to regulate their spheres of influence, stay out of each other's way, and legalise their claims to African land. The conference organiser was the cunning German chancellor, Otto von Bismarck. Once all the moustachioed bigwigs had scrawled loads of straight lines over the big map with their blue pencils, European control of African territory had shot up from 10 per cent to an obscene 90 per cent. These artificial, arbitrary, absurdly straight borders proved so powerful that, in the 1960s, the African independence movement was forced to keep them. And, thus, they remain today.

THE END.

Alas, history isn't so simple, and modern scholarship has challenged quite a lot of these assumptions, while still acknowledging European colonialism's damaging influence. So, let's rewind.

European meddling in Africa goes back a long way, not least because we get the name *Africa* from the Romans, though we don't know why they called it that. They only cared about its northern regions, but we mustn't repeat that mistake because Africa has an enormously rich and diverse history. In the west, there was Mansa Musa's Islamic Malian

Empire in the 1300s, and the subsequent Songhai Empire in the 1460s–1580s, both of which were astoundingly wealthy. A little earlier, Nigeria had played host to the Kingdom of Benin, with its beautiful bronze sculptures. And in the next question I'll discuss the Asante Empire, with its ornate gold-working, rich musical tradition, and stool culture. Further south, the medieval Kingdom of Great Zimbabwe had boasted a huge walled city that functioned as the centre of a powerful trading network.

Meanwhile, East Africa was especially diverse because of the influence of the Arab, Persian, and Ottoman worlds, giving rise to its Arabic name 'the Swahili coast'. These regions also had extensive links to India and wider Southeast Asia, with the Siddi people – who are descended from African Bantu peoples – still being a notable community in modern-day Pakistan and India. Of course, there was also Ethiopia, the long-standing bastion of African Christianity, which had embraced the faith in the fourth century and later developed its famous rock-cut churches in Lalibela.

So, that's the context to bear in mind when I say the European colonising project began long before the Berlin Conference. In 1488, the Portuguese Bartolomeu Dias rounded the Cape of Good Hope and witnessed the vast extent of the African continent. This gradually led to European powers in the 1600s embracing the despicable cruelty of transatlantic slavery to fuel their lucrative sugar and tobacco plantations in the New World. Over the next two centuries, an estimated 12.5 million human beings were forcibly enslaved (often having been captured and sold by other Africans), loaded onto cramped ships, and either died at sea or survived to face a life of dehumanising brutality.

Having established enslavement stations on the west

coast, Europeans started to gain footholds for other economic activity. The Portuguese brought maize, coffee, tobacco, and sugar cane over from their Brazilian colonies and planted them in Angola, as well as trading in ivory, fabrics, and gold. The Dutch *Trekboers* conquered farmland in the South African Cape, having fought the indigenous Khoikhoi clans, but then lost the Cape to the British in 1806, forcing these Boer trekkers further inland, where they established the Transvaal and Orange Free State (which later led to the Boer Wars against the Brits).

Meanwhile, the French had been in Senegal for ages, then invaded Egypt under Napoleon, and launched a devastatingly protracted assault on Algeria in the 1830s. Their arch-enemies, the British, got involved in South Africa early on, then Sierra Leone in 1821, and fought three separate wars against the Asante, eventually winning at the third attempt in 1874, then having two more wars for good luck. However, until the 1870s, such European involvement was focused on the north and western coastlines, and East Africa was still much more closely tied to the Arab Omani Empire.

But then came the sudden, notorious 'Scramble'. Why? The conventional interpretation is that Africa became a proxy political game, a second chessboard for the rival major powers to squabble over, with the European status quo having been recently upset by a newly unified Germany threatening France's borders, and with British politicians bouncing between contradictory policies of free trade and protectionism to maintain their economic superiority. Oh, and then you had little old Belgium . . .

Since the 1870s, the jealous King Leopold II of Belgium had felt embarrassed to rule such a tiny country. Having failed to acquire the Philippines, he spotted an opportunity in the public reaction to the work of British missionary David Livingstone, who became a posthumous celebrity for preaching against the evils of the slave trade in East Africa and the Indian Ocean. Writing to his ambassador in London, Leopold admitted: 'I do not want to miss a good chance of getting us a slice of this magnificent African cake.'

Whereas Leopold's motivation was obvious, historians such as Professor Richard Reid have argued that the other European powers were surprisingly reluctant to get involved. William Gladstone is now remembered as the UK Prime Minister who ramped up military involvement in Africa, yet, oddly enough, he and his Liberal Party tried to resist joining the Scramble. This phrasing suggests a ravenous hunger for advantage, but the Scramble was impelled more by fear of sudden disadvantage; what if rivals conquered Africa instead? Would it disrupt the global status quo? This was the real-politik logic of: 'we can't afford it, but we can't let *them* have it either!'

Richard Reid also stresses that cultural snobbery and ever-hardening racism were key motivators. In the early 1800s, the philosopher Georg Wilhelm Friedrich Hegel had declared Africa to be a continent without history, civilisation, or philosophical merit (apart from Egypt, which he admitted had been part of the cultured Greek and Roman world). Utter garbage! But to Western intellectuals, Africa was a blank slate. Oh, and then there was the racism . . .

An enslavement system that dehumanised Black Africans led to the ideology needed to defend it: this was scientific racism, which broadly divided into two camps. The *mono-genists* said that God had created all humankind simultaneously. Africans were thus 'primitive' because of their 'savage' environment, but they could be 'civilised' by exposure to the ideas and customs of a 'superior' race. The *polygenists* argued the different races were created at different times, either through divine deed or Darwinian evolution. Africans were therefore deemed to be inferior 'savages', whose only redeeming quality was a courageous warlike instinct. They couldn't be truly 'civilised', they instead needed to be subjugated by force.

Crucially, both camps agreed on Africa's untapped economic potential; there was gold in them there hills! Another important colonial driver was the moral righteousness of 'muscular Christianity'. By 1884, slavery had been widely abolished in the 'West', but it remained commonplace in parts of Africa. Despite several treaties between Britain and the Sultan of Zanzibar, the slave trade was also still happening in the coastal hubs controlled by the Omani Arabs. Having enriched themselves from embracing slavery, European powers could now play the role of slave abolishing superheroes, and feel good about it.

This was the spandex fig leaf worn by King Leopold II of Belgium. He cynically established a humanitarian organisation called the International Association for the Exploration and Civilisation of Central Africa, fronted by the British explorer Henry Morton Stanley, but Leopold used it to become a cruel colonial monster, responsible for the deaths of maybe 10 million souls when he mutilated, kidnapped, and starved the people of the Belgian Congo into working in his own personal rubber industry (it was his private empire until he was forced to cede it to the Belgian state after being outed by a newspaper scandal).

So, that's what drove the Berlin Conference of 1884-5, but what is the truth of its legacy when it comes to Africa's modern borders?

The famous story, that I believed until I contacted a noted expert in the field, tells us the African map was redrawn in Berlin, by people who had never been to Africa, and who had no clue what geographical features, or what ethnic groups, they were arbitrarily splitting asunder. In 1890, the British Prime Minister, Lord Salisbury, sardonically noted: 'we have been engaged in drawing lines upon maps where no white man's foot ever trod; we have been giving away mountains and rivers and lakes to each other, only hindered by the small impediment that we never knew exactly where the mountains and rivers and lakes were'. I suspect he intended it as a joke, because lots of modern scholarship now argues otherwise.

Intriguingly, this Berlin origin story wasn't the invention of lefty, post-colonial historians in turtleneck knitwear, or even African revolutionaries, but rather – as the historian Dr Camille Lefebvre has shown – French colonial administrators of the 1920s, who were trained in the new social sciences. They argued that *nations* should be territories based on shared language and ethnicity, and their predecessors had failed to recognise and foster such cohesive identities with their random borders. Ironically, the most famous anti-colonial myth was invented by European colonialists themselves.

In truth, the borders were not decided in Berlin; it actually took many years for these processes to be completed – 50 per cent of Africa's borders had been redrawn after fifteen years, according to the geographer Professor Michel Foucher. That's not to say there aren't obvious examples of border-drawing which now look completely absurd; the Gambia is a bizarrely long and narrow country with borders barely extending either side of a meandering river, resulting in what looks like a caterpillar crawling through Senegal.

In total, when looking at all of Africa's borders, Foucher argues:

> In 34 per cent of cases they follow lakes and rivers, while 13 per cent . . . follow the contours of physical geography. In 42 per cent of cases (compared to a global average of 23 per cent) they follow geometrical lines (astronomical, mathematical); other categories (ethnic, pre-existing boundaries) account for only 11 per cent of the total.

Indeed, ignoring the other European meddlers, just France and Great Britain alone were responsible for 60 per cent of Africa's border delineations. But numerous historians, such as Professor Paul Nugent, have shown that many colonial borders weren't arbitrary or artificial at all, and instead were the result of European bureaucrats beginning the process from afar, but leaving the field agents and soldiers to figure things out on the ground.

Some of these agents were undoubtedly shady operators. Professor Steven Press has argued in his book *Rogue Empires: Contracts and Conmen in Europe's Scramble for Africa* that individuals and private businesses descended upon indigenous communities wielding not weapons but contracts, hoping to assemble private empires of dubious legality. Press argues Africans were often manipulated into deals they didn't understand, and were given paltry goods in return. Not knowing what they'd done, they sometimes traded the same land multiple times to different parties, or sold mountains that didn't exist, accidentally sowing havoc among the competing agents.

But there is another branch of scholars, working under the banner of the 'African Borderlands Research Network', who

have argued for a much more complex story, in which negotiations also sometimes allowed for active African agency,
resistance, co-operation, and reinterpretation. Even if local
leaders were indeed later betrayed or trapped by legalities,
the initial deal-making could help those with an axe to grind
against their local enemies. Moreover, these new colonial
borders often reflected pre-existing ideas of space and territory; plenty of the straight lines rendered official what had
already been customary. And if they were indeed novel, some
Africans found ways to reinterpret, or simply ignore, them.

So, is it a myth that Africa's modern boundaries are purely
colonial legacies? Depends on who you ask! The French geographer Michel Foucher has ruffled some feathers by arguing:

> The time has come to put paid to the enduring myth
> that the scars of colonialism are responsible for all of
> Africa's troubles. This assertion about the disadvanta-
> geous consequences of Africa's borders is just one of a
> number of received ideas, others being the absence of
> any pre-colonial political boundaries, and the lack of
> consideration shown by Europeans to pre-existing geo-
> political realities.

Not all scholars agree with this revisionism. The eminent
Professor Anthony Asiwaju immediately pushed back against
Foucher's article. Despite the contested interpretations, I
should stress that none of these aforementioned historians
are letting the colonial powers off the hook for the pain
and suffering caused by colonialism; a land-grabbing policy
fuelled by racism easily tipped into indefensible cruelty at the
drop of a hat. And plenty of communities were traumatically
divided by new borders. The nomadic Maasai people were

split up into two colonies in Kenya and Tanganyika, while Somalis had their cattle-grazing lands stripped away, and they found themselves living as 'native aliens' in British Kenya. Indeed, this later caused arguments during independence negotiations, because Somalis requested a return to the old, borderless ways of nomadic existence, whereas a new Kenya wanted to define its territory in absolute terms.

As for the other claims, in the famous 'It All Happened in Berlin!' story, yes, European territorial control really did shoot up from 10 per cent in 1870 to 90 per cent by 1913. Of modern Africa's fifty-four nations, only Liberia and Ethiopia escaped colonialism, and even this fudges the fact that Ethiopia was thrice attacked by Italy – in 1887, 1895, and then conquered by Mussolini's forces in 1935 – while Liberia, which gained its independence in 1847, was founded in the 1820s as an American colony for people liberated from slavery. Meanwhile, the almost complete colonisation of the continent meant that, during both world wars, it became a literal battleground for European imperial ideologies, and so much African blood was spilled in the defence of foreign overlords.

However, these ruinous conflicts also helped spark independence. After decades of domination, African nations began to go it alone from the 1950s onwards. Cocoa-rich Ghana led the way in 1957, thanks to its charismatic Prime Minister Kwame Nkrumah. He was a pan-Africanist hoping for a socialist, borderless, United States of Africa, strong enough to defy Western influence (the Suez Crisis of 1956 was an obvious warning shot of what that might look like). Nkrumah's plan didn't work out. He became too big for his boots, declaring himself an authoritarian president for life, and he was deposed in 1966. However, the Organisation of African Unity, founded in 1963, tried to continue these pan-African ideals.

In some cases, regional unification did happen. After the First World War, Cameroon had been stripped from the defeated Germans and shared between France and Britain. In 1961, the people of British Southern Cameroons voted to join it back together, creating the Federal Republic of Cameroon. Not long after, in 1964, modern Tanzania emerged from the fusion of Tanganyika and Zanzibar. Mali and Senegal also briefly united to become the Mali Federation in 1960, following the Senegalese leader Léopold Sédar Senghor's long-standing arguments against the fractured weakness of a 'balkanised' West Africa. Alas, the political union immediately collapsed.

Similar attempts to form an East African political union in the early 1960s also failed, but the ideal of regional co-operation persisted. In 2000, an organisation known as the East African Community was revived from the ashes. If all goes well, your world atlas will soon need a big update, because Burundi, Kenya, Rwanda, South Sudan, Tanzania, and Uganda may merge into the East African Federation.

So, independence definitely changed the map. However, many colonial borders remained. The obvious justification for this status quo was a fear of political violence and refugee crises if peoples were shunted around – as had been the tragic fallout when the British partitioned India in 1947 – but pragmatism wasn't the sole factor. Many boundaries had acquired profound meaning in the passing decades, or their significance had long preceded Europe's incursions. Africans didn't necessarily want to redraw the map, even if they passionately desired independence.

Not everyone got the independence they desired. Since the 1960s, there have been bloody separatist conflicts in Nigeria, Angola, eastern Ghana, and Kenya. There's no doubting that these fissures are part of the ongoing repercussions of the

Berlin Conference. In which case, we can say that Africa's modern borders are indeed often colonial relics - even when they're newly installed, and might yet change again - but the rationale behind why these borders were created in the first place, and why they were often kept beyond the age of empires, goes way beyond the famous, simplistic story of the Berlin Conference, with its blue pencils and polished tables. The history of Africa is not one story, it is a tapestry of many interwoven stories. And that's what makes it fascinating.

CHAPTER 10:

WARS & BATTLES

39. Why did the Ashanti people keep a golden stool?
Asked by Nana Poku

Let's start with a little context. Situated in West Africa, on the coast of the Gulf of Guinea, Ghana is home to about 30 million people, and an extraordinary array of wildlife and flora. It is a beautiful country, rich in gold deposits - hence why the colonial British administrators called it the Gold Coast - and its mineral wealth and cocoa industry helped it become the first Black African nation to achieve independence from a colonial power, waving bye-bye to Britain in 1957. Confusingly, as with Mali, its proud new name of Ghana was taken in honour of a medieval African empire that had never actually held lands in the area.

OK, that's the modern history, but to tell the story of the Golden Stool we need to look a little earlier. In the 1600s, Ghana's dominant military power were the Denkyira, but within the region were numerous small substates ruled by members of the Asante (also known as the Ashanti) people - themselves members of a much larger ethno-linguistic group called the Akan. In 1701, an impressive ruler called King Osei Tutu managed to acquire guns from European traders and, through a combination of military conquest and diplomatic sweet talk, to unite these distinct Asante tribes into a single bloc, with his powerbase of Kumasi as its capital. Newly bemuscled, and assisted by his charismatic chief priest, Okomfo Anokye, Osei Tutu's warriors smashed the hated Denkyira, turning the tables to bring them under his control. And, as his reward, he took the title of *Asantehene* (ruler of the Asante Empire).

Osei Tutu now had a problem. Forging a shared cultural identity among former strangers often requires more than just top-notch admin. Having a shared enemy is handy, but what happens when you've defeated them? Instead, what you need is shared symbols and ideas. The British are supposed to bond over the Union Jack and 'God Save the Queen', yet we mostly prefer weather chat and TV shows about competitive baking, but for King Osei Tutu this symbol of unity was to be manifested in a seat of power: the Golden Stool, known in the Asante Twi language as the *Sika Dwa Kofi*. Charmingly, it's common custom in the Akan culture to name people after the day on which they were born, and royal furniture is afforded the same respect, so *Sika Dwa Kofi* translates as the 'Golden Stool Born on a Friday'.

Stools had been used as symbols of power for centuries, and local chiefs might have sat upon their own one carved from wood. Later on, senior royals of the Asante monarchy each had an ancestral stool that, when they died, was painted black with a mixture of egg yolks, soot, and spider webs, with additional offerings added of sheep blood, animal fat, and the nail clippings and hair of the deceased. These blackened stools were then enshrined in a sacred stool-house called *nkonnwafieso*.

But the Golden Stool was different. It was very much as advertised – a solid-gold stool, but not one of those three-legged stools you get in pubs, or movie scenes set in Wild West saloons. No, it was 18 inches high, created with a thin, curved, backless seat, a chunky central pillar, and a thin rectangular base. It came complete with accompanying bells and chimes, with each new king adding a new bell to represent their tenure in the political hot seat, or a major military victory. The stool also had its own official umbrella, the *Katamanso* (the covering of the nation) made of thick, colourful wool. This was furniture created with a purpose. And yet, it didn't serve the usual purposes that stools are designed for - namely, sitting, or hitting cowboys over the head in Wild West bar fights.

While the local chiefs took the weight off by plonking themselves down on their wooden stools, the Golden Stool wasn't a throne for the new emperor to perch upon in glorious dignity - in fact, nobody could even touch it, and nor could it touch the ground either; it apparently rested upon a carpet of camel skin, or the hide of an elephant which had died face-first without rolling onto its back. Sometimes, the stool even sat upon its own throne, next to the King's throne, during official ceremonies. And nor was this stool 'created' by a skilled craftsman, rather it was *summoned*. According to legend, Osei Tutu was gifted the stool by his loyal priest Okomfo Anokye, who pulled it down from the heavens with a magical incantation.

The Golden Stool was a pure symbol of the new Asante nation. The fact it was gold was proof of the King's legitimacy and military power, an example of his control over the region's mineral wealth, and so the stool was even consulted before battles and political decisions, giving it a certain inanimate sentience. Its uncorrupted status, remaining untarnished by human contact, served as a metaphor for the unending glory of the new Asante Empire, and the eternal idea of the new nation that would outlast its mortal kings. Okomfo Anokye also laid down a sacred sword in a river bank, and told people not to touch it, which sounds rather like the Arthurian legend of Excalibur being pulled from the stone and then returned to the Lady of the Lake.

Inevitably, Osei Tutu died. Yet the stool did its job, remaining as the enduring symbol of the ongoing nation, particularly during the nineteenth century when the British showed up, leading to five separate Anglo-Asante wars. They began in 1823 when an expanding Asante Empire tried to muscle in on the Fante region, which just happened to be under British protection. That conflict ended with British humiliation in 1831; the second ran from 1863 to 1864 and ended in stalemate; the third, in 1873-4, was much more violent. The British were led by the talented and ruthless commander Sir Garnet Wolseley, meaning the Asante were defeated at the third try. The victors burned the Asantehene's royal palace to the ground as a symbol of the power shift. The fourth Anglo-Asante War, in 1895-6, saw the pendulum swing emphatically towards the European superpower, which now wielded the devastating Maxim machine gun. The British troops captured the capital city of Kumasi, and forced the Asantehene King Prempeh into exile in the Seychelles. The Brits also demanded financial reparations for all the trouble they'd gone to in crushing the uprising, and captured many Asante royal treasures which were then shipped off to London. But one treasure remained out of their grasp . . .

Yes, the fifth and final Anglo-Asante war is perhaps the most relevant to Nana Poku's question because it involved the Golden Stool itself. In September 1900, having already been defeated, the Asante people rose up in rebellion, led by the sixty-year-old Yaa Asantewaa, who is now a great heroine in Ghanaian history. Those earlier British demands for reparations were a big factor, but the final straw was a tactless ultimatum from the Gold Coast's douchebag of a colonial administrator, Sir Frederick Mitchell Hodgson, who demanded that the sacred Golden Stool – which had been safely hidden from British looting – be handed over. According to popular belief at the time, he, and then Queen Victoria, wanted to sit on it as proof of their ranking superiority. This was pure incitement. No human had touched it in 199 years, and now a foreign invader planned to park his bum on the hallowed stool.

The subsequent war resulted in 1,000 British dead, which was quite the bloody nose, but twice as many losses for the Asante. Like King Prempeh a few years before her, Yaa Asantewaa was exiled to the Seychelles, where she died in 1921. The victorious British now formally annexed the Asante Empire into a British colony, but Sir Frederick never got his hands – or rather his backside – on the sacred Golden Stool, despite various undercover operations to track down its secret hiding place.

In the end, thieves stole and then buried it, only for it to be accidentally rediscovered and returned to political usage in 1935, when the Asante kingdom was partially restored. Its official flag, which still remains in use by the Asante people of modern Ghana, is a yellow stripe, black stripe, and green stripe with two thin white lines separating them. And in the centre, as had been intended by King Osei Tutu, is the Golden Stool – the eternal symbol of the nation.

40. Why are there so many penises shown on the Bayeux Tapestry, although mainly for horses? If the embroiderers were female, that would surely have 'raised' a few laughs!
Asked by Pat

Thanks, Pat, not least because you were the only person to include their own dick joke in the question itself – a bold move which I applaud. Right, first things first: have a quick google of the Bayeux Tapestry and familiarise yourself with its aesthetic style. Apart from the pedantic fact it's not actually a tapestry at all (it's a 70-metre-long embroidery), you'll see that it's a wonderfully vivid visual account of the events of 1066, which saw William, Duke of Normandy, earn his nickname of 'William the Conqueror' by defeating King Harold at the Battle of Hastings.

But yes, it's also a wonderfully vivid homage to the pendulous glory of the humble wang. Without doubt, the Bayeux Tapestry is chock-a-block with cock. There is a total of ninety-three phalluses on display, although only four are attached to humans, and it's the horses who possess the other eighty-nine. There's also a rogue pair of dangling testicles that appear to be flying solo because an axe handle conveniently covers the penis. And there's also a dead bloke being stripped naked whose todger is hinted at, but not fully shown.

Even without the genitalia, the Bayeux Tapestry is an absolute sausage fest. There are 626 people depicted in its scenes, yet only three of them are women. It definitely wouldn't pass the Bechdel test. Even worse, 66 per cent of these ladies (i.e. two of them) are gratuitously starkers, a ratio presumably only matched by the cast of HBO's *Game of Thrones*. And the only clothed member of the female trio - the mysterious Aelfgyva - is hardly the paragon of virtue; she's positioned cryptically close to a squatting, nude man whose very large penis and outstretched hand is anything but subtle. Are we meant to get this reference? Is it some topical joke about a sex scandal? Presumably everyone in 1066 knew who Aelfgyva was, but we don't. Her inclusion in his homage to martial conquest is baffling.

So, back to Pat's original question: *'why so many penises?'* Well, again, we're in guesswork territory. Having spent my teenage education at an all-boys grammar school, I am acutely attuned to the art of the puerile doodle; it may be an artistic masterpiece, but it's not beyond the realms of possibility the Bayeux Tapestry fell prey to a cheeky prankster drawing dicks on every available corner. The historian Professor George Garnett suspects that the design comes from the mind of a bloke with a priapic fixation. However, the dogs don't get genitals, so it's just men and horses who enjoy that phallic privilege. The fact the largest penis in the embroidery belongs to William the Conqueror's own stallion does seem rather symbolic. Presumably, it's a way of saying he's the alpha male in this story, and - unlike the joke about men who drive sports cars to compensate for their modest package - we're perhaps supposed to imagine that William, astride his powerful charger, is himself impressively hung.

Other historians argue that the nudity is only associated with the English characters, which might suggest this is the Norman propaganda machine making their enemies out to be crass, immoral perverts. The eminent art historian Professor Madeline Caviness wonders if the penises are meant to mirror the swords and spears, as symbols of penetrative, aggressive masculinity. Of course, it's entirely possible that it's just simply a work of honest naturalism, and the designer was unembarrassed by the biological reality of dangly body parts. Who knows!

There's long been a robust debate about who commissioned the design, and who then actually embroidered it. In the nineteenth century, the Bayeux Tapestry's patronage was often credited to the wife of William the Conqueror, Queen Matilda, and you'll still hear it referred to as 'La Tapisserie de la Reine Mathilde' in parts of France. Of course, the sheer number of penises shocked Victorian-era scholars, and so they couldn't see how such a distinguished woman would have given the OK to such a vulgar artwork. Personally, I'm not sure she did.

Instead, I lean towards the theory that it was commissioned by Bishop Odo of Bayeux, Duke William's half-brother, who is given a suspiciously overstated starring role in a key battle sequence; it's the sort of exaggerated prominence one might expect for the man writing the cheque. If so, it seems he may have had it made not in his native Normandy but in Canterbury, where – as Pat suggested in the question – it would have been embroidered by English nuns. I favour this theory because we can see several artistic tropes in the finished design which seem to be copied from illuminated manuscripts held, at the time, in Canterbury Cathedral's library. Essentially, I think the nuns ran out of ideas and started doing the medieval equivalent of flicking through magazines, looking for inspiration.

Some of those who oppose the Canterbury theory argue that virginal nuns wouldn't have known what penises looked like, so they wouldn't have embroidered ninety-three of them. Maybe. But not all nuns spent their entire life in the convent; these were also intellectually stimulating retirement communities for mothers and widowed wives, and so many members would've had sexual relations with men, and they certainly would've seen horses and bulls wandering past. Plus, no offence, but the humble penis isn't exactly difficult to draw. Just ask a teenage boy, or my university housemate who drew a massive cock and balls on our friend's essay, but forgot to tell him before it was submitted for marking. True story.

So, in conclusion, while we can say the Bayeux Tapestry is bountifully bestocked with bell-ends, we can't say *why* this is with total confidence. And, if you find such things off-putting, you can instead choose to enjoy the nineteenth-century facsimile produced by Elizabeth Wardle and her friends at the Leek Embroidery Society, which is now held at Reading Museum. It's exactly the same as the glorious original, except there are some tactical underpants added to the important bits, and the horses are much less excited.

41. What is the least consequential, but most famous battle that's entered the public consciousness?
Asked by Iain

As questions go, Iain, this one is booby-trapped – no matter how I answer, it will still explode in my face, because there is nothing that military history buffs enjoy doing more than arguing about the significance of battles. There are entire corners of the internet devoted to it, and if I boldly assert any opinion about the *least*-consequential-but-*most*-famous battle from history, I'm going to get angry emails. I'll need to legally change my identity and relocate my family to the remotest wilds of Montana. It is a reckless, foolhardy, stupid thing to publicly express strong opinions, because so many people care passionately about this stuff.

Saying that . . . the most famous, least consequential battle was the Battle of Agincourt in 1415.

Dammit! OK, it looks like I'm putting my head in the lion's mouth. Before I get it bitten clean off, let me just say that this isn't intended as my definitive, iron-clad truth that you should uphold as historical gospel. There simply isn't a single right answer to this question, and I've plumped for a very controversial one – which many historians will argue against – simply because I'm half-French, and I've always found this a fun thing to argue about.

You see, I grew up in a household where Agincourt and Waterloo weren't just famous battles, they were hilarious punchlines. As an infuriating teenager, I went through a petty and petulant phase of resisting my Frenchness and doing whatever I could to piss off my Parisian mother. Despite her having absolutely no interest in military history, I found I could still goad her into huffiness if Henry V or the Duke of Wellington were praised at the dinner table. Amusingly, my crowing smugness would be shot down with a righteous pout and the stinging reply: 'We still won the war. Also, you stupid English spelled it wrong – it's *Azincourt* with a "z"!'

Annoyingly, she was right on both fronts. The Battle of Agincourt (or *Azincourt*), fought on St Crispin's Day in October 1415, near the village of Azincourt, has become one of the most iconic battles in medieval history. I'm sure Iain, my question-setter, knows it very well. Of course, its reputation was undoubtedly burnished by William Shakespeare in his triumphal play *Henry V*, written in 1599, in which the titular king utters such magnificently quotable lines as, 'Once more unto the breach, dear friends, once more' and, 'We few,

we happy few, we band of brothers.' It is a great piece of political theatre, and its stirring power has often been hitched
to national causes. During the Seven Years' War of 1756–63,
and again during the Napoleonic Wars – when France was
the recurring enemy – *Henry V* was popularly restaged to great
acclaim; in fact, it was Lord Horatio Nelson's favourite Shakespeare play.

In 1915, during Agincourt's 500th anniversary year, Britain
was once again sending soldiers to France, though this time
the hated baddies were the Germans. British newspapers
were chock-full of commemorative references, and this
public fascination had already inspired Arthur Machen to
write a short story called 'The Bowmen' which he published
in the *Evening News* in 1914. It told of the Battle of Mons, in
which the British Expeditionary Force is vastly outnumbered
by the Germans but, in their hour of need, the ghosts of
the Agincourt longbowmen rise to their defence. It was, of
course, pure romantic fiction, but it soon inspired a popular
hoax that claimed guardian angels had been sighted at Mons,
as supposed proof that God was on Blighty's side in the war.

Agincourt proved its propaganda utility once again in 1944
when it was adapted by Laurence Olivier as a patriotic movie
intended to rouse public morale before D-Day (in actual fact,
it was released a few months after the Allied landings). The
film sanitised the less pleasant elements of Shakespeare's play,
making its hero a saintlier warrior than he really was. It was
also around this time that stories were told of the Welsh longbowmen flicking the V-sign to the French, therefore flaunting
their deadly bow-drawing fingers as a cheeky 'screw you!' to
those who would love to cut them off. It is, of course, absolute
tosh! There's zero medieval evidence for anything like this.
But Agincourt has always been something of a national myth,

especially when Brits want to bash those on the other side of the Channel.

I say *myth*, but of course the battle did happen. For much of the past six centuries, Agincourt was accepted as the tale of a huge French army, comprising the cream of its aristocracy, intercepting Henry V's small, retreating force of English and Welsh soldiers who'd besieged Harfleur and were now legging it back to Calais, naively hoping the French wouldn't notice them scurrying through their lands. The French very much noticed. However, through the combination of tactical ingenuity, courage, and Henry's heroic leadership, the smaller force all but annihilated the massed ranks of French attackers, handing Henry an almighty, unlikely victory in the Hundred Years' War.

Great story, right?

Modern historians have been kicking the tyres, and not all of them are totally convinced. The most sceptical has been Professor Anne Curry, who scoured administrative records to find out just how many men, and just how much cash, Henry had rustled up for his violent jaunt to Normandy. Typically, the French had been said to outnumber Henry's men by four to one. Curry's archival beavering led her to a much more cautious figure, putting the English and Welsh numbers at 8,700 men - an increase on the usual 6,000 - but drastically cutting the French forces from 24,000 to just 12,000. Other historians, like Dr Juliet Barker, have argued this hugely underestimates the French army, because each knight brought his own personal servant who Curry hasn't included in her count. Barker thinks there were 14,000 hardened troops and maybe another 10,000 light troops in reserve.

Technical debates aside, I'm not here to explode the myth of Agincourt as a battle. There's no doubting the Anglo-Welsh forces delivered a shock knockout blow from a position of apparent weakness. King Henry's army was weirdly lopsided in having no cavalry, and five times more Welsh archers than English men-at-arms. Ordinarily, that ratio was a calamity waiting to happen, but at Agincourt the vulnerable archers were shielded by a screen of protective trees at either side of them, and they hammered sharp stakes into the sodden ground, creating a nasty DIY fence to slow down the charge of French horses. Lodged in their defensive position, the archers then pelted the French from long range. Most of the arrows likely didn't puncture steel-plate armour, but French limbs and eyes were vulnerable, as were their horses; moreover, the French were wading through heavy, squelching mud, and they were probably knackered by the time they got to within stabbing distance.

Slowed down by the terrain, unable to mount a strong cavalry charge, prohibited from outflanking their enemy by the trees, and buffeted by arrows, the French then found themselves crushed from the rear by their own overeager comrades, who pushed forwards against the backs of their own men. Those in the front ranks then found themselves attacked from the sides by nimble, lightly armoured Welsh-men who daintily moved through the mud, while the English men-at-arms engaged them head-on.

Many French soldiers were likely killed before they even saw any action, being crushed and drowned in the mud by their own surging reinforcements barging into their backs. If we were being ungenerous, we might say the Anglo-Welsh troops didn't win the battle, the French found a way to lose it. Had Sky Sports been covering it like a football match, the pre-kick-off predictions would've hypothesised hundreds of casualties for the French side, but many thousands for the

Anglo-Welsh team. As it was, the opposite happened; the French lost 6,000-plus dead in the battle, with King Henry unheroically ordering further prisoner executions when he was worried about a second wave of attacks.

You're probably now thinking, 'Hang on! How is this an inconsequential battle, Greg? The French got completely mullered!' Yup, they absolutely did. Entire aristocratic families were wiped out in an afternoon; seven members of the French royal family lay dead, including three dukes. It was a brutal bloodbath that undoubtedly hurt the French morale and their fighting resilience. It also hurt national unity. Politically, France was divided between two rival factions - the Armagnacs and the Burgundians - who'd come together to oppose the English. But the defeat at Agincourt shattered their coalition. With the Armagnacs suffering most of the battlefield losses, the Burgundians seized their moment and marched on Armagnac Paris, attacking their own countrymen.

Meanwhile, King Henry V doubled down on his momentum, and made several territorial gains in Normandy over the next four years. But despite his battlefield brilliance, his political negotiations with John of Burgundy went awry, and somehow the two rival factions started to come back together. Then, out of nowhere, John of Burgundy was murdered by the Armagnacs, handing Henry another great opportunity to seize the initiative. True enough, he did a deal with John's vengeful son, Philip. In 1420, the Treaty of Troyes made Henry the rightful heir to the French throne, once the current king - Charles VI, who was plagued by mental health problems - had seen out his mortal years. Henry even married Charles's daughter, Catherine of Valois, to seal the deal. What a coup!

The problem was Charles VI's son, Charles the Dauphin, wasn't taking this lying down. He moved his followers to a rival court and stubbornly waited it out. Meanwhile, Henry discovered that it's all fun and games when you're only the English king, but the minute you become the French heir as well, suddenly Westminster loses interest in your foreign adventures. The vast sums of taxation and parliamentary grants that had funded his initial Normandy invasion – with its enormous naval investment to get the troops and supplies across the Channel – now dried up. If Henry wanted to keep fighting in France, he'd have to ask the French to cough up instead. Indeed, the English Parliament was actually rather grumpy that Henry's focus would now be elsewhere.

As Professor Gwilym Dodd has argued, Henry V now found himself waging extremely costly campaigns, which seemed to take forever to win, without his usual financial support. If he was as smart as Shakespeare later rendered him, it was at this point that he probably experienced a glum realisation: Agincourt had been a false dawn, and he had entangled himself in an unfixable conundrum. Since the late 1300s, it had been clear to contemporary commentators that the Hundred Years' War was unwinnable; neither side was strong enough to conquer the other. And yet Henry had recklessly tried it all the same, hurling himself around with the boisterous energy of a twenty-nine-year-old rugby lad on a stag do. But now, he was burning through money and men, with little to show for it.

He wouldn't have to suffer for long. In 1422, destiny played its darkly comic hand. While besieging Meaux, near Paris, Henry V contracted dysentery; the glorious battlefield titan gradually shat himself to death, which Shakespeare wisely left out of his final draft. A few weeks later, Charles VI of France perished too, after a lifetime of mental health problems. With the rightful heir dead, the French crown now technically passed to Henry and Catherine of Valois' son – another Henry who regularly shat himself, because he was a tiny baby. France was now governed by an infant, requiring a regent to step in. But the previous political divisions hadn't gone away; Charles the Dauphin's supporters refused to accept their new baby ruler. Much like a long-running TV soap opera, the intractable Hundred Years' War just carried on with a new cast.

The English, allied to the Burgundians, now expended huge resources on trying to crush the Dauphin's Armagnac supporters. And they were making some progress until a teenage girl with angelic visions popped herself into a pair of trousers and made a fool of them at the siege of Orléans. Joan of Arc turned the tide of the war, saw the Dauphin crowned in a sacred ceremony, and was then thrown under the bus by Charles once she'd served her purpose. The English burned her as a heretic, but, by then, she'd mostly achieved her goal. In 1453 - as my mother loved to point out over those tense dinners - France won the Hundred Years' War, a conflict of such protracted attrition that even its absurd name is an understatement, given that it lasted a depressing 116 years!

So, why is Agincourt my controversial choice for the 'most famous, but least consequential battle'? Because, in the grand scheme of things, it changed nothing. It was a decisive, shocking, rousing victory in a war that England was pretty much guaranteed to lose ... and then did lose. By winning it, and earning the title of heir to France, King Henry V only made his position harder; by moving the pendulum in one direction, he only gave it the impetus to swing back the other.

Of course, I'm not saying Agincourt had no historical impact, it clearly did! The French political situation became fascinatingly complex, and many lives were lost as a result. Moreover, would we know who Joan of Arc is - one of history's most famous figures – without Agincourt? Would she have risen up against King Henry, had he survived his bout of dysentery to take the French throne? Maybe, who knows?! But here's the thing I keep coming back to: had Henry lost at Agincourt, Charles VII would have ended up on the French throne. Instead, Henry won at Agincourt, and it still happened anyway. In the short term, Agincourt was un-doubtedly consequential, but, ultimately, it was just a surprise detour during a journey to a seemingly inevitable destination.

Agincourt has become talismanic of English, and Welsh, bravery over the centuries, and its invocation in times of crisis makes it a glorious martial trope. But the truth is, I was a bratty teenage arsehole and my long-suffering mother was spot-on; for all the pomp and ceremony, Azincourt ultimately proved to be of no lasting consequence. *Je suis désolé, Maman!*

42. A boyhood question to which I never received a satisfactory answer: how did knights in full armour satisfy their need to go to the toilet?
Asked by Peter

Hello, Peter, and thank you for this absolute classic question – one of the most commonly asked. I'll keep it really short, because I know not everyone likes hearing about bodily functions (if you do want to know more about the history of toilets, see my first book *A Million Years in a Day*). OK, as you've noted, Peter, it was the suit of *full* armour – known as a *harness*, or *panoply* – which likely proved particularly trouble-some, but the history of armour is the story of ever-increasing protection, so it sort of depends where in that story we look.

If we bounce to the Battle of Hastings in 1066, when William the Conqueror invaded England, his soldiers - and those of his opponent, King Harold Godwinson - were wearing long chainmail coats (*hauberks*) over cloth trousers, so it was easy-peasy to hoick up the mail and drop their kecks. We actually have a couple of nice medieval illustrations from a little later in history which show this process for defecation.

We then got the development of partial plate armour, in which the most obvious zones of the body were protected with a clanging sheet of steel, but chainmail remained visible in less vulnerable places. Generally, the groin and backside were protected with mail skirts, which were still easily liftable, or by strong steel skirts that flowed out around the front hips (*faulds*) and down over the buttocks (*culet*). This protected those sensitive body parts from a downward blow, but not from a low, upward strike, meaning knights also wore a lot of crotch padding to defend their crown jewels. This might have made going to the toilet perfectly feasible, but a bit of a faff, because the knight would have had to crouch down, bend over, and pull the padding away from themselves.

There were other complicating factors too. The way that plate armour was attached to the body might differ slightly, but, commonly, each piece was held in place by a strap looped around the rear of the respective body part, and the metal plates would then interlock and overlap, with pegs being pushed through holes to hold them in place. The heavy thigh plates, or *cuisses*, were suspended from garter belts around the waist, or from hooks on the knight's jacket; this ensured the weight was distributed through the warrior's back and core tummy muscles. Very sensible.

However, this also meant that a knight who needed to drop his trousers might have found it awkward to bend over without detaching his thigh protection first, particularly if he was using the garter belt system. In which case, he'd perhaps have beckoned for his squire to remove or lift the thigh plates and, if he was wearing one, the rear *culet*, so that he could squat down. But even then, going to the toilet was doable, if something of a palaver.

But things were certainly more complex when Italian and German craftsmen developed full suits of armour in the 1400s, which became ever more sophisticated into the early 1500s. Particularly used in jousting tournaments, such a *panoply* now fully encased the soldier with a tight bodyline shape, including plating for the crotch and buttocks; in short, they resembled Marvel's Iron Man, without the sarcasm. These interlocking plates would have made it virtually impossible to remove without some help, meaning a trip to the loo wasn't a one-man job.

And it's worth noting that toilet accidents were likely pretty common when knights frequently faced terrifying peril, surging adrenaline, and frequent problems with dysentery - due to poor food and water hygiene. In fact, it's likely that a great many chivalric champions soiled themselves on a regular basis, and then handed their filthy, squelching armour and leggings to their squires and washerwomen to scrub clean. Ah, the romance of the Middle Ages!

CHAPTER 11:

LANGUAGE &

COMMUNICATION

43. When was sign language first used in the UK, and when was the first hearing aid created?
Asked by Danalar

This is such an important question, because there have always been deaf people, but they often haven't been well remembered. If I asked you to name some famous deaf people from history, I'd imagine you'd struggle to get beyond Beethoven, Helen Keller, and maybe Thomas Edison. Truth be told, the history of disability isn't something most of us know much about, so, I'm grateful for the question, Danalar, not least because it's important in life to recognise the gaps in our knowledge and try to fill them.

Happily, there has been some fascinating modern scholarship by historians of deafness, such as Dr Emily Cockayne, Dr Jaipreet Virdi, Dr Esme Cleall, Dr Mike Gulliver, and Gerald Shea. They've looked at the experiences of deaf people, how they were treated by society, how they created modes of self-expression, and also have examined the medical and technological interventions that were designed to aid those with hearing loss. I'll start with the former, because gestural signing and formal sign language has a much deeper history than auditory assistive technology. Also, the second part is sadly more upsetting to read.

Signing is almost certainly older than human speech, as we know that our evolutionary cousins, apes, are highly skilled gestural communicators - until her death in 2018, Koko the gorilla could speak to her carers using around 1,000 different signs (she asked for ice cream by signing 'my cold cup'), and there is a very strong chance early species of humans did the same . . . well, apart from the ice cream thing. And even when *Homo sapiens* acquired spoken language way back in the Stone Age, perhaps around 100,000 years ago, it's extremely probable that signing remained in use for communicating between interacting groups who didn't share a common language.

However, in terms of usage by deaf people, the earliest evidence seems to be as far back as ancient Egypt, but we are absolutely certain of it by the time we get to ancient Greece, because Socrates (as reported by his protégé Plato) declared: 'Suppose that we had no voice or tongue, and wanted to communicate with one another, should we not, like the deaf and dumb, make signs with the hands and head and the rest of the body?'

In the UK, the earliest formal signing we know of wasn't intended for the deaf, but rather for those who'd taken a vow of silence. The medieval monks of Christ Church, Canterbury, followed the Rule of St Benedict, which meant a limit on everyday chat, other than during the reading of prayers or the singing of holy Psalms. A 1,000-year-old manuscript describes the signs they used, including 127 hand gestures for the most common things in daily monkish activity. For example, if a monk needed soap, he would rub his hands vigorously together; and if he wanted his underpants, he would stroke his thighs with both hands in an upward motion, as if pulling them on. Of course, if he'd done this too vigorously, he might have accidentally looked like a randy pervert, so moderation was presumably key.

One of the earliest written records of deaf signing is a rather beautiful snapshot, because it occurred at the wedding in 1575 of Thomas Tillsye and Ursula Russel. Our source states that Thomas was deaf and dumb, so he signed his marriage vows, including the 'until death do us part' bit:

> First he embraced her with his armes, and took her by the hande, putt a ring upon her finger and layde his hande upon her harte, and held his hands towards heaven; and to show his continuance to dwell with her to his lyves ende he did it by closing of his eyes with his hands and digging out of the earthe with his foote, and pulling as though he would ring a bell . . .

In fact, Dr Emily Cockayne has found lots of great evidence from this era, noting that: 'References to encounters with deaf people in diaries and literature suggest that through improvised languages composed of signs and gestures they managed to communicate crudely with strangers and elaborately with close intimates.' We also have observations by fascinated sixteenth-century polymaths such as England's Francis Bacon and France's Michel de Montaigne, the latter of whom noted: 'the deaf argue, disagree and tell stories by signs. I've seen some so supple and knowledgeable that, in fact, they are nothing less than perfect in their ability to make themselves understood.'

It seems that prior to the Early Modern era, many deaf people didn't usually belong to a separate group of their own.

Most were born into hearing families, and so probably developed their own private systems for communication, and deaf strangers meeting for the first time might not have been able to seamlessly chat with each other. But roughly five centuries ago, educational thinkers started to think more about standardised approaches. The first notable advocate for teaching sign language to deaf people was the Spanish monk Pedro Ponce de León in the mid-1500s, followed later by the work of Juan-Pablo Bonet in 1620.

However, Danalar has asked specifically about the UK's history, so let's turn to the physician John Bulwer who was an early advocate for an education programme for deaf people, and developed a manual signing system to represent letters. In his book *Philocophus: or, the Deafe and Dumbe Man's Friend*, written in 1648, Bulwer wrote: 'You already can expresse yourselves so truly by signes, from a habit you have gotten by using always signes, as we do speech.' He also confidently confirmed that 'men that are borne deafe and dumbe . . . can argue and dispute rhetorically by signs . . .', showing that deafness was no barrier to kicking arse in a high-level debate. However, he followed most philosophers of the day in assuming that those who didn't develop a system of language – either spoken or manual – could not develop rational minds. He believed communicating with others was a core tenet of being human.

In 1680, another book arrived entitled *Didascolocophus* – a bit of a mouthful, but it translated as 'teacher of the deaf'. Its author was a Scottish tutor and linguist named George Dalgarno, who put forward a signed alphabet which used the fingertips of the left hand to symbolise vowels. Intriguingly, Dalgarno wasn't just interested in deafness; he was also investigating whether there was such a thing as a universal language shared across humanity, which, if unlocked, might solve translation errors between foreign languages.

These books might seem surprisingly old to us, but Bulwer and Dalgarno were perhaps a thousand years late in the race for Britain's first speech therapist; that honour traditionally goes to St John of Beverley, Bishop of York, who died in 721 CE. He was canonised for his various miracles, one of which was popularly remembered as healing a deaf and mute person. But when we look at the details of the story - reported by the esteemed medieval monk known as the Venerable Bede - we see that St John of Beverley hadn't performed a healing miracle; rather, he'd patiently taught the man to articulate syllables, sounds, and then words, one at a time, in a similar way to the speech therapy techniques of the eighteenth century.

Indeed, it was in the mid-1700s that formal schools were established for educating deaf children, the most prominent pioneer perhaps being Thomas Braidwood. His school in Edinburgh was praised by the famed dictionary writer, Dr Samuel Johnson, who was impressed by the pupils' ability to pronounce difficult words. In this, we see that Braidwood was primarily an 'oralist' who wanted deaf people to adapt themselves to a speaking world.

However, his secret technique - which was only published after his death by his nephew, Joseph Watson, in 1809 - is better described as a *combined system*, as it taught sounds broken down into syllables, and then words, but also used finger-spelling and signs, as well as writing practice. Braidwood's pupils were privately wealthy, but Watson continued his techniques, refined them, and then taught at the first public school for deaf children, which helped to educate those without wealthy parents. This makes Watson an important early figure in the development of British Sign Language (BSL).

As well as increased provision for schooling, we also see that the English legal system was surprisingly comfortable with witness testimony being given in sign language. The Old Bailey's first ever deaf interpreter, who assisted with a case in 1773, had the amazing name of Fanny Lazarus, which I absolutely love! Not only does this show that deaf people were treated as reliable witnesses, but that the courts also had complete trust in the accuracy of third-party translation from signing to speech, even when the judge and jury couldn't directly understand the testimony for themselves.

While we've heard plenty about deaf people expressing themselves with gestures, we should turn our attention to the medical and technological attempts to cure deafness. Sadly, this bit is horrifically gruesome, and then gets pretty depressing, so prepare yourselves to feel somewhat bummed out.

Deafness was not medically well understood, and early treatments were crude. As Gerald Shea so chillingly reports in his important study *The Language of Light: A History of Silent Voices*:

> In the Middle Ages, hot coals were forced into the mouths of the Deaf to enable them to speak 'by the force of the burning'. These violent experiments continued into the eighteenth century and beyond, and included inserting catheters through the nostrils, twisting through the nasal cavity and into the Eustachian tubes and injecting burning liquids ... Other practices included drilling wide holes in the crown of the skull to enable a young Deaf girl to 'hear' through the openings; introducing ether or electric current into the auditory canal; perforating the eardrum and injecting burning agents into the middle ear cavity, leaving it permanently scarred; applying severe

blistering agents to the neck, scorching it from nape to chin with a hot cylinder full of supposedly magical burning leaves; applying adhesive cotton and setting it afire; using vomitories and purgative agents; and injecting hot needles into or removing the mastoids.

The less painful route to helping deaf people to hear was to design auditory aids. Since at least the 1550s, scholars had known that bone conducts sound and that clamping a rod in one's teeth might help noises better reach the ears. By the mid-1600s, several European natural scientists were writing about ear trumpets, the most notable being Athanasius Kircher, who designed a spiral trumpet based on the misguided idea that soundwaves would better bounce into the ear if they corkscrewed their way in, like screaming kids on a rollercoaster. Bone-conducting *tooth-rods* and ear trumpets were the most common types of mechanical hearing aids, and in the mid-1800s there were several patents issued for prototypes of such devices which might be better concealed behind the ear.

The electronic era of hearing aid technology arrived in 1898, arising from the acoustic engineering that went into designing the telephone and carbon microphone. The most notable phone wrangler was, of course, Alexander Graham Bell, but this prominent aspect of his career has somewhat masked his fervent commitment to eradicating deafness. His lifelong interest in sound technology stemmed from his mother and his wife both being deaf, and - being the pragmatist - he learned sign language to communicate with adults like them. But when he ran a school for deaf children, he was a staunch 'oralist' and insisted on ensuring that his pupils learn to speak using ear training and lip-reading techniques, as well as signing.

Like many thinkers of his day, Bell was a eugenicist who subscribed to ideas of biological purity; he believed society's breeding stock was something that could be improved or degraded, depending on the supposed quality of the people being allowed to reproduce. Though he didn't advocate sterilisation, he saw deafness as a threatening deformity spreading through American society, because deaf people had the temerity to be getting married, having kids, starting their own social clubs, and gathering with others like them. In doing this, Bell complained they were segregating themselves, and causing a schism in society. He believed the English language needed to be the unifying glue for the nation, and he argued that speech skills should be taught to all, including the deaf, saying: 'to ask the value of speech! It is like asking the value of life.'

Assuming he knew what was best for his young pupils, Bell also believed that, in using sign language, deaf people were drawing attention to themselves and making a scene: 'I think the spirit of the oral system is to make the deaf persons feel that they are the same as people, to make them object to exhibit[ing] their infirmity to the world; whereas on the special [signed] language method they glory in the defect, they glory in being deaf mutes, they glory in being distinct from the world.'

For Alexander Graham Bell - whose attitude to deafness is carefully charted in Katie Booth's book *The Invention of Miracles* - the powerful duet between speech education and electrical acoustic engineering would be the cure to what he saw as an unwanted ill. And he was a powerful lobbyist in the educational reforms of the 1880s, which emulated the pro-oralist outcome of the Second International Congress on Education of the Deaf, hosted in Milan in 1880. Sign language was all but removed from many deaf schools, and it wasn't until the 1980s that the policy started to change. Much damage was done to deaf people and their culture in the meantime. Consequently, BSL – a variant of which had been used centuries ago in wedding chapels and law courts – was only recognised as an official language in 2003.

44. How did empires from different continents communicate? Were there translators?
Asked by Thomas

Here's a challenge for you: name a famous interpreter from history. There are a few, so it's not an impossible request, but I won't judge you harshly if this stumps you. After all, who cares about interpreters? It's the bigwigs doing the hardcore negotiation that really matter, isn't it? And it's not as if we treat book translators, or the people who do the subtitles for moody Scandinavian murder dramas, any differently, is it? No, the job of the translator is to do a huge amount of work, and yet be as discreet as possible. We don't know their names. We don't really care about them. But, without them, the world would have been so different.

Interpreters and translators often make history, but they rarely make headlines. The most obvious exception I can think of is when the Libyan leader Colonel Gaddafi gave a rambling rant at the UN, and, after seventy-five minutes of translation, his despairing interpreter was reported to have cried: 'I just can't take it any more!' and collapsed. A different modern problem arrived when Donald Trump became President of the United States and Japanese interpreters struggled to make sense of his garbled nonsense, or were embarrassed by Trump's appalling crudeness, with one senior interpreter complaining they'd never had to translate 'nutjob!' or 'grab her by the pussy!' before.

Interpreting is an exceptionally difficult skill. It requires superb command of multiple languages, intense concentration, unflappable patience, and the judgement to defuse a potential crisis by choosing one's words very carefully. Thomas has thus asked a brilliant question, and I'm pleased to say we can trace the history of diplomatic interpretation back to the empires of the Bronze Age, which made a regular habit of invading foreign lands. Some 4,400 years ago, the Egyptians were trying to do deals with their neighbours, the Nubians, though we don't know who acted as interpreter. Presumably it was a merchant or scholar who'd spent time in the rival kingdom, learning the lingo, rather than just some guy shouting: 'Me Egyptian! Me want trade! You want trade?' insultingly slowly.

The Egyptians also gave us the earliest recorded peace treaty. It was drawn up between the mighty Ramesses the Great and his arch-rival King Muwatalli of the Hittite Empire. In 1274 BCE, their forces had clashed at the battle of Kadesh and, though it was a brutal stalemate, both claimed a triumph. Determined to shout the ancient equivalent of 'You should see the other guy!', both Ramesses and Muwatalli were eventually forced to negotiate a begrudging truce – the optimistically titled 'Eternal Treaty' – which was written on silver tablets, with the Hittite version inscribed in the international diplomatic language of Akkadian, and the Egyptian version rendered in hieroglyphs on temple walls.

Both kings also started writing faux-matey, passive-aggressive letters to each other, as did their wives, so we can probably presume that interpreters were involved in at least some of these processes. We know, for example, that fifty years earlier, the tomb of General Horemheb was decorated with a bas-relief depicting an interpreter taking the Pharaoh's words, turning to the gathered foreign delegates, and telling them whether it was good news or not. Clearly, there had been a few interpreters floating about the palace, at various points in ancient Egyptian history.

Nearly a millennium later, the Macedonian conquest-enthusiast Alexander the Great also hired interpreters, not least because he ended up with a massive empire and didn't know how to say, 'I own you all!' in the relevant dialects. One language he definitely needed to know was Persian; having smashed King Darius III in battle, Alexander helped himself to the mighty Persian Empire, but wasn't able to communicate with his new subjects. This didn't bode well for smooth administration of justice. Luckily, one of his new subjects volunteered to be his interpreter, having been born to a Persian mum and a Greek-speaking dad.

The Romans had a similar problem when they caught the empire bug. According to Cicero, interpreters were low-class functionaries; perhaps prisoners of war, enslaved people, travelling scholars, and merchants. He was forced to have one when he was made the governor of Cilicia, in modern Turkey. We also know from Pliny the Elder that the huge expanse of the Roman trade network meant that one Black Sea port alone needed 130 interpreters to handle the 300 different tongues spoken by the merchant seamen. Of course, in *Star Wars*, you only need one C3PO droid to cover 6 million languages, but the Romans were a little behind on their robotics.

We know the Romans had contact with the ancient Chinese, who referred to them as *Daqin*. As well as contact between artists and traders, Emperor Marcus Aurelius sent a large maritime diplomatic mission to the Chinese in 166 CE. The Romans also imported spices and black pepper directly from India, and Emperor Nero even dispatched an expeditionary team to trudge beyond Egypt and find the source of the Nile, although it ended in humiliation when the soldiers got bogged down in the Al-Sudd swamps. All of these missions presumably required skilled interpreters to negotiate with locals and keep things from turning violent (and also to retrieve swampy sandals).

Being an interpreter wasn't always the easiest, or safest, job. When the Persian king Darius the Great sent emissaries to the Athenians and Spartans, they allegedly chucked the defenceless messengers down a well; in some versions of the history, this was because the messengers were Greeks working for the enemy. Either way, it wasn't very diplomatic.

By contrast, a Persian interpreter called Bradukios had the opposite problem; when sent to negotiate with Emperor Justinian of the Byzantine Empire in 548 CE, he received the warmest of welcomes and even took pride of place next to Justinian at dinner. This generous treatment seemed suspiciously dodgy to the Persian king, as interpreters weren't allowed to sit beside even a minor official. 'Clearly, Bradukios is cosying up to the enemy!' he thought; he must be betraying me! When Bradukios returned home in triumph, having won Byzantine confidence, he was rewarded for his efforts with a death sentence.

Other diplomacy risks involved arduous travel to some faraway place, and people were at risk of dying on the way, as happened to Britain's first ambassador to China, Charles Cathcart, in 1788. His infamous replacement, George Macartney, arrived safely, but with only one Chinese Catholic monk, picked up in Italy, to translate for him. Unfortunately, that guy could speak Latin, but not English. Thankfully, Macartney had gone to a fancy school, and knew his *amo, amas, amat*. There were also some French Jesuits milling around the Chinese imperial court, who were presumably useful.

Frankly, however, it didn't really matter because the trade deal was of little interest to the Chinese emperor, who saw the British approach as the demands of a rival power rather than a trusted partner. Having left the court and travelled elsewhere in China, Macartney received the bad news and blamed the breakdown on his having refused to *kowtow* to the Chinese emperor, because he represented King George III, who was the emperor's equal, so prostrating himself on the floor was a humiliation to his mighty king. The whole collapse in trade talks was thus explained away as a squabble over manners, rather than a political failure, and historians accepted that story until very recently. Ultimately, therefore, this wasn't a failure of diplomatic interpretation, but rather a bad deal written up as one.

Macartney wasn't the first European to have conducted diplomacy in China, of course. The Venetian merchant Marco Polo is said to have arrived at the court of Kublai Khan in the early 1260s, and was tasked with various diplomatic missions back to Europe and around Asia. Historians squabble over whether he actually went there at all (some say it's all fairy-tale romance), while others argue about what languages he spoke: did Polo learn the imperial tongue of Mongol-Turkic, or administrative Persian, or local Chinese, or what? Chances are, he definitely picked up a few handy phrases in his seventeen years of service, even if it was just to order lunch.

Only a decade earlier, the Flemish Franciscan monk, William of Rubruck, had been sent by the King of France to convert the Mongols (known to Europeans as the Tatars) to Christianity. His subsequent travelogue, which is one of the most fascinating insights into Mongol customs, is surprisingly funny because his interpreter, Turgemannus, who was described as *Homo Dei* ('a man of God'), proved to be hilariously incompetent, and spent much of the journey unable to translate William's sermons. At one point, William had a Colonel Gaddafi moment, and exhausted his half-witted interpreter who became too knackered to remember any words. But the absolute punchline pinnacle was when they finally got a face-to-face with the great Mongol Khan, only for William to look over and see that his interpreter had been knocking back the free booze and was completely drunk on rice wine!

Christopher Columbus experienced a similar interpreter crisis when he went looking for a quicker route to the pepper-producing Indies in 1492. Expecting to meet Muslims and Mongols, he'd brought along Arabic speakers – such as Luis de Torres – who proved understandably useless when they blundered their way into Cuba instead. Hoping to train interpreters, Columbus tried to kidnap Indigenous people and transport them to Europe to learn Spanish, so they could convert to Catholicism and return home as useful interpreters. Unwilling to face such a prospect, some of them jumped overboard.

Frustrated, Columbus tried again on a different island, but this time seized both the men he wanted and women and children, perhaps assuming they wouldn't abandon each other. Though the captives weren't necessarily related, we do know of one man who desperately swam out, and climbed aboard, having seen that his wife and child were being taken from him. On his subsequent voyages, Columbus was able to lean on the interpretation services of one such captive, a young

Taíno man who'd been forced to go to Spain, christened as Diego Colón, taught Spanish, unofficially adopted by Columbus himself, and then returned to his native island to speak on behalf of his new European 'father'.

The Taíno were a newly encountered people and caused much excitement, but this forced language immersion class was a common tactic of the era. And that brings us full circle. At the start, I asked if you knew any famous interpreters from history? Well, in the USA, there are two Native American interpreting icons who regularly appear in school lessons. Sacagawea is the second. She was the young Lemhi Shoshone woman who helped guide Lewis and Clark's exploration mission across the lands of the Louisiana Purchase in 1804, assisting them with negotiations when they encountered other tribes. It was quite the complicated process, actually. Sacagawea spoke no English, but had learned the Hidatsa language after having been captured by them in childhood. They had then sold her in marriage to a French Canadian fur-trapper, Toussaint Charbonneau, who also spoke Hidatsa. If Sacagawea wanted to say something to Lewis and Clark, she had to tell her husband, who told it to a French-speaking member of the expedition, who translated it into English.

But the first interpreter was Tisquantum, known as Squanto, who was the Patuxet tribal member who greeted the *Mayflower* settlers, and helped bring about the famous Thanksgiving meal. He spoke in English because he'd been the victim of kidnapping by an English explorer called Thomas Hunt, who'd sold him to Spanish friars in Málaga. They'd set about converting him to Christianity, and then he ended up in England where, coincidentally, the famed princess Matoaka (by then using the English name Rebecca, but best known to history as Pocahontas) was also briefly living before her untimely death.

Tisquantum left England and returned home, only to learn everyone in his community had died of a deadly disease; he was the last of the Patuxet. So, he threw in his lot with the *Mayflower* mob, and taught them how to survive in their unfamiliar new surroundings. He too died of disease, soon after, and was greatly mourned.

Finally, a quick mention also of Malintzin (also known as Doña Marina) who was the enslaved Nahua woman given to the Spanish conquistador Hernán Cortés by the Chontal Maya people. He impregnated her, and she gave birth to his son, but she also served as his interpreter during the Spanish conquest of the Aztec Empire. This central involvement in a huge historical trauma meant Malintzin's reputation became extremely contested: she's famous in Mexican folklore as a scheming temptress and traitor to her people, who betrayed the Aztecs in revenge for their enslaving her, but she's also been radically reinterpreted as a tragic victim of enslavement and coercion. To others, she's simply the first to have fused the bloodlines of Mesoamerican peoples and Europeans, giving birth to the first mixed race *mestizo* child.

These stories are all a reminder that some of history's most significant events involved ordinary people whose language skills were utterly essential. And yet, they were rarely the heroes of the story. Sometimes, they were cast as the villains, but sometimes they were more like the victims.

45. Where do names for places in other languages come from? For example, London vs Londres, Munich vs München - is there an official system in place?

Asked by Georgia

As the child of a Parisian mother, I learned from a young age that London and Paris transformed into the glamorously sonorous '*Londres et Paree*' whenever we visited my French relatives. As children do, I quickly internalised this linguistic swap as normal. But I remember then being astonished when the football World Cup was on the TV, and all the teams had weird names that bore no resemblance to my atlas - 'Where the hell is Sverige?!' I remember thinking, and, 'What the blazes is a Magyarország!!??' Turns out, they're Sweden and Hungary. Who knew?!

I've read a few books since then, and now know who the Magyars were. But, even as a professional historian, I can still find these linguistic varieties somewhat mysterious. Paris becoming Paree is simple; the French don't pronounce the 's'. Case solved! But what's with Londres, huh? Linguists have wondered about this for ages, but, personally, I suspect it's the product of repeated abbreviations. Londinium was the ancient Roman name, and I can see how Londinium might perhaps have been shortened to Londrium, and then squeezed again into Londrum, before lazily stopping at Londre. But why the 's' on the end? Well, in fairness, Brits used to bung an unnecessary 's' on the end of Marseille, so maybe it's just vengeful payback! The French love to stick it to the English.

To hurl a couple of fancy words at you, Georgia, the names we give to foreign cities (that the people who live there don't themselves use) are called *exonyms,* a term coined in the 1950s by the Australian geographer Marcel Aurousseau. *Exonym* means 'outsider name', and the insider name is an *endonym*. For example, London is an endonym – that's what I call it when I'm working there – but Londres is the exonym used by my French auntie. When you start to look for them, exonyms are fascinating because so many cities have multiple names, and it's not always perfectly obvious why. Since the 1960s, the clunkily titled United Nations Group of Experts on Geographical Names have been holding conferences, roughly every five years, to help reduce the complexity, but it's a lot to unpick.

For example, if you were craving strudel and decided to hop on a plane to Vienna, you'd actually land in the city of Wien. But to the French it's Vienne, to the Dutch it's Wenen, in Polish it's Wiedeń, to the Chinese it's Wéiyěnà, and the Hungarians just chuck the entire system out of the window and plump for Bécs. I mean, what the hell, Hungary?! Well, it's because Vienna had once been on the edge of their medieval, Magyar empire, and Bécs means something like 'guardplace', 'treasury', or 'stronghold'. Basically, Vienna was their heavily bolted front door, so that's what they called it.

Of course, this process can be a very modern one, and some cities and nations adopted new names in response to independence or post-colonial rebranding – the Indian city of Bombay threw off its old British identity in 1995, becoming Mumbai, while in the 1970s the international adoption of the *Pinyin* system, which better converts Chinese into the Roman alphabet, saw Peking become Beijing.

Some cities don't have multiple alternatives, and I suspect that's related to the era in which they became international hubs. Ancient places likely entered foreign lexicons centuries ago, thanks to commercial and cultural links, and the names just stuck because people kept using them. Sometimes, they became ossified and widely known. Rome, for example, is spelled Roma in Italian, Portuguese, Norwegian, Spanish, Hungarian, Latvian, Romanian, and Turkish; various other languages go for something very similar, such as Rom (German), Rim (Croatian), and Rooma (Estonian). We get the sense here that the small differences in spelling are simply born of stressing the same syllables slightly differently in native tongues.

But constant interactions between peoples also would have affected linguistic change sometimes, bringing about really noticeable differences that grew over time. There's a myth that pre-modern people lived and died in the same smelly village for their entire, miserable lives, but historians now know so much more about the extraordinary movement of peoples and ideas. These journeys might have been religious pilgrimages, trading excursions, violent crusades, diplomatic contact, job-seeking, educational training, monastic exchanges, travel for the good of the soul, tourism, or the necessary fleeing from persecution, plague, pitiable hunger, and anything else that made staying at home seem suboptimal.

Such exchanges resulted in countless linguistic shortcuts and evolutions, as travellers with very different languages and alphabets tried to make sense of foreign words. Some places changed hands between conquering powers, and thus acquired new names and languages, resulting in multilingual cities with multiple endonyms. In medieval times, the Belgian capital was spelled Broeksele, but it is now either called Brussel (by Flemish speakers) or Bruxelles (by French speakers), but - because this causes tensions between those two groups - curiously, the exonymic English version, Brussels, is also sometimes used to keep the peace. Meanwhile, Aachen in Germany is confusingly called Aix-la-Chapelle by the French

- they sound so different, but both derive from the same Latin word for natural springs, *aquae*.

Brussels changed hands many times in the past 1,000 years, and such places likely witnessed centuries of linguistic drift, so that place names sharing a common linguistic root now appear bewilderingly confusing. Exonyms can be caused by changes in spelling, and changes in pronunciation, as time's passage introduces new ways of expressing old ideas. Take, for example, the pretty Welsh town of Monmouth, which perches on the mouth of the River Monnow. In 1086, William the Conqueror's Domesday Book listed it as 'Monemude'; say that 'mude' as a long *moother* sound, and you'll see it was basically 'Monnow-Mouth'. Over time, that contracted to Monmouth. Simple!

Back then, Monmouth was in English territory, but over the centuries it's been claimed by both nations, and the Welsh language renders Monnow as Mynwy (pronounced *Men-oi*) – not so different. However, medieval Welsh speakers also dropped 'mouth' off the back end and instead added *tre* ('town') on the front, making it Tremynwy – the town on the Monnow. To add further intrigue, around 400 years ago, the tell-tale 'm' evolved into an 'f', which is pronounced more as a 'v', so Tremynwy became modern Trefynwy (pronounced *Treh-van-oi*). Side by side, Monmouth and Trefynwy now look and sound totally unrelated, but they're pretty much the same idea, crowbarred apart by the passage of time and the charming nuances of language.

By contrast, then there's Manchester. To many Europeans, Manchester is just ... er ... Manchester. Spaniards might quibble and say it's spelled Mánchester, but that bonus accent isn't fooling anyone. The only exception I can think of is the Irish translation, Manchain; and I suppose things get somewhat trickier when you switch to the Cyrillic alphabet of Bulgaria and Russia, or the logographic writing systems of Japan, China, South Korea, etc. But, caveats aside, Liam Gallagher could Interrail around Europe, and he'd have no problem telling people where he was from. So, why is Manchester so lacking in exonyms?

Back in the early 1600s, when it was just a small community of a few thousand people, there was little reason for Europeans to have heard of Manchester, and so it didn't need an exonym. It only industrialised in the past 250 years, and thus acquired its international reputation during an era when new technologies were making communication easier, language was becoming standardised, literacy rates were shooting up, and state bureaucracy was getting more sophisticated. In short, by the time any foreigner had needed to spell Manchester, chances are there would have been a literate Mancunian to write it down for them; and being literate themselves, they'd have been able to absorb exactly how it was meant to be spelled. So, my suggested general rule is this: the younger a place, the fewer foreign exonyms it'll have.

With that in mind, let's look at the city in Georgia's original question: the medieval city of Munich, founded sometime around 1158 by Duke Henry the Lion (who sadly was not an *actual* lion). It began as a monastic marketplace next to a bridge on the River Isar, and its original name was Apud Munichen, probably meaning a place 'near the monks', although another theory suggests it meant 'place on the riverbank'. Gradually Munichen was shortened to München. But, because it quickly grew, and acquired its own role in the pan-European trade network, its original name, Munichen, reached British shores early on, and was adopted easily. It too was then shortened. That's why I call it Munich.

By contrast, Italians didn't accept the German word. They reached up to their exonym shelf and pulled down a literal translation of 'place of the monks', which in Italian is *Monaco*. Thus, the German city is known to Italians as Monaco di Bavaria, and the football team are known in Italy not as Bayern München, or Bayern Munich, but rather Bayern Monaco! Obviously, this is a hilarious misunderstanding waiting to happen, and I'm delighted to say that every year there are a couple of wry newspaper reports involving baffled tourists who aimed for the glamorous casinos of the French Riviera, but ended up at a Bavarian beer festival, listening to oompah music. I dunno, as mistakes go, that sounds like a fun one!

46. How do we know what people's accents and languages sounded like in the past?
Asked by Kat

This is a great question, Kat, and one I get asked a lot. As with most things in life, my first instinct is to turn to the genius of Eddie Izzard, who learned Latin at school by listening to audio tapes:

> It was pure lies because no one knew what the bloody accent was. They were trying to get you to learn the Latin accent, and they had NO IDEA! Because everyone was dead, it's a dead language; the Romans, for all they knew, could have said, [in ridiculous high-pitched voice] 'Hello, we're the Romans!' - Eddie Izzard, *Definite Article* (1996)

Eddie Izzard is one of my all-time favourite humans, and is responsible for about 34 per cent of my personality. But, on this question, Eddie is wide of the mark. We actually know plenty about how dead languages were pronounced. And seeing as Eddie's already brought it up, I'll start with Latin.

If you'd been dropped into an elite British private school in the 1850s - or a Boris Johnson press conference in 2020 - you'd have likely heard plenty of Latin being spoken in the classrooms and chapels, but in a distinctly unflattering English accent. Indeed, English was originally Germanic in its grammar, but its vocabulary boasts thousands of borrowed Latin words which arrived between the 1500s and 1900s, mostly to make British people sound proper fancy and highfalutin. The most pretentious of these Latinate acquisitions - some of which were newly coined words designed to seem impressively ancient - were called 'inkhorn terms' (named after the inkwells made of animal horn used by gentlemen scholars).

This Latinisation process was so influential that we don't even notice how richly sprinkled our dictionaries are with Roman linguistics: words like *alias, circa, agenda, appendices, sub, prefix*, etc. are all regulars in our mother tongue, but we pronounce them very differently to how ancient Romans would have done so. In fact, the most famous Roman of all - Julius Caesar - has been mercilessly mouth-mangled by English speakers for ages; we really should be pronouncing it *Yulius Kye-sahr*, much like the German *Kaiser*.

While the peculiarities of English Latin were powerfully dominant in the British Empire and North America, the French, Portuguese, Spanish, Italians, and Romanians all had their own versions, inflected by their own *Romance* languages - so called because these modern languages derive from Rome, and not because they're ideal for flirting. Meanwhile, the

Catholic Church uses a beautifully Italian-sounding Latin pronunciation variously dubbed Ecclesiastical/Church/Medieval Latin. You can spot it whenever the Pope namechecks Cicero, who acquires a sort of David Bowie-esque *'ch-ch-ch-changes'* vibe, becoming the much sexier *Chich-erro* instead of the authentic, ancient pronunciation of *Kick-air-oh*.

However, during the Renaissance era, humanist scholars started trying to recover and reconstruct Latin's ancient roots, with the most notable efforts being made by the sonnet-loving poet Petrarch and the big-brained polymath Erasmus. In truth, they had better luck moving the goalposts with Greek pronunciation than they did with Latin, and it wasn't until the 1870s that modern scholars properly undertook the tricky job of reconstructing *Classical* Latin as it was spoken by Caesar and Cicero (or, rather, *Kye-sahr* and *Kick-air-oh*).

These scholars are called philologists; their job is to understand how language evolves over time, and then use their linguistic detective skills to reverse-engineer the process. To communicate with each other around the world, they often work with a complex rubric called the International Phonetic Alphabet, established in the late 1880s, which breaks down sounds (known as *phonemes*) into textual symbols which are marked up with little *diacritics* to inform the reader how long the sounds are, which bits to stress, and where in the mouth to make them (for example, *fricatives* are made by forcing air through a narrow opening in the mouth, giving you the *ffff* sound in *frigid*).

Over the past 150 years, philologists have done a splendid job with Latin, often figuring out the true sounds of vowels and consonants by analysing the metrical rhythms of ancient poetry, or by studying the educational texts written by ancient grammarians – such as the great Quintilian – and sometimes by tracking down little asides and comments by ancient writers who pointed out quirks and rules in their own language. Philologists have been able not only to get back to what Latin originally sounded like, but to go back even further to find out how it got there in the first place.

Generally, Classical Latin was pronounced as it was written, but it had more rules than later Church Latin. The 'ae' double phoneme, usually pronounced *aay* by modern Catholic priests (and also The Fonz . . .), was originally a longer *ai/aye* sound. Ancient vowels could be both long or short, but the consonants 'c' and 'g' were always pronounced with a hard, short sound – even in front of 'a', 'o', 'u', or 'ae' – and 'v' was pronounced like a 'w'. In short, Julius Caesar's celebrated phrase *veni, vidi, vici* ('I came, I saw, I conquered') should be pronounced *wayni, weedi, weeki*.

OK, that's Latin done, so let's mosey on over to English, where a huge amount of work has also gone into understanding how the Old English language spoken by Alfred the Great and the Venerable Bede – both excellent names for lyrical rappers – morphed into the Anglo-Norman Middle English of Chaucer, before rounding out into Shakespearean English, then becoming the familiar modern English of Defoe and Dickens. Indeed, Professor David N. Klausner, an expert on medieval literature, has noted that English changed more between 1066 and 1750 than any other European language.

To be frank, Old English is virtually unintelligible to the modern ear, apart from a smattering of key words. Type 'The Lord's Prayer in Old English' into YouTube and you'll hear something strangely alien, punctuated by sudden recognisable jolts of 'father', 'heaven' and 'forgive'; it's a similar effect to watching subtitled Scandinavian crime dramas when suddenly you can make out the phrase 'Wi-Fi router' in the middle of impenetrable Danish chat. By contrast, the Middle English cadences of Chaucer's *Canterbury Tales* are still weird, because the words are pronounced phonetically, but if you concentrate it starts to feel eerily familiar. However, Chaucer is still harder for us to decode than Shakespeare, despite their being separated by only 200 years. So, how come so much changed in that short time?

We can blame the Great Vowel Shift which began sometime in the 1400s. Scholars argue vociferously over what caused it – some say everyone was trying to sound fancy and French, while others argue English people were hyper-correcting to *avoid* sounding French! In short, we're in the dark on that one. The Great Vowel Shift's most obvious impact was a lengthening of vowel sounds, which transformed words like *out* (pronounced *oot*), *mate* (*maht*), *moon* (*mohn*), *house* (*huuse*), *boot* (*bott*), knight (*kernicht*), queen (*kwen*), daughter (*dahrter*), and *bite* (*bitt*) into what we know today.

Unlike ancient Latin and Greek poetry, which didn't rhyme, Late Medieval and Early Modern poetry often did, which is a fantastically helpful guide to how words were meant to sound. For example, the arrival of French words with 'oi' in the middle – *foil, boil, toil, coil* – evolved away from the rounded sound of French and acquired an *aye* sound, meaning *boil* started to rhyme with *mile*. Shakespeare's lines tell us *blood* rhymed with *good* and *stood*. Even as late as the early 1700s, the famous poet Alexander Pope rhymed the words *obey, away* and . . . er. . . *tea*? From this we might deduce that, in his time, a nice cuppa was actually a nice cup of *tay,* although, by this point, he was *boiling* the kettle rather than *biling* it.

Poetry also helps us because so many poets stuck rigidly to a rhythm (called a *metre*). Shakespeare preferred *iambic pentameter*, with its five *feet* made up of ten syllables, with each foot being an unstressed syllable followed by a stressed one: it sounds like a heartbeat, a relentless pounding of *da DUM da DUM da DUM da DUM da DUM.* Because poets locked into these sorts of rhythms, it's obvious if old words don't fit our modern way of reading them. For example, Shakespeare uses the word *spirit* in Sonnet 129, but there's no room for its second syllable. We say *spir-it,* but he must have said it *sprit,* with only one sound.

Indeed, thanks to the research that accompanied the re-building of the Globe Theatre - and the outreach work of linguists like Professor David Crystal and his thespian son, Ben - there have been entire Shakespeare plays performed using original sixteenth-century pronunciation. What's fascinating about hearing them is the pronunciation sounds like several accents all at once. Even in just a short thirty-second clip, you'll detect elements of West Country rolling 'r's, Irish and Scottish lilts, the famous Lancashire 'a' which sounds more like *ehh,* the downward Brummie inflection at the end of sentences, the Yorkshire earthiness, and a whole bunch of other influences - it's as if the entire cast of *Game of Thrones* is trying to speak at once, but the Starks are nearest the microphone.

Another mega-handy source for philologists is the writing of so-called *orthoepists*, who were linguistic busybodies in the 1500s–1600s. These people had no interest in bones (nope, that's orthopaedics . . .), and were instead pronunciation gurus who got wonderfully grumpy about people saying things wrong. Or, as was the case with the playwright Ben Jonson, who was a compatriot of Shakespeare, they wrote a grammar guide in which was listed words and how to say them, including *move, love, approve* (pronounced *muvv, luvv, appruvv*).

However, it's also important to stress there were definitely regional variations in these periods too - not everyone sounded the same. Indeed, back in the 1300s, Chaucer famously had his northern characters pronounce words differently to his southern characters, and the Cornish writer John of Trevisa complained that people from Yorkshire spoke in a tongue that was 'shrill, cutting, and grating and ill-informed', although, ironically, I had to translate that into modern English because you'd possibly find his medieval phrasing equally shrill and grating.*

And as a final jolly thing to hurl your way, we have a good idea of how the American Founding Fathers sounded in the 1700s because the ingenious Benjamin Franklin created a phonetic dictionary in his attempt to improve literacy rates by getting rid of weird British spellings. Not only does he tell us that *when* was pronounced with an 'h' sound before the 'w' (*huen*), but we discover 'Founding Fathers' would've been pronounced *Fowhndin' Fathers* (to rhyme with *gathers*). What this means, of course, is that the musical *Hamilton* should sound less like Lin-Manuel Miranda and more like a drunk Sean Bean doing a dodgy Irish accent.

So, Kat, while there are certainly questions still to be answered about why pronunciation changed, we can be pretty confident in our estimations of how many people used to sound. But whether Caesar was himself a mumbling baritone, or Eddie Izzard's shrill squawker, will sadly require a time machine to figure out.

---

* His phrase was 'scharp, slitting, and frotynge and vnschape'.

CHAPTER 12:

HISTORY IN POP CULTURE

47. Which popular historical films are the most
accurate and do you get annoyed when you know
how wrong they've got something?
Asked by Chloe

Hooray! Thank you, Chloe, this is one of my absolute fave
subjects to talk about. Indeed, I've lectured on it in a couple
of British universities, and the typical theme of my impassioned rant is that historical movies are often judged far too
harshly, when it's historical documentaries - yes, proper
factual telly - that we should be yelling at instead, because
these programmes often pretend to be objective when they're
potentially just as constructed, subjective, and misleading as
the movies.

So, let me start with a bold assertion - perhaps even a
provocation: I don't think historical movies are meant to be
accurate. If that's what you're looking for, then you're always
going to be annoyed. Accuracy just isn't their purpose; their
job is to be an interesting work of dramatic art (ideally, one
that makes a ton of money, or is watched by 10 million
people on a chilly Sunday night). After all, we're very happy
to enjoy Shakespeare and his dodgy grasp of history, or the
Iliad with its cast of meddling gods, so there's no reason we

should demand that modern movies be held to any higher standards.

But let me run into my garden shed and wheel out the much larger philosophical defence too, because – without fail – whenever a historical drama is on the TV, I receive tweets from viewers complaining that it's inaccurate and lazy, and bemoaning that the filmmakers didn't hire expert historians to advise them, dammit! To which I reply: 'Hello! Any dramatist aiming for accuracy has failed the moment they start typing. It can't be done. There's no such thing as an accurate film about the past. Also, if you look in the credits, they did hire a historian. Kind regards, Greg.'

I realise I sound like I'm in the pocket of 'Big Cinema', but I get no brown envelopes stuffed full of cash to say this stuff. I just know that the past is incomprehensibly enormous, and messy, and we don't have nearly enough information about who was there, and what was said, and what they were thinking, etc. Do paying audiences really want all that doubt to be reflected on screen? How would you even make that into a watchable story? After all, movies are only two hours long (or three and a half hours long if you're Martin Scorsese), so how on earth do you cram the vast totality of the truth into such a small box? Obviously, you just can't.

A historian recounting the same story in a book will write over 100,000 words, but even that's not the full story. Not every history book is a dry tome on the economics of the fishing industry in fourteenth-century Grimsby; indeed, many historians write with flair, they give their book a narrative arc that corresponds to a genre – whether it's tragedy, romance, hubristic fall from grace, rise of the plucky underdog, etc. – and they might even end each chapter with a novelist's cliffhanger. Historians can be a bit like storytellers, sometimes.

But historians also stop every now and again to say, 'Sorry, we don't know the next bit!', or they present multiple versions of events, or they have arguments with themselves and other historians in the footnotes. They deliberately draw attention to the gaps in their knowledge.

But there are no footnotes in movies. And gaps in the story would just be maddeningly annoying for the viewer. Instead, there are rules about how stories work. They have beginnings, middles, and ends (or, as C. E. Lombardi quipped, 'a beginning, a muddle, and an end'). Stories need heroes and villains, protagonists and antagonists; they need to hit their narrative beats or the audience gets bored. Stories are deeply formulaic. The screenwriting how-to manual, *Save the Cat!*, breaks every story ever told down into fifteen beats. Some theorists argue there are only seven plots in all of world literature!

The past, meanwhile, is sprawlingly uncontainable, and frustratingly unknowable. True accuracy simply isn't possible. But we can certainly judge storytellers on their intentions: are they trying to capture the authentic spirit of the era, or are they being historically reckless? There are dramas that don't give a damn about the truth, and there are those that fastidiously put the main events in the right order, with the right characters in the right places, and which attempt to understand how people perceived the world at the time. Most dramas land somewhere between those two poles. They vaguely stick to the accepted story, but they invent exciting characters, cut out the dull ones, muck about with the timeline, conjure up faux romances to spice things up, decide the story needs a couple of dramatic action scenes, and, most crucially, they imagine all the snappy dialogue, simply because there weren't herds of court stenographers wandering around to capture the real conversations for us.

On top of that, you then have the craft of emotive film-making. The storytellers try to make you feel a certain way about what you're watching, manipulating your emotions with bombastic orchestral scores or sombre ballads, when - obviously - the real historical events never had the benefit of parping tubas or plinky-plonky piano soundtracks. The crash zooms and editing choices all influence how we, as audiences, react to the people and events on screen. This is an editorialising of the past which has little to do with the historical reality. It's about sensory experiences and sensational thrills.

Questions of dramatic accuracy fascinated me when I was a young history student, and, to my great joy, I now get to work as a historical adviser on TV dramas, comedies, and movies. It's a job where you have to pick your battles - and you might even win a couple - but there's so much you have to compromise on, usually for the sake of budget but also for audience enjoyment. For example, in medieval battle scenes, key actors will be running around without a helmet on, so we can see their faces, otherwise the audience doesn't know who is fighting whom. Of course, doing this in a real battle would've been as idiotically dangerous as smearing oneself in blood and leaping into a shark tank. We'll also put soldiers in colour-coded uniforms, so we can tell the good guys from the bad guys - even though standardised uniforms are a modern invention - and swords don't make that *shiiiing* noise when you pull them from scabbards; that sound is added in post-production to remind you that the sword is lethally sharp and your fave character is in mortal peril.

And then, of course, you have the language problem. Would you watch a movie set in the Middle Ages if all the actors spoke in authentic Chaucerian dialect? I would, but I'm obviously a tedious nerd. Surprisingly, the most notable director to try this sort of thing wasn't some highbrow auteur, but rather Mel Gibson. Both *The Passion of the Christ* and *Apocalypto* were entirely shot using archaic languages. My publisher's lawyers won't let me say what I think about Mel Gibson as a human being, but he managed to make two very successful box-office smashes that contained not a single word of modern English, and that's no mean feat.

There are several reasons filmmakers didn't copy him. Firstly, it's hard to convince English-speaking audiences to read subtitles; as a student, I worked in Blockbuster Video (R.I.P.) and regularly had to contend with customers angrily storming back into the shop, demanding a refund when their South Korean horror movie had the temerity to be filmed in the Korean language. But it's also a logistical nightmare for the production team to make a film in a different language.

Early in my career, I worked on a TV drama about the events of 1066 where our Viking, English, and Norman characters all spoke in their respective archaic tongues for a few minutes before the drama switched to modern English. Translating those lines into three dead languages, and teaching it to the actors, was my responsibility, and pushed me to the very extreme edges of my limited abilities. More annoyingly, nobody else except me knew if the actors had flubbed their lines and needed to do another take. We had an entire team filming something they didn't understand. I did it for just a couple of days. Imagine doing that for months on a whole movie production!

The internal logic of communication between characters is also a head-scratcher. When I worked on the children's comedy, *Horrible Histories: The Movie - Rotten Romans*, one of our first script conversations was how should the characters talk to each other? How does a Roman, who speaks Latin, chat to a Celt, who doesn't? Would he shout louder and slower, like a British person ordering egg and chips in a Spanish café? Or would we have a shared tongue across the movie, understood by all? What language should the street signs be in – modern English? A more olde worlde, Latiny sort of English? And what about when a gladiator trainer says to his men: 'I want you to give CX per cent out there!'? This is a joke that made us all chuckle, but it actually broke the linguistic logic of our film because elsewhere we don't then have characters say 'V' instead of 'five'. These are the tiny, pedantic headaches historical advisers endure on a daily basis.

Another telling facet of the accuracy conversation is that we, the audience, are often wrong ourselves. We commonly hold received ideas of what the past should look like, and we might get upset if we think a drama is inaccurate, even though sometimes the filmmakers have done their homework and we're the ones with the outdated view. The BBC drama *Taboo* got into hot bother because of its extensive use of swearing – journalists and viewers felt it wasn't in keeping with the genteel spirit of the eighteenth century that they expected. In fact, swearing in the eighteenth century was extensive and vulgar (my fave curse word being the emphatic 'f**kster!'), but a ceaseless diet of Jane Austen adaptations has warped our linguistic sensibilities. Often, we demand a new thing must resemble a previous thing, even though that thing was probably inaccurate too.

What I really want to stress, however, is that – above all else – historical dramas are always fascinated by the present. As a society, we tell stories that reflect our current interests, and we use history as a frosted mirror into which we can gaze at who we've become, or who we wish we were. The past is harnessed for dramatic entertainment to either make us feel wistful and nostalgic, or to make us feel lucky to live in the twenty-first century. One of my party tricks is being able to tell you what decade a film was made in, just by looking at the costumes and hair, regardless of what year it's meant to be set in.

So, I'm not one for nit-picking. I notice things that are anachronistic and I either forgive them as easy mistakes, or I assume they were deliberate choices made in the service of better storytelling. And that brings me to my choice of Most Accurate Movie About The Past *cue the trumpets!* – ladies and gentlemen, I give you . . . *Monty Python and the Holy Grail.*

Yes, obviously, it's very, very silly and very, very 1970s. It boasts Knights Who Say 'Ni!', a ruthless killer bunny, jokes about the airspeed velocity of an unladen swallow, and a holy hand grenade. None of this would get you any marks in a GCSE history exam. And yet, it's also full of very niche jokes that medieval historians enjoy; jokes about palaeography (deciphering old handwriting), about the French origins of the Arthurian grail narrative, and about the evolving canonical reputations of Lancelot and Galahad. It is a surprisingly rich text that manages to combine overtly modern references to anarcho-communism with genuinely lovely nods to the medieval Arthurian tradition.

And I know that historians genuinely love it because I wrote my MA thesis on how medievalists react to movies about their own period (spoiler alert: they're way more critical of anything treading on their patch than movies about a different era). *Holy Grail* was the most beloved of all the films I polled, perhaps because its overt silliness ensured viewers didn't take it seriously, so it wasn't a threat to the integrity of the past, but also because so many of its jokes reveal a deep well of learning among the Pythons. Sometimes, being deliberately subversive is an act of accuracy, for it means you must understand the thing before you can tear it apart. *Holy Grail* is full of absurdly brutal violence and misunderstandings, but so is the fifteenth-century Arthurian text *Le Morte d'Arthur*.

So, in answer to your question, Chloe, no, inaccurate films don't annoy me. I would much rather let filmmakers tell the stories they want to tell. Obviously, some of my colleagues find this a terrifying shirking of my sacred duties as public historian. And yes, I absolutely recognise that misleading popular history can be dangerous and disrespectful. Medievalists have realised much too late that white supremacists and neo-Nazis have weaponised the Middle Ages, turning Viking warriors and Crusader knights into symbols of their hateful cause. Pop culture has undoubtedly been part of this, and there are clearly real-world ramifications to popular representations of the past. We must fight this dangerous abuse of history.

But my riposte isn't to demand censorship of popular culture. Some films will be a pile of utter guff, but, rather than ignoring or attacking them, I'd much rather use them as launchpads for public conversations. Yelling at someone, and saying their fave thing is stupid, doesn't tend to make them very receptive listeners. But Wikipedia data shows that historical movies and TV shows are enormous drivers of public curiosity. People often want to know the facts behind the romantic fantasy. So, my approach is always to welcome that opportunity to redirect someone's enthusiasm to the quality scholarship, rather than chastise them for liking a bad thing.

In conclusion, *Braveheart* is a hot, sweaty pile of historical garbage, but it's a very decent movie and a great way to begin a conversation. Just don't get me started on how I feel about Mel Gibson, because that guy is an absolute [REDACTED] . . .

48. What did *The Flintstones* get right about the Stone Age?

Asked by Anonymous

Let's start with the most important thing – 'Yabba-dabba-doo!' is a fantastic catchphrase and I'm genuinely saddened that I forgot all about it, having not seen *The Flintstones* for nearly three decades. Apparently, it was improvised by the voice actor who played Fred Flintstone, and I wish I was as blessed with such creative prowess to conjure up such an iconic, joyous bit of nonsense off the cuff.

Anyway, with the yabba-dabba-doos out of the way, I suppose I should cater to the yabba-dabba-don't-knows. For those of you who haven't seen it, *The Flintstones* was a hugely successful American animation that ran from 1960 until 1966, and then had various spin-offs, plus two modern movie reboots in 1994 and 2000. It's a boisterously energetic family sitcom set in the Stone Age town of Bedrock, apparently in the year 10,000 BCE. But, in reality, it's a show about suburban life in 1960s America, but with bonus mammoths.

Not wanting to be a boring pedant, let's just get the obvious factual clangers out of the way before we move on to the vaguely accurate stuff about Stone Age life. Clanger numero uno is obviously the fact that Fred, Wilma, Barney, Betty, Pebbles, and Bamm-Bamm quite happily cohabit with actual dinosaurs, which had died out tens of millions of years before humanity even existed. Indeed, by 10,000 BCE, North America had already experienced another mass extinction, with the collapse in *megafauna* diversity (megafauna meaning 'very large animals'). This was either thanks to human overhunting, or due to climate change. In which case, the mammoths, giant sloths, and sabre-toothed cats you see in *The Flintstones* would have had to be among the last remaining survivors in continental America.

Other things that obviously don't tally up in the show include the emphasis on nuclear families of two parents, one kid, and a pet living in self-contained housing. It's possible our prehistoric ancestors did have pets – there's evidence they bred wolves into dogs, kept tame foxes, and even had young bear cubs on a leash – but Stone Age living was likely communal, and they certainly didn't have nice gardens that required a munching array of dinosaurs, tortoises, and birds to trim their lawns and hedges. These gags, based on animals being tools, are among the most memorable things from my childhood recollections of the show, whether it's the woolly mammoth trunk as the shower, a swordfish for a breadknife, a camera containing a bird that engraves stone polaroids with its beak, or another bird beak used as a needle to play LP records.

The Flintstones also gives humans plenty of recognisable technology that hadn't been invented yet, such as modern musical instruments, vehicles with wheels and axles (a Bronze Age invention), domestic ovens and cooking hobs, chimneys for extracting smoke, and forks (seventeenth century) to eat their spaghetti (a medieval food). The male characters are also clean-shaven, and the female characters are impossibly glam, with up-do hairstyles and immaculate makeup. It's a quintessentially 1960s look, complete with Fred wearing a large kipper tie over his fur tunic. Needless to say, grooming and self-beautification probably weren't that easy when you lived in a cave, though that's not to say people didn't try their best.

And, of course, there was no way a major animation about the prehistoric world wasn't going to fall in line with the classic Hollywood obsession with aliens. Yes, sorry to return to my old bugbear from before (see page 22), but, when ratings needed a boost in 1965, best friends Fred and Barney stumbled upon an alien called the Great Gazoo, who had been exiled from his home planet for creating a terrifying superweapon capable of destroying the universe. Gazoo is a tiny, green, big-headed biped who floats, and who has various magical powers to freeze time, make stuff disappear, and do whatever else the writers needed to liven up a faltering sitcom. Oh, and not all the characters can see him, which causes much hilarity.

OK, obviously, *The Flintstones* was just a bit of fun and I'm guilty of taking it too seriously. Actually, when you watch it back, it's not quite as fun as you remember – there's ongoing domestic violence between Fred and Wilma, and a very sad infertility storyline that nearly drives Barney Rubble to a dramatic suicide. But, above all, this was not a show that had any interest in archaeological research; it was just a cartoonish – in both senses of the word – excuse to do a family sitcom with a unique visual aesthetic. Where else could you have dinosaurs and mammoths in a scene at a bowling alley? And yet, surprisingly, there are some things *The Flintstones* did get right, even if these were accidental.

To find out what, I turned to archaeologist Dr Rebecca Wragg Sykes, the author of the marvellous book *Kindred: Neanderthal Life, Love, Death and Art*. We chatted for more than an hour about what she could spot in a few *Flintstones* clips on YouTube, and her expert eye detected a lot more than I expected. The first thing she noticed was the characters' clothing. Fred wears his distinctive orange animal pelt with black markings, suggesting he'd skinned a powerfully built scimitar-toothed cat (*Homotherium*), which did exist at the time. The fact he also owns one as a pet, called Baby Puss, provides the rather grim possibility that Fred is wearing the skin of its predecessor. I'm not sure any of us would get away with turning up to work in a shirt made of Tiddles and Fido.

More interesting to Dr Rebecca was the stitching visible in some of the other clothes and fabric canopies. This is spot-on. We now know that sewing needles date back at least 40,000 years; though, in *The Flintstones,* Wilma instead uses a sewing-machine-bird, of course! There's also some limited evidence from 28,000 years ago in Central Europe for dyed plant fibres being twisted into cords and perhaps woven into rough fabric, meaning Wilma and Betty's colourful dresses weren't beyond the realms of possibility. The pristine white and blue colours are obviously modern, but they did have vibrant mineral dyes, used in their astonishing cave art, so the notion of dyed fabric isn't ludicrous.

Speaking of cave art, the Flintstones go to the cinema to watch the moving pictures – obviously intended as a gag, but this isn't so far-fetched either. The astonishing sophistication of Palaeolithic cave art, found at such places as Chauvet or Lascaux, depicts animals and humans in dynamic scenes that might well have appeared to move in the flickering flames of firelight. And, sticking with artsy pursuits, we also know of Stone Age jewellery, including decorative necklaces of ivory, shimmery shells, antlers, and threaded beads, meaning Wilma's chunky pearl necklace is archaeologically legit.

As for the stuff inside the home, Dr Rebecca and I had a bit of a back-and-forth on how to square *The Flintstones'* apparent chronology with what we know of the era. Awkwardly, the show seems to be set in 10,000 BCE, which the creators clearly thought meant the days of so-called *cavemen*. Actually, this is a rather vague conclusion, and there's a scene where Wilma is waiting for her dishwasher to finish (it's a monkey, tortoise, and water-shooting mastodon working in unison) and she's putting up her feet reading a magazine called *Today's Woman 3,000,000 BC*.

Admittedly, whenever I go to the dentist, the magazines in the waiting room are always very out of date, but not by 3 million years! Assuming the show is supposed to be broadly set in the time of cave-dwelling, our Stone Age ancestors weren't permanent settlers in any one place for long; they perhaps used caves as base camps while hunting mobile prey, but the idea of creating a permanent home, let alone a town called Bedrock, simply wasn't sustainable when their favourite migratory protein source had an annoying habit of wandering off to pastures new.

However, the jolly opening theme tune calls the Flintstones 'the modern Stone Age family', and that allows me to be slightly cheeky in my definitions: 10,000 BCE in North America might have been the late Palaeolithic era (though archaeological evidence of cave-dwelling is limited from this time), but in Turkey it was roughly around the time of the Neolithic (New Stone Age) when things were radically changing. This was when humanity began early experiments with farming, domesticating animal species, building monumental religious architecture, and settling into small communal villages.

The oldest town yet excavated, Çatalhöyük in Turkey, seems to have flourished around 7000 BCE. If we wanted to be generous, this town of 5–10,000 people, living in mud-brick houses, is not a million miles away from Bedrock, with its stone houses, leisure facilities, and places of work. That's where a *modern* Stone Age family would perhaps have lived. So, the Flintstones should actually have been Turkish.

What's more, if we jump forward to 4,500 years ago, to the Orkney Islands (off the coast of Scotland), here we find a famous Neolithic settlement called Skara Brae which resembles the Hobbit dwellings in *Lord of the Rings*. These eight fascinating, adorable homes – covered over by grassy mounds – were single-room spaces connected by passages, suggesting they were shared by a community of perhaps one hundred people.

The extraordinary thing that strikes us immediately is the surviving prehistoric furniture; though carved from stone, we can recognise beds, sideboard dressers with shelving, storage areas, and a central cooking hearth. It's not so different from a tiny city apartment, although the rent was probably cheaper; not so much Bedrock as bedsit. This was a modern Stone Age home that looks and feels oddly familiar to our own, and in this we can see something more akin to *The Flintstones,* not least in how Fred and Wilma sleep on stone slabs with stone headboards.

The people of Skara Brae seem to have had very limited access to wood, but when I asked Dr Rebecca to watch clips from *The Flintstones,* she noticed a lot more usage of wood in furniture and everyday design – annoyingly, organic materials such as wood, leather, and animal skins don't tend to survive well in the archaeological record. But what evidence we do have shows that Neanderthals and early *Homo sapiens* were skilled with woodwork, and might well have been able to build things with tree trunks, ropes, and animal sinew; perhaps not a foot-powered car – they had no wheels or axles, remember? – but maybe a dugout canoe, animal cage, or fishing boat.

The other most famous thing about Fred Flintstone is that he works in a stone quarry. This might well seem like an obvious joke about blue-collar employment in post-war America, but it's not totally off base. Stone Age tool manufacture required a lot of raw material, and while Dr Rebecca told me that much of it was sourced from secondary sites - perhaps river gravel, or places where glacial erosion had deposited it - there are some indications that Neanderthals and later *Homo sapiens* did indeed locate rock outcrops, and quarry whatever they needed. This would then have been taken to secondary sites where the tool-making process, known as flintknapping, took place (for more on this, see answer 34).

In short, Fred Flintstone can keep his job at the quarry - Yabba-dabba-dooooo! Alas, he'll have to do without the aid of his dinosaur crane . . . Yabba-dabba-*doh*! Oops, sorry, wrong American cartoon; that's *The Simpsons*. My bad.

49. Why do we care so much about the Tudors in England?
Asked by Nick

You can't see me, Nick, but I'm vigorously nodding my head, laughing, rolling my eyes, and gurning a bit too. I regret to inform you that you have landed on one of my pet peeves, and, as such, I cannot be held responsible for the length of this response. Indeed, if left to my own devices - and if I didn't have a very patient book editor, gently nudging me back on track - this answer would easily run to 4 million words of incoherent ranting. The simplest answer, Nick, is that we all do them at school, meaning they form the bedrock of our historical thinking. This means we gravitate to TV docs and books about them because we know enough to be interested, but not enough to know it all.

When I became the host of my BBC podcast, my first tyrannical edict was 'no Hitler, no Tudors', at least for the first couple of series. It's not that they're not interesting, but – much like Henry VIII in his portraits – they dominate the focus of attention to the detriment of pretty much every other historical period, and I wanted to broaden people's knowledge. The Tudors' grip on the public imagination is intractable and vice-like, which means popular culture creatives keep scrambling to give us more of what we crave – books, movies, TV, games, podcasts, posters, memes, touristic experiences; we are insatiable in our appetite for the same thing, over and over, like little kids who demand to watch Disney's *Frozen* nine times in a row before they'll go to bed.

As a public historian, I find this fascinating and frustrating in equal measure. The Tudors hoover up so much of the airtime, it's hard to find room for all the other stuff that's ever happened, of which there is a fair bit. One of my biggest disappointments is the public's shrug towards seventeenth-century radicalism. In France, America, Italy, and Russia, their revolutions and civil wars are held aloft as talismanic moments of national significance; and yet, in the UK, we seem to frown at the century in which the King's head was sliced off, devastating civil wars erupted, Ireland endured a genocide, plague ravaged the land, and an anti-Catholic coup forced the introduction of a weird, compromised, constitutional monarchy whose rules are so arcane that during the Brexit debate nobody knew if the Queen was legally allowed to shut down Parliament or not. Every time I've tried to tell these stories on TV, I get the same response: 'Sorry, the 1600s doesn't rate well with viewers - have you got any Anne Boleyn? People *love* Anne Boleyn!'

So, apart from the primary school thing, why else are we so Tudor-obsessed? Let's start with the personalities. As a dynasty ruling from 1485 until 1603, the Tudors have managed to become shorthand for sex, drama, power, tyranny, beauty, glory, and hubris. They arrest our attention because each member is so different from the next, and yet they were tethered together by their screwed-up family bond; one forged through a merry-go-round of marriages, deadly divorces, religious conflicts, and sibling tensions.

Edward, Mary, and Elizabeth were half-siblings, each of whom had a different mum; they were rivals and allies in a deadly court game where nobody was safe. In fact, the two sisters were declared illegitimate bastards when their mothers fell out of favour, and Mary eventually cycled through the bizarre experience of having five different stepmothers. Meanwhile, Elizabeth's mum was executed on her dad's orders - surely that must have messed her up a bit? These siblings didn't even share the same religious faith; I bet Christmas was super-awkward. In fact, when I watched HBO's brilliant drama *Succession* - a bleakly funny parallel of the Murdoch family's power struggles - I didn't just see Murdoch and his billionaire brood, but also the psychologically damaged Tudor children wrestling to escape the shadow of their warlike patriarch.

In truth, this wasn't a uniquely Tudor dynamic. The Plantagenets were also a total shitshow when it came to family loyalty; as were the Julio-Claudians of Imperial Rome, but there's something seductively pure about the way the Tudors have been branded as both individuals and as a collective. When I'm in flippant mood, I like to think of them as a classic nineties boy band, with each member having their own role in the group:

• **Henry VII** - underrated talent. Writes the songs, but dances like your dad at a wedding.
• **Henry VIII** - charismatic, sexy, dangerous. Out on bail for punching an air stewardess while off his face on prescription meds.
• **Edward VI** - the pretty one who's yet to shave.
• **Lady Jane Grey** - dropped by the record label after the first single flopped.
• **Mary I** - tries hard but seems a little too intense.
• **Elizabeth I** - the breakout star looking to go solo; speaks only through her publicist.

The truth is, this line-up boasts only two true stars: the tyrannical, toxic, truculent Henry VIII - he of the infamous six wives - and his daughter Elizabeth I, the heroic, stoic, strategic Virgin Queen who transformed herself into the old-but-ageless Gloriana. It's blindingly obvious why they dominate our imaginations; both reigned for decades, they hired the best artists to pimp their image, executed their trusted friends, had complicated love lives, took provocative lines on religious affairs, waged war with European powers, and built/stole glorious palaces with fancy giftshops which we still get to poke around today.

Henry and Elizabeth were power players whose exploits - whether reckless or prudent - shaped the course of British history. Some historians would argue that the most significant developments of the 1500s were the sectarian scars inflicted by theological radicalism on a traditionally Catholic population; and yet, in popular culture, the Tudor era often isn't marketed as a century of contested ideas and religious conflict, but as a quasi-secular era of personality politics where the huffy whims and urgent desires of the ruler took precedence over moral beliefs.

In fact, Henry and Elizabeth have often been portrayed as opposite sides of the same coin. If Henry was all libido, appetite, rage, and kneejerk instinct – a man (wrongly) famed for tearing hunks of meat from the bone with his teeth – then Elizabeth was all virginity, self-control, forgiveness, and cautious stalling. He was the majestic tyrant, she the stoic saint who undid his mess and built upon her grandfather's prudent foundations. This, of course, is hugely reductive; both were much more complex figures, and their political legacies are not easily summarised.

Personally, I like to annoy everyone by ignoring both Henry and Elizabeth and instead highlighting the importance of the dynastic originator, King Henry VII, whose low-key reputation belies an extraordinary level of cynical ruthlessness as the ender of a civil war and the founder of a powerful, financially solvent nation state. Henry VII was a sharp-elbowed upstart who stole a bedraggled turkey of a kingdom and somehow turned it into a golden goose. The only reason Henry VIII got to be a glamorous, messy drama queen is because his daddy had been the sensible, unyielding bastard who built up the power of the monarchy after the crisis of the Wars of the Roses.

Let it be clearly stated for the record, lest the pitchforks be raised against me, that I'm not anti-Tudors. They were very important! I do find them interesting, honest! The sixteenth century was an era of enormous social, political, cultural, religious, and military transition. The population rapidly grew, London doubled in size, the navy received record investment,

England began building its overseas empire, Ireland was brutally suppressed, Catholicism was supplanted by the Church of England, monasteries were sacked and sold off, the common land was enclosed, gunpowder technology killed off knightly prestige, Holbein, Shakespeare, and Spenser blossomed into cultural heavyweights, and fashion went through an absolutely iconic spell of bigger-is-better hyperbole that essentially turned humans into those birds of paradise which fluff themselves up in exotic colours to impress a mate. The Tudor era was full-on!

However, we've also been seduced by a potent brand. The Tudors were cunning mythmakers, and they benefited from later mythmaking too. In fact, they would have *hated* to be called Tudors at all. It was a lowly, Welsh name and a source of great embarrassment to Henry VIII, who did everything he could to connect himself back to heroic, legitimate kings rather than his dad's minor family which had somehow risen from regional Welsh politics to steal the bloodstained crown in a shock battlefield upset. The very fact we call the dynasty 'the Tudors', let alone the millions of people who lived in the country at the time, is pure retroactive mislabelling.

Though the big personalities really matter - probably more so in our era of visual media - Tudormania's deep-rooted potency also lies in the propagandised myth of Merrie England that arose in the 1700s and endured well into the 1900s. This was a bucolic, romantic fairy tale of English political exceptionalism, hived off from the rest of Europe, with its hale and hearty folk enjoying country pubs, timber-framed houses, rolling green landscapes, mince pies, jesters, hey-nonnynonnies, and cheery ballads.

The Victorians - and judging by his speeches in Parliament, also Jacob Rees-Mogg MP, who somehow still seems to live in the 1800s – delighted in venerating this misty-eyed fantasy of national greatness. They drew particular attention to the naval heroes of Francis Drake and Walter Raleigh, who were eulogised as chivalrous progenitors for Britannia ruling the waves; and they championed the poetical genius of Shakespeare, Spenser, and Sidney, who were seen to have breathed life into a new, distinctly English language which was to be exported throughout the colonial empire as a 'civilising' influence on the natives. Here, as proof, is how Charles Dickens – the quintessential Victorian – described the era:

> That reign had been a glorious one and is made for ever memorable by the distinguished men who flourished in it. Apart from the great voyagers, statesmen, and scholars, whom it produced, the names of Bacon, Spenser, and Shakespeare, will always be remembered with pride and veneration by the civilised world, and will always impart (though with no great reason, perhaps) some portion of their lustre to the name of Elizabeth herself. It was a great reign for discovery, for commerce, and for English enterprise and spirit in general. It was a great reign for the Protestant religion and for the Reformation which made England free.

We also see in the writings of nineteenth-century historians, like J. A. Froude, that a deeply anti-Catholic bigotry lurked in this fabricated past of Good Queen Bess: the sensible Protestant batting off Johnny Foreigner's galleons, while tolerating the Catholics in her own kingdom as an act of wise mercy. Her elder sister, Queen Mary I, meanwhile, was the Protestant-burning monster who acquired the epithet 'Bloody

Mary', even though Henry and Elizabeth shed far more blood in their reigns.

Mary's bad rep was born in the 1560s, when John Foxe published his influential book of Protestant martyrs, but it endured well into the twentieth century, not least because the establishment continued to revile Catholics. In fact, it wasn't until 1829's Catholic Emancipation Act that British (and Irish) Catholics were allowed to take an active role in politics. Co-incidentally, around the same time, some MPs had debated whether, upon her accession to the throne, the young princess Victoria should one day take the regnal name of Queen Elizabeth II, giving the naive trainee monarch a glorious, historical figure to emulate. As it happens, she decided against it, but we still did eventually get a QE2, and she's had quite the interesting innings . . .

In short, our current obsession with the Tudors isn't a modern addiction, but rather a long-standing habit. And when we look through the recipe's ingredients, we see it's a rich broth made from big personalities, easy branding, casual xenophobia, and a deeply embedded hankering for some idyllic golden age. But if you ask novelists and screenwriters why they're drawn to the sixteenth century, they'll tell you that the Tudor court was a deadly gladiatorial arena where the smart and the beautiful could advance to the highest of stations, but the axe constantly dangled over their necks, not least because the rulers were a messed-up bunch of capricious, paranoid despots with daddy issues. Needless to say, that makes for brilliant drama. There's a reason people keep making telly, films, and books about them. I just wish some of the other historical stories would get a look-in . . .

50. Which people from history would you hire for an *Ocean's Eleven*-style heist?
Asked by Anonymous

This is the final question in the book, and I've saved it till last because it was so much fun to ponder, but I also spent way too long assembling a massive list of potential accomplices. Most didn't make the cut. For example, Jack Sheppard was an eighteenth-century burglar who became a huge celebrity by escaping from jail an incredible four times; such skills are certainly useful when breaking *into* a place too, but Sheppard had a bad habit of immediately being recaptured, and I'm not looking for a charming idiot who leads the cops to my door.

I'm also not looking to work with anyone violent. I want a nice gang of rogues, please! That obviously rules out one of history's most infamous bank robbers, a chap by the name of Joseph Stalin. Long before he was a terrifying tyrant, a young Stalin was one of the brains behind a series of robberies, including the dramatic 1907 job in the main square of Tiflis (now known as Tbilisi in Georgia). The raid was a fundraising exercise for the revolutionary Bolsheviks, and Stalin helped put the team together. The heist was extremely violent. Bombs were used, many people were killed, and the stolen money was basically unusable – the authorities were able to track the serial numbers – meaning the deaths were tragically futile. Also, Stalin was a monstrous psychopath who lacked the cheery bonhomie I'm looking for in my gang of cheeky rascals. He's definitely the gang member who betrays everyone else at the end of the movie. No thanks!

All right, so who is making it onto my hypothetical, historical crew then? Well, after way too much debate, here's my wish list:

THE MASTERMIND: MUHAMMAD IBN-AMMAR

This brainiac was a famed eleventh-century poet and court adviser to the famously cultured ruler of Seville, Abbad III al-Mu'tamid. So, why him? Well, according to the medieval Moroccan historian Abdelwahid al-Marrakushi, Ibn-Ammar was a dazzling poet, an impressive administrator, and an unbeatable chess master. And what is chess if not a plan of action that requires patience, foresight, and – when things go wrong – quick adaptability to a new plan? Yes, a chess genius is the perfect mastermind for planning a complex heist on a casino that knows it's going to be under attack.

Also, his chess career was properly impressive. Allegedly, he saved the city of Seville from invasion by defeating the invading King of Castile, Alfonso VI, in a chess match. According to the story, he challenged Alfonso using a gorgeously hand-crafted chess set. If Alfonso won, he could keep the set, if Ibn-Ammar won, Alfonso would have to grant any request. Naturally, Ibn-Ammar was victorious and demanded a full military retreat. The story might be apocryphal, but, frankly, I don't care – Ibn-Ammar sounds to me like a big-brained strategist who can remain cool under pressure. Welcome aboard! Let's draw up some plans . . .

THE TECH GURU: SU SONG

I'm going to need a top-level nerd to help me crack the casino's security. Obviously, history offers up many scientific geniuses

- Tesla, Edison, Brunel, Turing, Babbage and Lovelace - and, if you were to ask me who my fave person in history is, I'd get fanboy-excited about Leonardo da Vinci, a genius of astonishing, multifaceted brilliance. But Leonardo was famously allergic to deadlines; I'd be trying to break into the vault and he'd be off in the corner, building a mechanical lion.

So, instead, I'm plumping for an equally brilliant polymath who was a lot less prone to procrastination: the eleventh-century Chinese bureaucrat Su Song, who was a ridiculous overachiever in so many fields, including poetry, medicine, astronomy, maths, mapmaking, art theory, but most notably clockmaking. His ingenious water-powered astronomical clock - a huge feat of engineering which boasted a self-driving waterwheel to power the clock's escapement - was so sophisticated, even modern scholars have struggled to make a scale model. He may have lived 1,000 years before Wi-Fi, but I'm willing to bet he could still crack the casino security cameras.

THE DIVERSION: JOSEPHINE BAKER

In *Ocean's 8*, Anne Hathaway plays a superstar celebrity who begins as the mark but ... SPOILER ALERT ... ends up as part of the gang, not least because her fame gives her access to the priceless jewels. I'm stealing this idea, but I'm going one better because my real superstar celebrity was an actual spy. Josephine Baker was one of the most extraordinary people of the twentieth century, a poor, young, African American dancer from Missouri who ended up as the sensational jazz queen of Paris.

Baker was extremely funny, beautiful, risqué, went to the cinema with her diamond-adorned pet cheetah, was a revolutionary performer in both dance and song, and then – when the Nazis invaded France – used her celebrity status to spy for the French Resistance, managing to pass messages through checkpoints because who would dare search Josephine Baker? As if that wasn't enough, she later became a leading light in the American civil rights movement, giving her own impressive speech to a million people before Martin Luther King Jr stepped up to say, 'I have a dream.' Everywhere she went, people stared, which makes her the perfect distraction for getting my crew past the security guards. She's hired!

THE MASTER OF DISGUISE: MARY JANE RICHARDS

The perfect robbery needs someone on the inside. My undercover eyes and ears will be Mary Jane Richards, often wrongly known as Mary Bowser. She too was a talented Black woman. Born into slavery, she was liberated, educated, and recruited by Elizabeth Van Lew into her espionage network during the American Civil War. Richards went undercover in the household of Jefferson Davis, the President of the Southern Confederacy, and on at least one occasion rifled through his documents looking for vital military intelligence. There are plenty of exaggerated myths about Mary Jane Richards, such as her having perfect memory recall, or trying to burn down Davis' house, but the simple truth is she did her job well, and never got outed as a spy. Good enough for me!

THE CON ARTIST: GEORGE PSALMANAZAR

I'll need a smooth-talking trickster to talk their way into private areas, so I'm recruiting George Psalmanazar. In 1703, he arrived in London pretending to be from the mysterious island of Formosa (Taiwan). To fool Londoners, he invented a fake language, fake calendar, fake religion, fake cultural practices, and utterly convinced the most learned gentlemen of the day. His bestselling book was full of richly detailed information, every word of it pure fantasy. And even though people were naturally suspicious, Psalmanazar could talk the hind legs off a donkey. Even after he was eventually unmasked, and was discovered to be French, he still remained well respected. If ever there was a chap to charm his way out of a dodgy situation, it was George Psalmanazar.

THE COMMUNICATIONS DIRECTOR: NANCY WAKE

I suspect a flawless heist needs a production manager with expert people skills. And I can think of no greater organisational badass than Nancy Wake, the New Zealand-born intelligence officer who played a key part in both the French Resistance and British SOE (Special Operations Executive), helping to wreak havoc against the Nazi occupiers in France, and getting downed Allied airmen out of the country.

Wake was, by all accounts, an absolute hoot - funny, fierce, determined, and a crack shot when things went sideways. Her job was logistics and comms, but she also planned and fought in lethal battles, killing enemy soldiers when necessary. At other times, she simply flirted with them to get past the guards. Famously, she cycled 500km in a mere seventy-two hours to relay a vital message back to London. Even when the bad guys figured out who she was, nicknaming her the White Mouse, she managed to get out of the country with extraordinary cunning. Nancy Wake was a hell of a woman, and I have no doubt she'd make my team tick.

THE INSIDE MAN: HENRY 'BOX' BROWN

I'm not a skilled burglar; in fact, I've not so much as stolen any pick'n'mix in my criminal career. But I've seen *Now You See Me,* and it strikes me that I probably need a magician, if only for some narrative glamour. The first to come to mind is, of course, the great Harry Houdini – a master escapologist with extraordinary strength, agility, breath control, and focus. But he had something of an inflated ego, and I'm looking for team players. There was also Jasper Maskelyne, a magician recruited into the British Army during the Second World War, who claimed to have fooled the Nazis with massive deceptions, including making Cairo vanish and fake armies appear. On the face of it, he sounds perfect, but modern scholars think he was an absolute chancer who made most of it up. What a cad! No thanks . . .

So, I'm going for Henry 'Box' Brown. He was born into slavery in Virginia in 1815. When his wife and children were sold, he vowed to escape, and made contact with abolitionists who helped him get out of the state by hiding in a small wooden box. For twenty-seven hours, he was shunted and bounced around various trains and carts, in agonising discomfort and with only a small bottle of water and some biscuits* to eat. But, finally, he made it to safety and freedom. Brown became a famous hero in the abolitionist movement and ended up touring Britain, demonstrating how he hid in his box to delighted audiences. Over time, he transitioned into being a touring magician, giving him the skills to dazzle and deceive. And, of course – if he was OK with it, and we'd ensured his comfort – perhaps Brown could get back in his

---

* The American sort of biscuits. What Brits might call scones.

box to be delivered to the casino vault, ready to jump out and start robbing the place!

THE SAFECRACKER: AMENPANUFER

Sometimes you just need a hardened crim; a safe pair of hands who not only knows how to steal stuff, but also how to deal with the cops. So, while there are many brilliant thieves from history, I'm putting the responsibility of breaking into the vault in the hands of this ancient Egyptian labourer. He's 3,000 years old, so he's got plenty of experience. Indeed, Amenpanufer was a regular tomb raider, though probably not as photogenic as Angelina Jolie. We know about him because his confession is recorded in the Mayer Papyri written in 1108 BCE, meaning he did eventually fall foul of the law, but in his interview he claimed to have robbed many tombs, and, when caught, had bribed officials to let him go so he could rob another one. Yes, please!

THE GETAWAY DRIVER: GAIUS APPULEIUS DIOCLES

If things get hairy, and we need to make a quick escape, I want someone fast, aggressive, and able to dodge any onrushing obstacles. Enter Diocles, the celebrated Roman charioteer whose winnings, when converted into modern money, made him the wealthiest sportsperson of all time. Not only was he a brilliant driver, with 1,462 wins under his belt, but he was an extraordinary survivor in a sport renowned for its terrifying dangers. Remarkably, he retired after 4,257 races, when most drivers had been crushed to death long before that. Diocles was either a genius or incredibly lucky. Either way, he's getting my car keys.

So, there you have it: my team has been assembled, so bring on the heist! Just please don't tell Joseph Stalin, or else we're all dead . . .

Acknowledgements

Writing books is hard. Writing them in the midst of a terrifying pandemic even more so. Suddenly, we were anxiously glued to the news headlines and government briefings, hoping that a vaccine would come and that those we loved would be spared the terrible cruelty of Covid-19. Tragically, too many precious lives were lost, and too often my social media timeline was filled with messages of heartfelt grief, as the people I'd chatted to for years announced the deaths of those they cared most about. It has been a year of exhausting sadness and fear, and trying to write enjoyable, lively, cheery prose hasn't always been so easy.

The other unexpected thing about pandemics is the workload. My schedule unexpectedly doubled overnight. I suddenly found myself writing two books, hosting three podcast series, and trying to care for a young baby who was almost constantly bedevilled by erupting teeth. Needless to say, we didn't get much sleep.

So, without doubt, my biggest debt is to my amazing wife, Kate, whose superhuman endurance, patience, and care - doing so much to look after me and our wonderful daughter, all the while juggling her own career - allowed me to tackle a daunting mountain of work, one fourteen-hour shift at a time. I'm a very lucky man to have such love and support in my life.

I'm also hugely grateful to my friend and colleague Henri Ward, who helped me research this book. I've worked with Henri for several years on the TV show *Horrible Histories*, and, as well as being a dogged historical researcher, he's a constant source of enthusiasm and positive energy. We hadn't planned to work together; I had initially intended this to be a long-term project slated for a 2023 deadline, but then along came Covid . . . and the rest, as they say, is history.

I must also say a big thank-you to my brilliant, long-suffering agent, Donald Winchester, who calmly and kindly endures my overlong phone calls and emails without ever telling me to shut up (even though he really should). I'm also greatly indebted to my editor at Weidenfeld & Nicolson, the marvellous Maddy Price, who took me to lunch and pitched the idea for this book, not realising I'd been pondering doing something similar as a podcast idea. I had slight reservations over whether it would work. Turns out, it does (well . . . I hope so, anyway!).

Maddy was also wonderfully supportive and flexible when I begged for that aforementioned deadline of 2023, explaining that I was 'VERY TIRED AND DID NOT WANT TO WRITE A BOOK FOR AT LEAST TWO YEARS!', only to phone her up two months later and say: 'Change of plan, can I do it now?' Yes, I'm a pain in the arse. Maddy is a kind, supportive, insightful, and trusting editor, meaning her proverbial red pen was most welcome in its mission to sharpen up my meandering waffle.

As with my previous book, *Dead Famous*, my grateful thanks once again go to Jo Whitford and Lorraine Jerram, whose job it was to tidy up the typos, blunders, and grammatical crime scenes that I left behind. It takes remarkable attention to detail to spot errors in 95,000 words of text, and they found plenty, I can tell you!

Writing a book both feels like, and outwardly looks like, a mammoth task solely reserved for the lone author, because only one person's name goes on the front cover, but books are always the precious child of many collaborations. Please do read the Credits on pages 331-2, so you can see just how many people, and how much work, is required to publish something. I'm very grateful to absolutely every one of these people for their hard work and support.

As you can perhaps imagine, a book of this type, with its unwieldy thematic range, is somewhat tricky to fact-check. So, I hereby perform a formal bow of respectable gratitude to all the historians who so kindly gave up their precious, pandemic-inflected spare hours to read through my manuscript and point out how best to fix my errors or improve my arguments. In no particular order, this pantheon of scholars comprised Professor Peter Frankopan, Professor Suzannah Lipscomb, Dr Tineke D'Haeseleer, Dr Campbell Price, Professor Sarah Bond, Professor Llewelyn Morgan, Dr Seb Falk, Dr Janina Ramirez, Dr Jaipreet Virdi, Dr Annie Gray, Dr Fern Riddell, Dr Jonathan Healey, Dr Moudhy Al-Rashid, Dr David Veevers, Dr Eleanor Janega, Professor Catherine Fletcher, Dr Lindsey Fitzharris, Olivia Wyatt, Professor Arunima Datta, and Dr Caroline Dodds Pennock.

Also, I must extend particular thanks to Dr Rebecca Wragg-Sykes, for her fantastic help in answering both the Stone Age tools and the *Flintstones* questions, and to Professor Emma Hunter for her superb assistance in tackling the hardest question in the book, the historical roots of Africa's borders (a question which I only later discovered had been posed by my own agent, Donald, perhaps as sweet revenge for all my rambling emails . . . in which case, touché, Donald!)

My profound thanks to all the people – not including Donald! – who so kindly sent in their questions. I received hundreds of entries, and choosing the questions that would go in the final book took a lot of deliberation, so please accept my apologies if yours isn't here. It's always so nice to see what people want to know, and I hope that I did them all justice in my answers.

And, finally, my thanks to you, dear reader, for sharing your time with me. I hope you found this book as enjoyable and interesting to read as I found it enjoyable and interesting to write. If it's whetted your appetite for more, you may like my previous books, or my BBC podcasts, but please also take a look at the Recommended Reading section, and pluck out a follow-up tome to carry on your journey of historical appreciation. The wonderful thing about History is there's always more of it to enjoy. Until next we meet . . .

With warmest wishes,

Greg Jenner,

April 2021

Recommended Reading

If you've enjoyed this book, and you'd like to know more about the subjects covered, here are some reading recommendations you might like. I've tried to prioritise things that are affordable, accessibly written, and available without a university library login, but sometimes the only sources I consulted were academic journal articles or PhD theses. Happy reading!

CHAPTER 1: FACT OR FICTION?

1. Did Anne Boleyn have three nipples? My history teacher said this was used as evidence of witchcraft against her at her trial.

Stephanie Russo, *The Afterlife of Anne Boleyn: Representations of Anne Boleyn in Fiction and on the Screen*

Susan Bordo, *The Creation of Anne Boleyn: In Search of the Tudors' Most Notorious Queen*

2. Is it true that a dead Pope was put on trial?

John Julius Norwich, *The Popes: A History*

Chris Wickham, *Medieval Rome: Stability and Crisis of a City, 900-1150* (this book is more scholarly in tone)

3. Who is the richest person that ever lived and what made him or her so rich?

John Kampfner, *The Rich: From Slaves to Super-Yachts: A 2,000-Year History* (this is more of a satirical, journalistic sweep through the story of modern oligarchs and how they compare to history's wealthiest people, but it has some enjoyable stories)

Modern biographies of Mansa Musa tend to be a bit sensationalist, and repeat debunked myths, so may I instead recommend François-Xavier Fauvelle's book *The Golden Rhinoceros: Histories of the African Middle Ages*, which is very readable

Greg Steinmetz, *The Richest Man Who Ever Lived: The Life and Times of Jacob Fugger*

Philip Beresford and William D. Rubinstein, *The Richest of the Rich: The Wealthiest 250 People in Britain since 1066* (this is a little dated now, but it was compiled by a history professor and the editor of the *Sunday Times* Rich List)

4. Are you fed up with people saying, 'Atlantis proves aliens are real'?

Ronald H. Fritze, *Invented Knowledge: False History, Fake Science and Pseudo-religions*

Stephen P. Kershaw, *A Brief History of Atlantis: Plato's Ideal State*

CHAPTER 2: ORIGINS & FIRSTS

5. When was the first jokebook written and were there any funny ones in it?

Mary Beard, *Laughter in Ancient Rome: On Joking, Tickling, and Cracking Up*

Jim Holt, *Stop Me If You've Heard This: A History and Philosophy of Jokes*

6. When was the first Monday?

Eviatar Zerubavel, *The Seven Day Circle: The History and Meaning of the Week* (this is scholarly stuff, but interesting)

7. What conditions did the Windrush generation meet when they arrived in the UK?

David Olusoga, *Black and British: A Forgotten History*

Peter Fryer, *Staying Power: The History of Black People in Britain*

Amelia Gentleman, *The Windrush Betrayal*

8. When did birthdays start being a thing people celebrated or even remembered?

Katheryn Argentsinger, 'Birthday Rituals: Friends and Patrons in Roman Poetry and Cult', in *Classical Antiquity,* October 1992, Vol. 11, No. 2 (sorry, properly academic, this one!)

CHAPTER 3: HEALTH & MEDICINE

9. How did women manage their periods before the twentieth century?

Elissa Stein and Susan Kim, *Flow: The Cultural Story of Menstruation*

Sara Read, *Menstruation and the Female Body in Early Modern England* (an academic book, and priccy too, but really interesting)

Look up Professor Helen King for lots of interesting work on ancient ideas of medicine and women's medicine – she blogs and broadcasts regularly, even if her academic writing is harder to access

10. Has hay fever always been an allergy, or do we only suffer from it now that we live in cities?

Mark Jackson, *Allergy: The History of a Modern Malady*

11. Did European people really eat ground-up mummies?

Richard Sugg, *Mummies, Cannibals and Vampires: The History of Corpse Medicine from the Renaissance to the Victorians*

12. What is the strangest (and on the surface most incredulous) medical procedure that turned out to be medically sound?

Charles G. Gross, *A Hole in the Head: More Tales in the History of Neuroscience*

Harold Ellis, *A Brief History of Surgery*

13. Apart from the modern age, in which period in history would we have been best able to deal with a zombie-causing virus?

Neil Price, *The Children of Ash and Elm: A History of the Vikings*

CHAPTER 4: FOOD

14. Who was the first vegetarian?

Colin Spencer, *Vegetarianism: A History*

15. How old is curry?

Lizzie Collingham, *Curry: A Tale of Cooks and Conquerors*

Yasmin Alibhai-Brown, *Exotic England: The Making of a Curious Nation*

Arunima Datta, 'Curry Tales of the Empire', *Journal of Victorian Culture*

16. Who invented meringue and why?

Alan Davidson, *The Oxford Companion to Food*

17. How did early humans discover how to make bread?

William Rubel, *Bread: A Global History*

CHAPTER 5: HISTORIOGRAPHY

18. I'm a zoologist and we like dinosaurs A LOT. But these are 'prehistoric'. So, when did 'history' begin?

Chris Gosden, *Prehistory: A Very Short Introduction*

E. H. Carr, *What Is History?* (a definitive classic, but a little dry)

Helen Carr and Suzannah Lipscomb (eds), *What Is History, Now?* (a new book featuring thoughtful essays from lots of eminent public historians)

19. Who names historical periods? And what will future historians call us, given that 'Elizabethan' is already taken?

Helen Carr and Suzannah Lipscomb (eds), *What Is History, Now?*

Jacques Le Goff, *Must We Divide History into Periods?*

20. What are some of the greatest 'lost texts' from history that we know existed, but haven't survived?

Stuart Kelly, *The Book of Lost Books: An Incomplete History of All the Great Books You Will Never Read*

21. What's your favourite historical what-if?

Mark Millar, *Superman: Red Son* (a classic comic book, asking what would have happened if Superman had crash-landed in Soviet Ukraine instead)

Catherine Gallagher, *Telling It Like It Wasn't: Counterfactual Imagination in History and Fiction*

Richard J. Evans, *Altered Pasts: Counterfactuals in History* (not the easiest to read, but Evans is a powerful thinker)

CHAPTER 6: ANIMALS & NATURE

22. Why is the Devil a goat?

Robert Muchembled, *A History of the Devil: From the Middle Ages to the Present*

23. When and why did we start keeping hamsters as pets?

Michael R. Murphy, 'History of the Syrian Golden Hamster', in H. I. Siegel (ed.), *The Hamster: Reproduction and Behavior*

24. How much horse faeces and urine were created per day in London during the reign of Henry VIII, and what was done with it all?

Peter Edwards, *The Horse Trade of Tudor and Stuart England*

Leona J. Skelton, *Sanitation in Urban Britain, 1560–1700*

Hannah Velten, *Beastly London: A History of Animals in the City*

25. When and where were seeds first sold in packets, and by whom? What did people use before then?

Roderick Floud, *An Economic History of the English Garden*

Peter Frankopan, *The Silk Roads*

Amy Bess Williams Miller, *Shaker Herbs: A History and a Compendium*

Thomas J. Mickey, *America's Romance with the English Garden*

Malcolm Thick, 'Garden seeds in England before the late eighteenth century – II, The Trade in Seeds to 1760', *Agricultural History Review*, Vol. 38, No. 2 (1990)

26. Are there any trees in history that have had a big impact/ funny stories?

Simon Wills, *A History of Trees*

Jonathan Drori, *Around the World in 80 Trees*

CHAPTER 7: FASHION & BEAUTY

27. What are some of the strangest qualities ever considered signs of great beauty and why?

Gretchen E. Henderson, *Ugliness: A Cultural History*

Umberto Eco, *On Beauty: A History of a Western Idea* (written by one of the great intellectuals of the twentieth century, it's not an easy read but it is fascinating)

Rebecca M. Herzig, *Plucked: A History of Hair Removal*

28. Why do Greek statues have small penises?

David M. Friedman, *A Mind of its Own: A Cultural History of the Penis*

Paul Chrystal, *In Bed with the Ancient Greeks*

29. When did high heels come into fashion and why are they found mainly on women's shoes?

Elizabeth Semmelhack, *Shoes: The Meaning of Style*

30. Which beauty treatment ended up becoming the most dangerous or deadly?

Sarah Jane Downing, *Beauty and Cosmetics – 1550 to 1950*

Elizabeth Haiken, *Venus Envy: A History of Cosmetic Surgery*

Sander L. Gilman, *Making the Body Beautiful: A Cultural History of Aesthetic Surgery*

CHAPTER 8: IDEAS & TECHNOLOGY
31. Who invented maths?
John Stillwell, *Mathematics and Its History: A Concise Edition*

Eleanor Robson and Jacqueline Stedall (eds), *The Oxford Handbook of the History of Mathematics* (pretty academic stuff, this . . .)

This is a great website: https://mathshistory.st-andrews.ac.uk/

You may also enjoy the writing of Alex Bellos, who has the knack for making maths lively for the uninitiated

32. When were mirrors invented and did people know what they looked like before then?
Mark Pendergrast, *Mirror Mirror: A History of the Human Love Affair with Reflection*

Sabine Melchior-Bonnet, *The Mirror: A History*

33. Who first had the idea of actually going to the Moon or another planet? Did they have any idea how?
Barbara J. Shapiro, *John Wilkins, 1614-72* (an old book that you might need to get second-hand, but it's a good study of his ideas)

John Wilkins, *A discourse concerning a new world & another planet in 2 bookes* (you can read this online)

34. How can you tell that the earliest Stone Age tools are actually tools, and not just rocks?
John C. Whittaker, *Flintknapping: Making and Understanding Stone Tools*

CHAPTER 9: NATIONS & EMPIRES
35. China is massive. If the emperor died, or a new law was passed, how long did it take for news to reach everyone?

Mark Edward Lewis and Timothy Brook, *China's Cosmopolitan Empire (History of Imperial China): The Tang Dynasty*

Timothy Brook, 'Communications and Commerce', in Denis C. Twitchett and Frederick W. Mote (eds), *The Cambridge History of China, Vol. 8: The Ming Dynasty, Part 2: 1368–1644*

36. Did Genghis Khan plant trees wherever he went?

Peter Frankopan, *The Silk Roads*

John Man, *The Mongol Empire: Genghis Khan, His Heirs and the Founding of Modern China*

37. Why is Italy called Italy?

Vincent Cronin, *Italy: A History*

Charles L. Killinger, *The History of Italy*

David Gilmour, *The Pursuit of Italy: A History of a Land, its Regions and their Peoples*

David Abulafia (editor), *Italy in the Central Middle Ages*

38. How did the modern boundaries of African nations come to be?

Paul Nugent, *Boundaries, Communities and State-Making in West Africa* (a chunky academic publication, but the most up-to-date scholarship)

Steven Press, *Rogue Empires: Contracts and Conmen in Europe's Scramble for Africa* (a bit too reliant on the European sources and perspective, but worth a read)

See also academic articles by Camille Lefebvre and Anthony Asiwaju

CHAPTER 10: WARS & BATTLES

39. Why did the Ashanti people keep a golden stool?

M. D. McLeod, *The Asante* (out of print and a bit dated, but worth a look)

My BBC podcast *You're Dead to Me* has an episode about the Asante featuring the museum curator and art historian Dr

Gus Casely-Hayford and the British-Ghanaian comedian Sophie Duker

You can see beautiful examples of Asante stools in the online collections of many major museums

40. Why are there so many penises shown on the Bayeux Tapestry, although mainly for horses?

David Musgrove and Michael Lewis, *The Story of the Bayeux Tapestry: Unravelling the Norman Conquest*

Carola Hicks, *The Bayeux Tapestry: The Life Story of a Masterpiece*

41. What is the least consequential, but most famous battle that's entered the public consciousness?

Anne Curry, *Agincourt: A New History*

Juliet Barker, *Agincourt: The King, the Campaign, the Battle*

Stephen Cooper, *Agincourt, Myth and Reality 1415–2015*

42. A boyhood question to which I never received a satisfactory answer: how did knights in full armour satisfy their need to go to the toilet?

Christopher Gravett and Chris McNab, *The Medieval Knight* (suitable for younger readers too)

Donald Larocca, *How to Read European Armor* (Metropolitan Museum of Art) (an art historian's guide to the history of how armour evolved)

CHAPTER 11: LANGUAGE & COMMUNICATION

43. When was sign language first used in the UK, and when was the first hearing aid created?

Gerald Shea, *The Language of Light: A History of Silent Voices*

Jaipreet Virdi, *Medicalizing Deafness: Aural Surgery in Victorian Britain*

Katie Booth, *The Invention of Miracles: Language, Power, and Alexander Graham Bell's Quest to End Deafness*

Marc Marschark and Patricia Elizabeth Spencer (eds), *The Oxford Handbook of Deaf Studies, Language, and Education*

44. How did empires from different continents communicate? Were there translators?

Frances Karttunen, *Between Worlds: Interpreters, Guides, and Survivors*

Ruth Rowland, *Interpreters as Diplomats: A Diplomatic History of the Role of Interpreters in World Politics*

Lucas Christopoulos, 'Hellenes and Romans in Ancient China', *Sino-Platonic Papers*, No. 230, August 2012, p.44

Rachel Mairs, 'Translator, Traditor: The Interpreter as Traitor in Classical Tradition', *Greece and Rome*, Vol. 58, No. 1 (2011)

Kayoko Takeda and Jesus Baigorri-Jalón (eds), *New Insights in the History of Interpreting*

45. Where do names for places in other languages come from? For example, London vs Londres, Munich vs München – is there an official system in place?

John Everett-Heath, *Place Names of the World: Historical Context, Meanings and Changes*

Adrian Room, *Placenames of the World: Origins and Meanings of the Names for 6,600 Countries, Cities, Territories, Natural Features, and Historic Sites*

46. How do we know what people's accents and languages sounded like in the past?

Melvyn Bragg, *The Adventure of English: The Biography of a Language*

David Crystal, *The Oxford Dictionary of Original Shakespearean Pronunciation*

Joshua C. Kendall, *The Forgotten Founding Father: Noah Webster's Obsession and the Creation of an American Culture*

W. Sidney Allen, *Vox Latina 2nd edn: A Guide to the Pronunciation of Classical Latin*

CHAPTER 12: HISTORY IN POP CULTURE

47. Which popular historical films are the most accurate and do you get annoyed when you know how wrong they've got something?

Alex von Tunzelmann, *Reel History: The World According to the Movies*

48. What did *The Flintstones* get right about the Stone Age?

Rebecca Wragg Sykes, *Kindred: Neanderthal Life, Love, Death and Art*

Roland Ennos, *The Wood Age: How One Material Shaped the Whole of Human History*

Francis Pryor, *Scenes from Prehistoric Life: From the Ice Age to the Coming of the Romans: One Million Years of Life in the British Isles*

49. Why do we care so much about the Tudors in England?

Cliff Davies, 'Is Tudor England a Myth?', University of Oxford: https://www.ox.ac.uk/news/2012-05-29-tudor-england-myth

Basil Glynn, 'The Tudors', in Mandy Merck (ed.), *The British Monarchy on Screen*

50. Which people from history would you hire for an *Ocean's Eleven*-style heist?

Henry 'Box' Brown, *Narrative of the Life of Henry Box Brown*

Simon Sebag Montefiore, *Young Stalin*

Maria Rosa Menocal, *The Ornament of the World: How Muslims, Jews and Christians Created a Culture of Tolerance in Medieval Spain*

Joseph Needham, *Heavenly Clockwork: The Great Astronomical Clocks of Medieval China* (an old book in reprint, rather dated but full of fascinating technical info)

Bennetta Jules-Rosette, *Josephine Baker in Art and Life: The Icon and the Image* (there are countless books about this extraordinary woman, but they are all unreliable. This is a better attempt to analyse her life and how she portrayed herself)

An essay on Mary Jane Richards (Mary Bowser) by Lois Leveen, the novelist who wrote about her: https://lareviewofbooks.org/article/the-vanishing-black-woman-spy-reappears/

Michael Keevak, *The Pretended Asian: George Psalmanazar's Eighteenth-century Formosan Hoax*

Russell Braddon, *Nancy Wake: World War Two's Most Rebellious Spy*

CREDITS

Weidenfeld & Nicolson would like to thank everyone at Orion who worked on the publication of *Ask a Historian*.

Agent
Donald Winchester

Editor
Maddy Price

Copy-editor
Lorraine Jerram

Proofreader
Clare Hubbard

Editorial Management
Jo Whitford
Kate Moreton
Charlie Panayiotou
Jane Hughes
Claire Boyle
Jake Alderson

Audio
Paul Stark

Contracts
Anne Goddard
Paul Bulos

Design
Lucie Stericker
Debbie Holmes
Joanna Ridley
Nick May
Clare Sivell
Helen Ewing

Production
Hannah Cox
Fiona McIntosh

Finance
Jennifer Muchan
Jasdip Nandra
Rabale Mustafa
Ibukun Ademefun
Levancia Clarendon
Tom Costello

Marketing
Brittany Sankey

Publicity
Virginia Woolstencroft

Sales
Jen Wilson
Victoria Laws
Esther Waters
Lucy Brem
Frances Doyle
Ben Goddard
Georgina Cutler
Jack Hallam
Ellie Kyrke-Smith
Inês Figuiera
Barbara Ronan
Andrew Hally
Dominic Smith
Deborah Deyong

Lauren Buck
Maggy Park
Linda McGregor
Sinead White
Jemimah James
Rachael Jones
Jack Dennison
Nigel Andrews
Ian Williamson
Julia Benson
Declan Kyle
Robert Mackenzie
Imogen Clarke
Megan Smith
Charlotte Clay
Rebecca Cobbold

Operations
Jo Jacobs
Sharon Willis
Lisa Pryde

Rights
Susan Howe
Richard King
Krystyna Kujawinska
Jessica Purdue
Louise Henderson